THE GREAT INVASION

The mark of the invader. Aerial view of Watling Street, looking south-east from Hockliffe, Bedfordshire.

THE GREAT INVASION

by

LEONARD COTTRELL

LONDON
EVANS BROTHERS LIMITED

To Graham Webster

In appreciation of his
kindness and patient help.

Printed in Great Britain by
The Camelot Press Ltd., London and Southampton
Z.5074

CONTENTS

ACKNOWLEDGEMENTS

THE author wishes to express his grateful acknowledgement of the help he has received from the following books, and, in the case of those marked with an asterisk, to thank the authors, translators and publishers for permission to make quotations.

The Roman Army, by Graham Webster (Grosvenor Museum, Chester); *Roman Britain*,* by I. A. Richmond (Penguin Books); *Prehistoric and Roman Wales*, by Sir Mortimer Wheeler (Clarendon Press); *The Roman Occupation of South-western Scotland*,* by Clarke, Davidson, Robertson and St. Joseph, edited by S. N. Miller (Glasgow Archaeological Society); *The Stanwick Fortifications*,* by Sir Mortimer Wheeler (Society of Antiquaries, London); *Fourth Report of the Excavation of the Roman Fort at Richborough, Kent*,* by J. P. Bushe-Fox (Society of Antiquaries, London); *The Roman Frontier in Wales*, by V. E. Nash-Williams (University of Wales Press); *The Roman Occupation of Britain*, by F. Haverfield and G. Macdonald (Clarendon Press); *The Geographic Background of Greek and Roman History*, by M. Cary (Clarendon Press); *The Annals of Imperial Rome*,* by Tacitus, translated by Michael Grant (Penguin Books); *Dio's Roman History*,* translated by H. B. Foster (William Heinemann); *The Geography of Strabo*, translated by H. L. Jones (William Heinemann); *The Conquest of Gaul*,* by Julius Caesar, translated by S. A. Handford (Penguin Books); *The Twelve Caesars*,* by Suetonius, translated by Robert Graves (Penguin Books); *The Romans were Here*,* by J. Lindsay (Frederick Muller); *Tacitus on Britain and Germany*,* translated by H. Mattingly (Penguin Books); *Agricola and Roman Britain*, by A. R. Burn (London Universities Press); *Roman Britain and the Roman Army*, by E. Birley (Titus Wilson & Son); *Roman Britain*,* by R. G. Collingwood (Clarendon Press); *Caesar's War Commentaries*,* translated by John Warrington (Dent); *Corbridge Roman Station*,* by Eric Birley, and *Maiden Castle*,* by Sir Mortimer Wheeler (H.M.S.O., by permission of the Controller); *Roman Colchester*,* by M. R. Hull (Colchester Town Council).

Grateful thanks are also due to Mr. Graham Webster, M.A., F.S.A., and Dr. John Morris, B.A., Ph.D., for their help and advice; to Messrs. Evans Brothers, publishers of the author's book, *Seeing Roman Britain*, for permission to quote from it; and to the British Broadcasting Corporation for allowing the use of certain material from the author's B.B.C. documentary programmes on the Roman Army.

ILLUSTRATIONS

The mark of the invader. Aerial view of Watling Street, looking south-east from Hockliffe, Bedfordshire (*Curator of Aerial Photography, Cambridge*)   *frontispiece*

facing page

MAPS

Author's Note

The sketch-maps in this volume have been prepared purely to help the reader follow the general course of the Invasion. Owing to the complete lack of precise contemporary documentation these maps can only give the approximate lines of advance, and many points, e.g. the presence of certain legions in particular areas, are in dispute. The maps should be regarded only as a very rough guide.

PROLOGUE

AMONG the readers of this book may be some who have known what it is to wade on to an enemy beach under heavy fire. Others may have commanded troops in such an action, and experienced that nerve-racking moment when all hangs in the balance, when the defenders have the advantage of protected positions, and the attackers have not had time to establish their fighting formations; a moment like this:

> . . . the troops, besides being ignorant of the locality, had their hands full; weighted with a mass of heavy armour, they had to jump from their ships, stand firm in the surf, and fight at the same time. But the enemy knew their ground, they could fire their weapons boldly from dry land . . . our fellows were unable to keep their appointed standards, because men from different ships were falling in under the first one they reached, and a good deal of confusion resulted. The enemy, of course, knew all the shallows; standing on dry land, they watched the men disembark in small parties, moved down, attacked them as they struggled through the surf, and surrounded them with superior numbers while others opened fire on the exposed flanks of the isolated units. . . .

Those words were written by Julius Caesar 2,000 years ago; yet, apart from the mention of "standards", and the absence of firearms, they could almost describe an attack on the Normandy beaches, or a Japanese-held island in the Pacific. Again and again, when gathering information for this book, I have been struck by the extraordinary similarities between the Roman Army and those of today.

Here is a Roman unit pitching camp:

> They march straight into the place, and each section or group of ten men dumps off kit. They put down the tents, one or two men sit busy cooking the evening meal. The rest are detailed for various duties. A couple go out on guard duty outside the area, and a

couple get busy digging a trench and throwing up earth behind. . . .

Here are some of the compulsory stoppages from a Roman
private's pay (in drachmae):

Bedding . . . 10
Food . . . 80
Boots and straps . . . 12
Annual Camp Dinner . . . 20. . . .

Basic training of recruits; (*a*) marching:

In the beginning of their preparation . . . the recruits must be
taught the military pace, for there is no point which must be
watched more carefully on the march or in the field than the
preservation of their marching ranks by the men. The result is
impossible to achieve unless by continual practice . . .

(*b*) weapon-training:

Single stakes, six feet high, are fixed to the ground. The recruit
attacks them as if they were an enemy, with a wickerwork shield
and a wooden sword . . . using all the strength and skill needed
in real battle;

(*c*) the C.O.'s comments after watching an exercise:

Your javelin-throwing was accurate and good, and that in spite
of the javelins being of a type difficult to grasp. Your spear-
throwing too was in many cases excellent, and the jumping was
neat and lively. I would certainly have pointed out to you any
deficiencies if I had noted them.

The Emperor Hadrian said that after reviewing troops in North
Africa. Among the great Roman generals there were "characters"
of whom Julius Caesar was one:

He never gave warning of a march or a battle, but kept his troops
always on the alert for sudden orders to go wherever he directed.
Often he made them turn out when there was no need at all,
especially in wet weather or on public holidays. Sometimes he
would say, "Keep a close eye on me!" and then steal away from
camp at any hour of the day or night, expecting them to follow.
It was certain to be a particularly long march, and hard on
stragglers.

And Vespasian, who, when a young, newly-promoted officer
came to offer his thanks, reeking of perfume, dismissed and
demoted the man with the remark "I wouldn't have minded if it
had been garlic. . . ."

On the other hand, Caesar, when his men had fought well,
would "let them run as wild as they pleased, remarking to one of
his critics, 'My men fight just as well when they are stinking of
perfume.' " In return, they repaid him with a loyalty so intense
that, when he was temporarily without means to pay them they
served him without payment, and many, when captured, preferred to die rather than agree to fight against their old commander.

Even in their off-duty hours their activities were not unlike
those of a modern private soldier. The equivalent of the "Naafi"
was the regimental bath-house, where they could drink and
gamble for their pay with dice or a game rather like draughts; or
they boxed, swam and watched regimental sports.

Among the young officers there were the "Military Tribunes"
—usually high-born sprigs whose duties were like those of a
modern A.D.C. Among these were some, who, in the rather
pompous words of Tacitus "turned their military career into a
debauch" and made "their staff-captaincy and inexperience an
excuse for asking long leave with its relaxing pleasures". But
others, like Agricola, who later became Governor of Britain,
"got to know his province and be known by the army. He
learned from the experts the best models to follow."

The careers of these young officers, from staff-captain up to
regimental commander and sometimes to Governor, provide an
absorbing study, and there is no better way of understanding
them than by following the invasion and occupation of Britain.
That invasion, because it was so remote in time and apparently
unconnected with our subsequent history, misleads some people
into thinking that Roman Britain was not very important. The
Romans did not think so, once they had established a foothold
and realized how tough the opposition was to become. Britain
was the northernmost frontier of their Empire and remained so
for 400 years. Apart from Syria, it was the only Roman province
which was permanently occupied by three Legions; the Gover-
norships of these provinces were the two "plum jobs" of the

Roman Army, held by some of the ablest commanders the Roman system produced; men such as Aulus Plautius, Suetonius, Agricola, and Platorius Nepos.

Some years ago, I tactlessly suggested to the late Professor Nash-Williams, who had just returned from Italy, that digging for Roman remains in Britain must be dull compared with archaeological work near the heart of the Empire. "Rubbish!" he replied. "*This* was the Roman frontier. Here you can see what the Romans were capable of when they were really up against it."

Of course, he was right. Apart from the Roman *limes* along the Rhine and Danube frontiers, there is probably no better place to study the Roman military system than Britain. Other countries can show better-preserved cities, villas, theatres, aqueducts and other civil monuments. But—again apart from Germany—no former Roman province is as rich as Britain in remains of forts, encampments, and military roads; nor can any country match the lonely splendour of Hadrian's great wall, snaking over the Northumberland fells for mile after mile, overlooking country which, in many parts, is still as wild and forbidding as it was when the Romans knew it.

This, then, is essentially a "war-book", concentrating mainly on the military aspects of the invasion and occupation, as far as they can be known. There are many gaps in the story which professional historians hesitate to fill, and I shall certainly not attempt to do so. For it is a disappointing fact that the Roman invasion of these islands is but sparsely documented. A few ancient authors, such as Dio Cassius, Suetonius and Tacitus, give us glimpses; and Julius Caesar set down his terse, soldierly account of the raid which preceded the full-scale invasion. But for the rest we have to rely largely on the evidence revealed by the spade, which increases year by year.

In writing the book I have kept in mind the needs of people like myself—people who are interested in the early history of our homeland, and who enjoy personally exploring some of the places which figure in the story. I have therefore drawn liberally on the excavation reports of archaeologists who have examined sites directly associated with the invasion; for instance, that of Sir Mortimer Wheeler, whose excavations at Maiden Castle lifted the veil of the centuries and showed us the defenders of a British hill-fort still lying where they had been hastily buried, with the wounds inflicted by the Second Augustan Legion still visible on their skeletons.

We shall visit, in the course of our journey, the training camps at which newly-recruited Britons were drilled by Roman N.C.Os. before being sent abroad to defend other Imperial frontiers, and the marching-camps which mark the path of Petilius Cerialis as he moved north-westward against the turbulent Brigantes. We shall try to see Hadrian's Wall, for centuries the northernmost frontier of the Empire, as it was in Hadrian's day, and try to reconstruct the life lived within the forts which lay behind it. We shall follow Agricola into Scotland, and Frontinus into Wales. We shall visit the great Legionary bases at Caerleon, York and Chester, and study the system by which Britain was garrisoned and defended during the long, relatively peaceful years before the Legions withdrew.

A word concerning the general plan of this book. I have tried, first, to describe Britain as it may have looked before the Romans came. What kind of people were the Britons, and what was the quality of their civilization? And how did they appear to the Romans, already established in Gaul? What were the reasons, real or ostensible, for the invasion, first by Caesar, and later by Claudius? And what of the invaders themselves? What was the Roman Army like; how organized, officered and disciplined? How was the attack mounted, and what manner of men took part in it?

The second part of the book describes the forty-year campaign which eventually brought about the subjugation of all Britain south of the Tay, though only after bitter fighting and many setbacks. We follow in turn the advance to the Severn-Humber line, the Boudiccan revolt, the invasion of Wales, the march into Brigantia and the north, and Agricola's advance into Scotland, where the invasion ended. And this is essentially the story of the Invasion, which occupied 41 years. No attempt has been made to describe the Occupation, which requires a volume to itself.

Whenever possible, I have quoted concrete archaeological evidence, partly because such evidence puts us into immediate contact with the past, and also because it contains a promise of a story yet untold. The Roman historians tell us tantalizingly little; yet who knows what still remains to be found under the peaceful turf which now covers a British hill-camp in the Midlands, or an Auxiliary Fortress in the Welsh Mountains, or on the Northumbrian fells? Antiquaries and archaeologists have been uncovering Roman Britain for 200 years, yet every year brings new discoveries, and many more still await the spade.

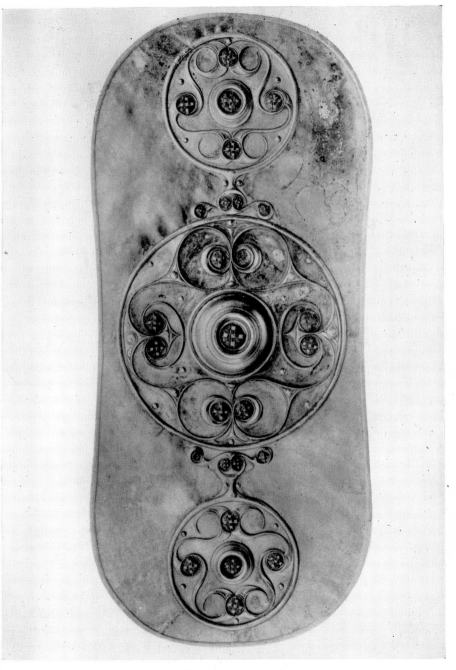

1. The art of the Celt. Decorated bronze shield (La Tène style) first century B.C

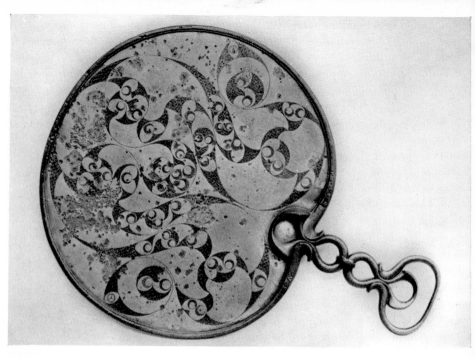

2. The art of the Celt. The Desborough Mirror, first century A.D.

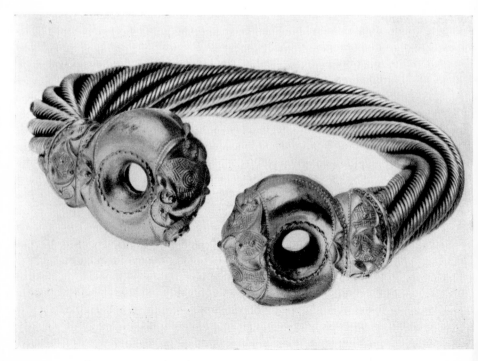

3. Electrum torc from the Snettisham Treasure, first century B.C.

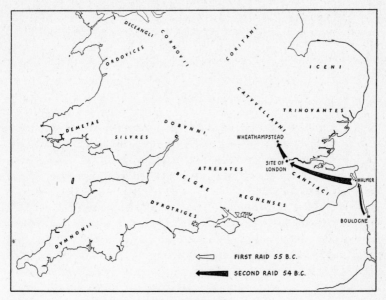

DECEANGLI
CORNOVII
ORDOVICES
CORITANI
ICENI
CATVVELLAVNI
TRINOVANTES
DEMETAE
DOBVNNI
SILVRES
WHEATHAMPSTEAD
ATREBATES
SITE OF
LONDON
CANTIACI
BELGAE
WALMER
REGNENSES
DVROTRIGES
BOULOGNE
DVMNONII

FIRST RAID 55 B.C.
SECOND RAID 54 B.C.

Caesar's Raids.

B

CHAPTER ONE

CAESAR'S RAID

A T about 9 a.m. on an autumn morning, over 2,000 years ago, eighty ships appeared off the cliffs of Dover. On the cliff-tops thousands of charioteers, horsemen and spearmen, looked down on the Roman fleet as it rolled and pitched in the Channel swell.

"I saw the enemy forces standing under arms along the heights" writes Caesar. "At this point of the coast precipitous cliffs tower above the water, making it possible to fire directly on to the beaches. It was clearly no place to attempt a landing, so we rode at anchor until 3.30 p.m. awaiting the rest of the fleet. I summoned my staff and company commanders (centurions), passed on to them the information obtained by Volusenus, and explained my plans. They were warned that, as tactical demands, particularly at sea, are always uncertain and subject to rapid change, they must be ready to act at a moment's notice on the briefest order from myself. The meeting then broke up; both wind and tide were favourable, the signal was given to weigh anchor, and after moving about eight miles up channel the ships were grounded on an open and evenly shelving beach."

Thus speaks the dry voice of the commanding officer, appraising the situation, making decisions, giving orders. But how did the landing appear to the other thousands taking part—the legionaries crammed in the rolling hulks, with the cold sea-spray dashing on their helmets, men from Italy and Gaul who had marched two thousand miles behind their brilliant commander, land-soldiers hardened by a score of campaigns, but unaccustomed to the sea, and fearful, perhaps, of what lay beyond the white cliffs which towered above their little ships? Caesar had led them out of many tights spots, often "snatching victory from the jaws of defeat". But had he gone a little too far this time?

And the Britons on the cliff-tops, wheeling their horses and chariots and, under the shouted orders of their commanders

moving steadily westward, keeping watchful eyes on that flotilla
as it coasted towards Walmer, seeking a landing-place. What was
in their minds? Some of them knew the Romans, had fought them
in Gaul; they were familiar with those indomitable phalanxes of
armed men who stood unmoved against the rushing chariots,
hurling their deadly throwing-spears which stuck in one's shield
and then bent at the head, so that one had to throw away the useless shield and rely on the sword; that slashing-sword which the
Romans despised, trained as they were to kill with the thrusting-
point. The Romans were men, like themselves, but a different
kind of men; all dressed and armed alike, and moving in disciplined formations, as if 1,000 bodies were impelled by only one
brain.

When they advanced, with shields interlocked above their
heads, it was as if one was fighting, not beings of flesh and blood,
but some metal monster without a soul. One had seen them
marching through the passes of the Ardennes with their baggage-
trains, wagons, tents and equipment, moving and halting at the
word of command, building their fortified camps at night, camps
which were like small cities, with earthworks surrounding neat,
tented enclosures. One fought them, and was defeated. They
moved on to the banks of the Seine, the Meuse and the Sambre,
where one's fathers had lived. And after they had moved on,
there followed, inevitably, the officials and tax-gatherers. . . .

And now they are here, on the coast of Britain to which one
had hoped they could not follow. The young men are confident,
as young men usually are, though among the older warriors there
are some who doubt if the wild, undisciplined courage of the
Celt can ever prevail against these men of steel. But now, from
the vanguard of the British army comes a roar. The Romans have
grounded their ships, and are coming ashore.

"On account of their large draught", wrote Caesar "the ships
could not be beached except in deep water; and the troops,
besides being ignorant of the locality, had their hands full;
weighted with a mass of heavy armour, they had to jump from
their ships, stand firm in the surf, and fight at the same time.
But the enemy knew their ground, they could hurl their weapons
boldly from dry land or shallow water, and gallop their horses
which were trained for this kind of work. Our men were terrified;

they were inexperienced in this kind of fighting and lacked that dash and drive which always characterized their land battles."

If only one had but one account by a Legionary of that moment! The shingle beach at Walmer, where the Romans landed, shelves steeply. The heavy wooden hulls dug their prows into the beach many yards from the shore. On the beach and behind it were the massed tribesmen, shouting and hurling their spears into the Roman ships, which canted over. The flap of sails mixed with orders, curses, words of command. A rain of spears fell among the packed troops. A man fell backwards on the deck, vomiting blood. Another pitched into the sea, a spear in his back. Confused cries from the other ships drifted down on the wind, mixed with the crash of breakers and the long-drawn hiss of the undertow. It was a moment of panic and uncertainty.

"Then", writes Caesar, "the standard-bearer of the 10th Legion, calling on the Gods to bless the Legion through his act, shouted: 'Come on, men! Jump, unless you want to betray your standard to the enemy! I, at any rate, shall do my duty to my country and my commander.' He threw himself into the sea and started forward with the eagle. The rest were not going to disgrace themselves; cheering wildly they leaped down, and when the men in the next ships saw them they too quickly followed their example."

At first the fight was bitter; the Legionaries and their auxiliary troops, accustomed to fight in disciplined formations, were confused.

> . . . our fellows were unable to keep their appointed standards, because men from different ships were falling in under the first one they reached, and a good deal of confusion resulted. The Britons, of course, knew all the shallows, standing on dry land, they watched the men disembark in small parties, galloped down, attacked them as they struggled through the surf, and surrounded them with superior numbers while others opened fire on the exposed flanks of the isolated units. I therefore had the warships' boats and scouting vessels filled with troops, so that help could be sent to any point where the men seemed to be in difficulties. When every one was ashore and formed up, the legions charged. . . .

This was the decisive moment. Once ashore, the Romans

could fight as units under their commanders. The Britons retired in disorder, but Caesar was unable to follow up his advantage, since, as he tells us "the cavalry transports had been unable to hold their course and make the island. That was the only thing that deprived us of a decisive victory."

*   *   *

Thus began the first Roman attack on the British Isles, the prelude to the full scale invasion which followed nearly a century later. It is an exciting story, but before we attempt to follow the Romans into the hinterland of the island it will help us if we try to understand what Britain was like before the Romans came. I propose to look at this from two aspects; first, pre-Roman Britain as it has been dimly revealed by geologists and archaeologists; second, the mysterious island which the Romans knew vaguely from the reports of traders and the few ancient travellers who had left records of it.

Round about 10000 B.C. begins the period which geologists have labelled the Old Stone Age (Palaeolithic). It was a time when the ice-caps were steadily retreating northward, and the climate of Europe became comparatively temperate, though we would probably have found it cold enough, but to the increasing human population of Europe it must have seemed almost paradisical. There was an abundance of game; buffalo, reindeer, wild horses and mammoth. Technical advances in weapons had produced the throwing spear, enabling hunters to kill at a distance; beautifully-made spears were made from bone and stone. Hunting was the main occupation, and was linked with magico-religious rituals of which we find evidence in such caves as those of Altamira in Spain, and at Lascaux in France. Here, and in other places, are vigorous paintings of animals, with figures of hunters. Sometimes the animals are pierced by weapons. There seems little doubt that, by a process of sympathetic magic, primitive man hoped in this way to obtain power over the wild beasts upon whom he depended for his food.

No such cave-paintings have yet been discovered in Britain, though some caves, such as Wookey Hole and Cheddar in Somerset, Kent's Cavern in Devon, and others in Yorkshire and Derbyshire, were occupied by men of the Middle Stone Age.

"Throughout our history", writes Graham Clark, "whether as an island or as an extension of the continental land-mass, it has been our lot to sit at the corner of Europe and receive influences from many directions, from east, south and south-west. Hardly a major wave of civilization has surged across Europe but sooner or later it has broken upon our shores."[1]

By examining sites, by noting "culture-spreads", as revealed by characteristic tools and weapons, archaeologists have traced these successive waves of invasion, though the people concerned have left no written records to guide us. To those whose interests lie mainly with the great civilizations of western Asia, whose material remains offer a more ample appeal to the eye, these relics of pre-historic-Britain—bits of pottery, corroded weapons, crouched skeletons in grass-covered tumuli—may seem unimpressive. The damp soil of Britain has destroyed or damaged most of the fragile objects of antiquity, and only the trained minds of the archaeologists can interpret for us the things which have survived. For instance, they tell us that, round about 2500 B.C., just after the period of the first Pyramid-builders in Egypt, and the beginnings of the Minoan civilization in Crete, waves of new-comers began to land in Britain. These people had reached a much higher level of culture than the men of the Middle Stone Age. As Clark points out, we were always on the fringe of Europe. As far back as 3000 B.C. there were highly developed urban civilizations in Egypt and Mesopotamia, but the customs, crafts and skills learned in these cradles of western culture took centuries to percolate to the remote periphery of Europe.

Some 4,500 years ago they began to reach Britain. Which race, or races, brought them we cannot be sure. Some may have come direct from the Mediterranean via the Straits of Gibraltar and the coast of Spain. They settled mainly in Ireland and west Scotland. Others reached us via what are now France and the Low Countries but they came by sea; that is certain, since in 2500 B.C. Britain had been an island for some 6,000 or 7,000 years.

These people were farmers rather than hunters, a fact of great significance. They brought sheep, cattle and the seeds of wheat. It is generally believed that the development of wheat from wild grasses, an invention of revolutionary importance in the human

[1] Clark, Graham, *Prehistoric England*, Batsford, 1940.

story, took place in western Asia. How it came about no one knows, but, like the domestication of wild animals, it may have been due to the womenfolk of the tribe.

But all these developments had taken place thousands of years before the newcomers arrived in Britain, 4,500 years ago. They also brought with them certain techniques and skills which, though a commonplace in the eastern Mediterranean for centuries, were new to this country: weaving, and pottery-making.

In those days we must imagine that most of the lowlands of Britain were forest and marsh, suitable only for hunting, but the hills of southern and south-western Britain, the downlands of Sussex, Hampshire, Wiltshire and Dorset, were unforested; the soils were light, and therefore amenable to the primitive digging-tools of the time; they were also suitable for cattle-grazing. Here, therefore, these early invaders settled, and we can find ample evidence of their occupation even to this day. Hunting now became relatively unimportant. There was an abundant supply of wheat and dairy produce, and the use of pottery—also invented in the Middle East—meant that not only was cooked food more nutritious, but also more palatable.

The sheep and cattle grazed on the hills, while the pigs were left to rootle in the oak forests on the lower ground.

Meanwhile, while these newcomers, ultimately of Mediterranean origin, were occupying the hills of the south and west, people belonging to the Middle Stone Age culture were living in what is now East Anglia. To these areas, from time to time, new elements arrived from Scandinavia. They were on a more primitive level, still relying mainly on hunting, as their ancestors had done.

Weapons and tools, such as axes for tree-felling, were made by specialized craftsmen; there must have been, at this time, a sizable industry to produce the great quantities which have been found. In the southern part of Britain, however, flint was the staple material. Flint-mines, some of them seventy feet deep, with radiating galleries, still exist on the Sussex Downs and elsewhere. In one of these, at Grime's Graves in Norfolk, was found a carved phallus and a primitive figure of a woman with prominent breasts. This again suggests a link with the Mediterranean and western Asia, where the cult of the Mother-Goddess was famous; e.g. in Minoan Crete.

It is interesting to reflect that the great megalithic monuments of this period, the stone-chambered Long Barrows of Dorset, Wiltshire and the Cotswolds, link us, however remotely, with the stone-built sepulchres of Minoan Crete. There seems to be no doubt that the New Stone Age inhabitants of Britain practised a fertility cult, linked with the dead. Tumuli with such homely names as Hetty Pegler's Tump, and Belas Knapp, in the Cotswolds, may be remotely related to the tombs in which the Minoan kings and nobles were buried.

Metal-working may have been introduced into Britain by later waves of these same Mediterranean invaders. Bronze-working, had, of course, been known in the Middle East since the third millennium, and was probably spread across Europe by travelling craftsmen. Copper was available in Ireland and once the art of bronze-working was established, the tin-mines of Cornwall became famous, even as far as Phoenicia.

The next great wave came from France and the Low Countries in 1800 B.C., about the end of the Middle Kingdom in Egypt, when the Hittites were moving into Asia Minor and the early Greek-speaking peoples into Greece. We have no ethnic or philological name for these peoples; we have no idea from which race they came or what language they spoke. They are known simply as the "Beaker Folk" from the characteristic drinking-cups or "beakers" found in their graves and settlements. From their remains, however, we can establish certain facts: (*a*) that they used the bow; (*b*) that they carried stone battle-axes and (*c*) that they understood metal-working and may even have brought metal-working equipment with them. They also came early into contact with Irish craftsmen, who already understood bronze-working, and who provided them with bronze weapons. The Bronze Age had reached Britain.

From an examination of their skulls, archaeologists have deduced that most of the Beaker people came from the same northern, Indo-European stock from which Homer's warrior aristocracy were drawn. Their great men, like Homer's heroes, also had a taste for luxury, especially in weapons and adornment. Golden ornaments made by Irish craftsmen have been found in their graves. Though they left few traces of domestic settlements, they were responsible for some of the greatest prehistoric monuments in Britain; religious temples such as Avebury, with its vast ring, Maumbury Rings near Dorchester, Stennis in the Orkney Islands, the Rollright Stones in Oxfordshire, and many others. The most splendid of all, of course, is Stonehenge.

About 1700 B.C. came another wave of invaders, who settled in Wessex; these may have been reinforcements of the earlier warrior stock. It is interesting to note that in graves of this period we begin to find goods imported from Europe and even the Near East; amber from the Baltic, and—most fascinating of all, perhaps—little cylindrical beads of blue faience, which undoubtedly came from Pharaonic Egypt. Nor was this a one-way traffic. There is evidence which suggests that the islanders even exchanged goods with the far-off Myceneans of Greece. This does not mean, of course, that the barbaric chieftains of Britain had any direct cultural contact with the rich civilizations of the Mediterranean, but trade-goods undoubtedly passed between them. Did, perhaps, Agamemnon's ancestors wear ornaments of British gold?

It may be thought that this brief summary of the prehistory of Britain has little relevance to the Roman invasion of A.D. 43. It has for me, because, just as one cannot understand the Britain of 1958 without regard to the peoples who have made our nation—British, Roman, Anglo-Saxon, Danish, Norman—so the Roman conquest of Britain can only be understood with reference to the history of the island before the legions set foot in Kent. For Britain had been invaded many times before the Romans came, indeed, long before the Romans existed; if the invaders had been literate we might have had epic poetry as moving as that of Sumeria and Greece.

The Mediterranean settlers of 2500 B.C., the Beaker Folk of 1800 B.C., the bearers of the Iron Age culture who came eight or nine centuries later—what were they like? All they have left to tell their story are their weapons, cooking-pots, drinking vessels, and graves. Yet these people made the Britain which Caesar knew, just as much as the later, Celtic folk who were the Romans' chief rivals for possession of the island.

When Vespasian marched into Somerset at the head of the 2nd

Augustan Legion he must have seen, breaking the outline of the
Mendip Hills, the grave-mounds of chieftains who had died 1,700
years before he was born, and concerning which the Celtic
warriors who opposed him, themselves newly-arrived in Britain,
were as ignorant as he.

As new elements in the population were gradually submerged
in the older stock, a single, unified culture spread across Britain;
we call this the Urn Culture, which extended northward over the
country after about 1500 B.C. It was an amalgam of "the con-
tributions brought by all the various groups of peoples who had
crossed to Britain during the past millenium, together with sur-
vivals from the still earlier aborigines".

Five more centuries passed, in which the predominant culture
of Britain was Indo-European; that of small farmers and stock-
raisers. But trade was an important source of wealth. In particular,
Irish goldsmiths and weapon-makers provided articles which
were bartered far afield. There is one particularly splendid
example of such work found at a place called Grunty Fen in
Cambridgeshire; a gold *torc* or bracelet, comparable in richness to
the finest work found in the Mycenean graves by Schliemann.

So we come to the period *c.* 1000 B.C. when, once again,
according to archaeological evidence, another wave of newcomers moved across the Channel and fought their way into
Britain. It is a curious fact that these "waves", of which the archaeologists are so fond, seem to coincide with the movement of
peoples in Western Asia and Eastern Europe.

From the twelfth to the tenth centuries B.C. there seems to
have been a continuous stir of movement in southern Europe, in
Asia Minor and the Levant. What caused it? And was there any
relationship between it, and the arrival in Britain, after about
900 B.C., of yet another flood of warlike invaders, this time of
Celtic stock, the first of many which were to surge into southern
Britain up to the time of the Roman invasion.

Who were these Celts? "The name is used confusedly, some-
times for warrior peoples of the early Iron Age north of the
Alps, sometimes for later peoples who spoke or now speak Celtic
languages. It is in fact a linguistic form", writes Mr. H. J.
Fleure. "The pre-Roman warrior peoples of what is now south
Germany appear to have had a Celtic language in the early part

of the last millennium B.C. They spread their conquests to Cata-
lonia about the seventh century B.C., and later took possession
of north-western Spain. On the way thither they spread their
language in France, and the short, round-headed, moderately
dark-coloured French peasants of the interior have often been
called Celtic or Alpine. . . . In the west they spread into the
British Isles at all events with the La Tène culture, perhaps
earlier. . . ."[1]

All we can be certain of is that, after about 800 B.C., immigrants
of Celtic stock began to move across the Channel into Britain.
From this period onwards appears that characteristic weapon of
the Continent, the broad-bladed, double-edged sword designed
for a slashing stroke. The bronze industry flourished and developed. The metal was more plentiful. Copper ore was found in
Wales, in northern Britain and in Scotland. Professional smithies
came into use, and furnaces, casting-pits, etc., replaced the
primitive domestic hearths. Weapon and tool manufacture had
become a specialized occupation, and with it rose a new class of
craftsman. Merchants travelled from place to place selling these
weapons and tools. They may be compared to the itinerant
tinkers of much later times.

Then came the so-called Iron Age. In the Mediterranean area,
iron had been used, since the beginning of the last millennium
B.C. Practical iron-smelting was developed, originally, by an
obscure tribe called the *Kizwadana*, in Armenia, from which it had
spread rapidly throughout western Asia and the eastern Mediterranean. But the technique of iron-smelting did not penetrate
north of the Alps until about 800 B.C., a time when, possibly,
Homer was making his first draft of the *Odyssey*.

To us it may not sound very exciting, but to the European
peoples of the ninth century B.C., the new technique and the new
metal—which was readily available in thousands of iron-bearing
rocks—brought about a revolution as drastic as that which
occurred in the mid-twentieth century A.D., when electronically-
guided rockets suddenly made the military aeroplane as old-
fashioned as the stage-coach.

Iron ore was abundant and widespread; it did not need alloying
(as did bronze) and its use revolutionized society;

[1] *Chambers's Encyclopaedia*, Vol. 3, p. 224. 1955.

From now on anyone could have durable weapons with a hard cutting edge, far superior to the expensive bronze swords which had been practically a monopoly of the war-lords. Any little farmer could have iron ploughshares which enabled him to tackle land which had been uncultivable before, axes for felling trees, and clearing new ground, and iron scythes for reaping. All these made his work easier and his land more productive. . . .[1]

The archaeologists date this revolution from the discovery in Austria, of an Iron Age settlement at Hallstatt, hence the term "Hallstatt culture". The people who lived at Hallstatt in the ninth century B.C. had clearly learned how to fashion tools and weapons of iron. In time the technique spread across western Europe, reaching Britain round about 450 B.C.

But there was another interesting link with the ancient civilizations of the eastern Mediterranean. The so-called "Hallstatt culture" was followed by the "La Tène culture", named after the village in Switzerland, near which its objects were found.

The "La Tène" was begotten on the "Hallstatt" culture; pre-classical Greek influences permeated north of the Alps, bringing to western Europe a school of art which eventually reached the shores of Britain. These influences reached the Celtic peoples via their trade with the Mediterranean; they sent furs and slaves, and received, in return, wine and "luxury goods", such as ornamented arms, bracelets, necklaces and other adornments, of which the designs were derived from pre-classical Greece. The Celtic craftsmen copied these, and ultimately derived their own native art. Thus, we find that the art of Celtic Britain, although it betrays no obvious Greek influences, none the less has its roots in the Mediterranean.

Some of these "La Tène" invaders arrived in eastern Scotland, and then swept westward to the Atlantic. Another group penetrated into south-western Britain. Yet a third settled in what is now Yorkshire. These were the *Parisi*; that was their real name—not an archaeological label stuck on thousands of years later, as was the case with the "Hallstatt" and "La Tène" cultures. "Parisi" was the name by which these people were known among themselves, and among their neighbours. It is a Gaulish name, still preserved in that of the best-loved city in Europe.

[1] Cottrell, Leonard, *The Anvil of Civilisation*, Faber and Faber, 1958.

It was the Parisi who introduced the war-chariot to Britain, and that fact in itself unfolds a vast historical panorama, for the chariot and the horse came from Asia. The Pyramid builders of Egypt, in 2700 B.C., knew neither. They did not arrive in Egypt until after 1700 B.C., introduced, in all probability, by the invading *Hyksos* tribes from Asia. The heroes of *The Iliad*, in the time of the Trojan War (*c.* 1180 B.C.) fought from chariots, and representations of these occur in stelae of the Mycenean period (1500 B.C.). Yet we know, from Hittite inscriptions that, round about 1500 B.C., a king of the *Ahhiyawa*—who may be identified with Homer's Achaeans—sent his son to Asia to be trained in the use of that new-fangled weapon, the horse-drawn chariot. A thousand years later it reached Britain via Gaul, and was to prove a formidable weapon against the Romans, who did not use it for warfare. Neither, for that matter, did the "classical" Greeks of the fifth and fourth centuries B.C., who, like the Romans, were infantrymen.

Trappings from these magnificent vehicles, bits, horse-armour, helmets, shields and personal ornaments have survived in Celtic tombs. "These Yorkshire Celts", writes Miss Hawkes, "beyond all other groups seem to have been responsible for establishing the tradition of La Tène art, which must have been so brilliant a feature in this country." Such objects as the famous Desborough Mirror and the wonderful bronze shield found at Battersea prove that the Britons were not mere woad-painted savages.

After the coming of the Yorkshire Parisi, other bearers of the La Tène culture appeared in south-western Britain. The Cornish tin-mines had by this time become famous; centuries earlier the Carthaginians had traded there, and the mines were mentioned by the Greek traveller Pytheas who wrote in the fourth century B.C. By this time Britain has begun to emerge from the mists, and is occasionally mentioned by travellers who have ventured out from the civilized Mediterranean world. Pytheas has a strange, evocative passage which has perplexed many historians, including Strabo, the geographer, who pours scorn on his predecessor:

There, in the north, where ice, water and air mingle, is, without doubt, the end of the earth. There I have seen the lung of the

sea, for across those vast sandy foreshores and wide, desolate
creeks, the sea moves in and out with a slow breathing rhythm.

Whatever region Pytheas was describing, there is no doubt
that he shared the attitude of all Mediterranean men to the
mysterious seas which lay beyond the Pillars of Hercules. To the
ancient Greek and Roman geographers the earth was surrounded
by "the river of Ocean" which marked the limit of the habitable
world. Homer has a powerful passage in which Odysseus describes
his visit to this region. Is it pure legend, or does it perhaps
embody the tale of some traveller who had ventured into the
North Sea?

> We had attained Earth's verge, and its girdling river of Ocean,
> where are the cloud-wracked and misty confines of Cimmerian
> men. There no flashing Sun-god shines down a living light, nor
> in the morning when he climbs through the starry sky, nor at the
> day's end, when he rolls down from heaven beyond the land.
> There an endless dreadful night is spread over its melancholy
> people.

Nevertheless Britain, or at least south-western Britain, was
certainly known to some ancient navigators. The Carthaginians
traded with the people of the *Cassiterides*—the "tin-islands", by
which Cornwall is probably meant. From about 500 B.C. these
merchant adventurers controlled the Straits of Gibraltar and
monopolized the profitable tin-trade; they were careful not to let
the Greeks know where the "tin-islands" were. Later, when
an alternative route was opened from the Greek colony of
Marseilles, overland via Carcassonne and Narbonne to the mouth
of the Loire, the Greeks did not realize that Cornwall was in
fact the ancient *Cassiterides*, which were thought by Pliny and
Diodorus to be off the coast of Spain. So vague was ancient geography, as far as the Atlantic coast was concerned. And this
vagueness continued right down to the Roman period; for, until
Agricola's fleet circumnavigated Britain in the first century A.D.,
the Romans were not even certain that Britain was an island.

CHAPTER TWO

EYES ACROSS THE CHANNEL

THE latest peoples to settle in Britain before the Romans came were Celtic tribes, some of whom had already begun to cross over from France and the Low Countries as early as 800 B.C. They were not, of course, a united people under a common leadership, but groups of independent tribes, loosely related ethnically, and speaking a language which, though it had a common root, must have had a wide variety of dialects. There were many such peoples, the names of which are given by Roman historians; names such as the Allobroges, the Cimbri, the Nervii, the Helvetii, the Belgae, and others; some, such as the Belgae, though they spoke a Celtic language, had their origins in the forests of Germany, and retained some German customs.

The Celts were already established north of the Alps by the ninth century B.C. and, as we have seen, traded fur and slaves for the products of the Greek world. By the fifth century they were spread over a vast region which included northern Italy, Switzerland, parts of Germany, Holland, Belgium and France. The Romans called this area Gaul, and its people the Gauls. It is sometimes imagined that Roman Gaul was roughly equivalent to modern France; in fact the Gaulish tribes covered a much larger area. It is also sometimes forgotten that, although the Romans eventually conquered Gaul, the Gauls attacked Rome first; in fact, just before 400 B.C., certain Celtic tribes, the Boii, Insubres, Cenomani and others came over the Brenner, entered Italy, defeated the Etruscans in the north and founded such cities as Milan and Bologna. In 390 B.C. they beat the Roman army and sacked Rome itself. This, of course, was centuries before Rome had developed into a powerful state.

If we try to discover what these Celts looked like we encounter a difficulty, because in physical type they varied a great deal. A common fallacy is that they were small and dark like some of the Welsh today. In fact many were large, fair, and powerfully built as we can see, for example, in the well-known statue of the "Dying Gaul". Many Scotsmen are descended from this stock, and in the tall, big-boned Highlander with his ruddy complexion and fair or reddish hair we see one type of enemy which the Legions had to face. In the small-framed, wiry Welshman with his dark hair and eyes, we see another. And in the Scottish clan system we may, perhaps, recognize the type of tribal organization which bound these people together and divided them. On one point the Roman historians are agreed; it was intertribal jealousy, often breaking into open war, which prevented the Gauls from presenting a united front against the Romans, and made their conquest easier.

Their settlements were primitive; clusters of timber buildings stood within a banked enclosure; the tribal leaders were slightly better-housed, and both they and their womenfolk were fond of magnificent personal adornment; gold and enamelled brooches for their cloaks, beautifully-fashioned and decorated swords and shields, bracelets and necklaces of pale Irish gold, chased and enamelled hand-mirrors. A Celtic nobleman in full regalia must have been a splendid sight.

Some of them, the Veneti, for example, who settled in Brittany, were skilful seamen, able to maul the Roman fleet; the same tribe built enormous multi-banked hill-forts of great size with complex barbican gates and cunningly-sited defences. It is possible though not proven, that they moved across to Britain in the first century B.C. and built similar fortresses in south-western England, e.g. at Maiden Castle, a monument as mighty in its way as the Egyptian Pyramids.

Like the Homeric warriors of *The Iliad*, the Celtic nobles fought from chariots, which they handled with miraculous dexterity.

"Their skill", wrote Julius Caesar, "may be judged by the fact that they can control their horses at full gallop on the steepest incline, check and turn them in a moment, run along the pole, stand on the yoke, and get back again into the chariot as quick as lightning."[1]

These and other passages from Caesar's "War Commentaries" show that the Gauls (and their British relatives) were not mere painted savages but skilful and experienced warriors.

Caesar also says of the Gauls:

[1] *Caesar's War Commentaries*, translated by John Warrington, Dent, 1953.

4. Walmer Beach, where Caesar is believed to have landed.

5. Bust of Julius Caesar.

6. Model of an Iron Age chariot.

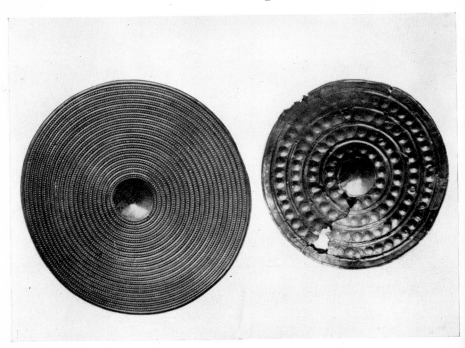

7. Round bronze shields used by Celtic warriors.

. . . not only every tribe, canton and subdivision of a canton, but almost every family, is divided into rival factions. At the head of these factions are men who are regarded by their followers as having particularly great prestige, and these have the final say on all questions that come up for judgement and in all discussions of policy.

He also has an interesting comment on their rulers, temporal and religious.

Everywhere in Gaul there are only two classes of men who are of any account or consideration. The common people are treated almost as slaves, never venture to act on their own initiative, and are not consulted on any subject. Most of them, crushed by debt or heavy taxation or the oppression of more powerful persons, bind themselves to serve men of rank, who exercise over them all the rights that masters have over slaves. The two privileged classes are the Druids and the Knights. The Druids officiate at the worship of the gods, regulate public and private sacrifices, and give rulings on all religious questions. . . . They act as judges in practically all disputes, whether between tribes or between individuals. . . . The Druids are exempt from military service and do not pay taxes like other citizens. . . . The Knights . . . when their services are required in some war that has broken out, all take the field, surrounded by their servants and retainers, of whom each Knight has a greater or smaller number according to his birth or fortune.

The Celts of Gaul had a more highly developed culture than the British Celts. The pattern of Gaulish society seems to have been a military aristocracy whose power was balanced by a privileged priestly class, who also had judical functions. Of the Druids it should be remembered that they had no connection with the much older religion of the New Stone Age peoples. To the Celtic invaders of the first century B.C. Stonehenge, Avebury and the other great religious temples were already nearly 2,000 years old; as ancient to the Celts as the Celts are to us. They may, however, have used them for their own ceremonies which, according to Caesar, sometimes involved human sacrifice.

"Some tribes have colossal images made of wickerwork", he writes, "the limbs of which they fill with living men. They are then set on fire, and the victims burnt to death. They think that

c

the gods prefer the execution of men taken in an act of theft or brigandage, or guilty of some offence; but when they run short of criminals, they do not hesitate to make up with innocent men."

The Romans were very shocked by such practices, and eventually abolished them, yet they themselves enjoyed the spectacle of men torn to pieces by wild beasts in their arenas.

We are now approaching the climactic point in our story; the moment when Rome, which had already subdued most of the known world, stretched out her hand to the British Isles. The date is 55 B.C. We have tried to look at the development of Britain during the 2,500 years preceding that moment. Let us now try to narrow our focus and look at Britain from two viewpoints; first, that of Rome, then that of the islanders.

When the first Celtic settlers were landing in Britain in about 750 B.C. Rome was an obscure city in middle Italy. The Etruscans, probably Oriental invaders, ruled most of the land; the Latins were a tribe of primitive farmers who had established themselves, with some difficulty, beside the Tiber. Round about 600 B.C. the farming communities established on the Quirinal, Esquiline and Palatine hills drained the low-lying land which later became the Forum, and founded the "city of the four regions", an act of union which marked the historic founding of Rome.

Kings ruled at first; the legendary Romulus, then Titus Tatius, Numa Pompilius, Tullius Hostilius and others. There were struggles with the Etruscans, who were the dominant power, but, bit by bit the Latin race won a local independence, and began to expand. They borrowed freely from the Etruscans, as from other peoples with which they came in contact. By 509 B.C., when she signed a treaty with Carthage, Rome was able to represent the coastal cities as well as herself. Greek influence, which reached Rome via the Greek settlements in Italy, was strong, as was that of Etruria, but the Romans remained a Latin community. They were farmer-soldiers, tough and self-reliant, organized in a society based primarily on the family (*gens*) under its head (*patronus*) and to which were attached retainers (*clientes*) who were morally bound to fulfil certain obligations.

It was a rudimentary social system, strong, unsophisticated, and puritanical, with an emphasis on hard work, duty and the honouring of the gods. Roman religion, which ranged from household to state gods, was highly ritualistic, a religion of sacrifice and expiation. Perhaps because the Imperial Age is so much better documented most of us tend to think of Rome only in its heyday of vulgar wealth and power. By contrast with Nero and Domitian the primitive forefathers of the Republic seem a dull lot, and none too clean at that. But they laid the foundations on which the Empire was built.

In the beginning they were probably not a particularly aggressive or warlike people, but they were surrounded by enemies; first the Etruscans, and when they became weakened by internal divisions, and ceased to be dominant, lesser Italian tribes such as the Samnites, Oscans, and others warred with the Latins. Stubbornly fighting for their independence, the Roman people extended their frontiers north, south and east. Adversity hardened them, but it did more than that. It brought out in them a capacity for political, social and military organization such as the world had not seen before. Gradually, over the centuries, the soldier-farmers from the Tiber brought the whole of Italy under their control. They threw back the invading Gauls from beyond the Alps. They came into conflict with the empire of Carthage and defeated it, annexing Sicily in the process.

During these struggles the Romans forged a military and political machine which was to bring the whole civilized world under its control. Beginning as a citizen army it became in time a purely professional force, superbly equipped, disciplined and led. It was no mere ravaging horde, but a constructive force, which included in its ranks engineers and craftsmen. It built roads and bridges; it cleared forests, drained swamps, dug canals, and, in time of peace, acted as a police force. But the Romans' greatest gift was for colonization; when they conquered new territory they exacted tribute, and were often guilty of exploitation. But they did not try to exterminate the population, which was encouraged to become part of the Roman system. In time some Spaniards, Gauls, Africans and Germans could attain high positions, becoming consuls, governors of provinces, and even Emperors. The great Hadrian himself was a Spaniard.

In ruling these newly-won territories the Romans developed their genius for administration; their generals had to be not only soldiers, but diplomats, statesmen and judges, able to administer a province. And they were not ashamed to learn from the people they ruled. Intervening in a war between the Ptolemies and the Seleucids they found themselves, eventually, in control of Greece, Egypt, Asia Minor and Syria-Palestine. From their old rulers, the Etruscans, they had learned engineering, town-planning and political organization. From the Greeks they took art and philosophy, from Egypt and the east certain religious practices, some of which corrupted rather than improved their own culture. But they made their own contribution to civiliza-tion, mainly in the fields of literature, portraiture, law, administra-tion and military science.

These well-known facts are worth repeating because when one narrows focus to a short moment of time—the invasion of Britain —the Romans appear unsympathetically as a great power ruth-lessly crushing the semi-barbaric tribes which resisted them. It is worth remembering that, when the first Celtic peoples began to cross to Britain in the eighth century, the Romans themselves were only an unimportant tribe settled near the Tiber. When, in 55 B.C., they looked across the Channel to the white cliffs of Kent, there lay behind them some 600 years during which they had struggled from obscurity to the status of a world power.

Western Europe was the last great region to come under their control. First they had thrown back the Gaulish tribes who swept into Italy in the fourth century. After 190 B.C. they advanced be-yond the Alps, and by 125 B.C. had made themselves masters of the lower Rhone and formed the province of Transalpine Gaul. Thus the area which is now Provence and the French Riviera was opened to Roman culture. All who have visited that delect-able part of France will have seen the numerous relics of Roman civilization; the amphitheatres at Nîmes and Arles, the theatre at Orange, and that enormous monument to Roman engineering, the Pont du Gard. Incidentally, one of the greatest Roman Governors of Britain, Gaius Julius Agricola, was born in one of these small Provençal towns, Forum Julii, nowadays known to thousands of holidaymakers as Fréjus.

The Romans had to fight many battles to make their hold secure. Only a few years after their conquest of Transalpine Gaul German tribes, the Teutoni and the Cimbri, crossed the Rhine and conquered most of central and northern Gaul. Three times, between 109 and 105 B.C. they destroyed Roman armies and even began to threaten Italy. Gaius Marius, the great reformer of the Roman army, brought the Teutoni to battle near Aix-en-Provence and routed them. Later, with Quintus Lutatius Catullus, Marius defeated the Cimbri in northern Italy. There was a breathing-space, but not for long. Thirty years later Gaulish tribes rebelled against the rapacity of Roman tax-gatherers, and fresh threats arose from Germany, where a powerful confederacy of tribes—the Suebi—began to move westwards. Western Europe, at this period, must have been a chaos of warring tribes, and though Roman power now extended from Spain to the eastern Mediterranean, there could be no security while northern and western Europe remained unconquered.

As at other crises in human history, the hour produced the man. In 59 B.C. the Roman Assembly passed a law giving command of Cisalpine Gaul (i.e. northern Italy between the Apennines and the Alps) to a Roman aristocrat, Gaius Julius Caesar. He was then about forty-two and had already proved himself as a soldier, statesman and administrator. Like other members of his class, he had passed through the usual stages of advancement; military tribune (aide-de-camp), during which he won distinction in Asia Minor; *questor* (financial officer) under the Governor of southern Spain; *aedile* (a civil post rather like that of Commissioner of Public Works); *praetor* (chief civil justice) until, in 61 B.C., he became Governor of southern Spain. He resigned this post, however, in order to take part in the political struggles which followed the return of Pompey the Great to Rome after his conquest of Syria. With Pompey, the soldier, and Crassus, the wealthy financier (though he also was a distinguished military leader), Caesar formed a triumvirate which exercised, at first secretly, a powerful influence on Roman politics.

Rome was, of course, still a republic, but the Senate was becoming increasingly inefficient in dealing with the vast administrative problems consequent upon the Roman conquests. The old republican system, which had served well enough when Rome was a small state, was proving inadequate to the new situation. Rome had grown from a city-state into an empire, but the Senate still tried to rule it as if it were a city-state. Simple city governors, equivalent to a modern provincial mayor, were sent out to rule provinces of the size of Spain. Many of them became corrupt, and farmed out their provinces to financiers. There was ruthless exploitation, vice and violence. In some ways the records of Roman provincial rule under the Republic—in Spain, for instance—remind one of the gangster rule in Chicago. The Republican period does not deserve the praise afforded to it by some former scholars.

Able and ambitious men such as Caesar, Pompey and Crassus realised the true situation and were determined to alter it; but their manœuvres were watched jealously by the Senate and Assembly. Caesar, however, had learned the lesson which has since been applied by other successful dictators; the art of appealing to the ruled over the heads of the rulers. During his term of office as *aedile* he had won great popularity with the Roman mob by his lavish patronage of public entertainments. This was bribery, but his capacity for inspiring the loyalty of his troops, which was to show itself during the eight years' campaign in Gaul, was due to sheer power of personality.

It is important to try to understand that personality because, apart from being one of the most extraordinary human beings who ever lived, it is through Caesar's eyes that we get our first clear picture of Britain and its inhabitants. For Caesar, besides being one of the greatest generals of all time, was also a vivid prose writer and, according to his contemporaries, an orator second only to Cicero. Unfortunately, like other great figures of the past, he has tended to stiffen into a stereotype. The severe, finely-modelled head of the well-known portrait bust gives us the man of power, but no hint of the charm he must have exercised.

Plutarch's study is unflattering: a man corrupted by power, degenerating by degrees into a tyrant and a monster. Suetonius, drawing on Imperial and Senatorial archives and contemporary memoirs, gives us some human details:

> Caesar is said to have been tall, fair, and well-built, with a rather broad face and keen, dark-brown eyes. . . . He was something of a dandy, always keeping his head carefully trimmed and shaved; and has been accused of having certain other hairy parts of his body depilated with tweezers. His baldness was a disfigurement which his enemies harped upon, much to his exasperation; but he

used to comb the thin strands of hair forward from his poll, and
of all the honours voted him by the Senate and people, none
pleased him so much as the privilege of wearing a laurel-wreath
on all occasions—he constantly took advantage of it.

He was also "a most skilful swordsman and horseman, and
showed surprising powers of endurance. He always led his army,
more often on foot than in the saddle, went bareheaded in sun
and rain alike, and could travel for long distances at incredible
speed in a gig, taking very little luggage. If he reached an unford-
able river, he would either swim or propel himself across it on an
inflated skin; and often arrived at his destination before the
messengers whom he had sent ahead to announce his
approach. . . . "

> It is a disputable point which was the more remarkable when
> he went to war; his caution or his daring. He never exposed
> his army to ambushes, but made careful reconnaissances; and
> refrained from crossing over into Britain until he had collected
> reliable information . . . about the harbours there, the best course
> to steer, and the navigational risks. On the other hand, when
> news reached him that his camp in Germany was being besieged,
> he disguised himself as a Gaul and picked his way through the
> enemy outposts to take command on the spot.[1]

"He judged his men", continues Suetonius, "by their fighting
record, not by their morals or social position, treating them all
with equal severity—and equal indulgence; since it was only in
the presence of the enemy that he insisted on strict discipline.
He never gave forewarning of a march or a battle, but kept his
troops always on the alert for sudden orders to go wherever he
directed. Often he made them turn out when there was no need
at all, especially in wet weather or on public holidays. Sometimes
he would say, 'Keep a close eye on me!' and then steal away from
camp at any hour of the day or night, expecting them to follow.
It was certain to be a particularly long march, and hard on
stragglers."

I make no apology for these lengthy quotations, because they
bring Caesar and the Roman army vividly before our eyes, and
prove that modern methods of military training, toughening

[1] Suetonius, *Lives of the Caesars*, translated by Robert Graves, Penguin Books,
1957.

courses and so on were all in use 2,000 years ago. Sometimes, when reading Suetonius or Caesar's own *War Commentaries*, one seems to be reading about Montgomery or Wingate. For instance: "When his troops were in a panic before the Battle of Thapus at the news of King Juba's approach, he called them together and announced:

> 'You may take it from me that the King will be here within a few days, at the head of ten infantry legions, thirty thousand cavalry, a hundred thousand lightly armed troops, and three hundred elephants. This being the case, you may as well stop asking questions and making guesses. I have given you the facts, with which I am familiar. Any of you who remain unsatisfied will find themselves aboard a leaky hulk and being carried across the sea wherever the winds may decide to blow them.'

But if he could be tough and severe, he could also be indulgent. He never addressed his troops as "My men", but as "Comrades", which pleased them; and if, after a particularly hard-won victory, he felt they deserved relaxation, he let them run as wild as they pleased, remarking to one of his critics, "My men fight just as well when they are stinking of perfume."

Regimental pride and "a smart turn-out" were also encouraged. "The silver and gold inlay of their weapons both improved their appearance and made them more careful not to get disarmed in battle. . . . By these means he won the devotion of his army, as well as making it extraordinarily gallant."

It is details such as this which help to explain the fact that, during the eight years when Caesar commanded in Gaul, years of "hard fighting, hard digging, and hard living", his soldiers "gave him everything he asked of them. There was never a sign of mutiny. At the start of the civil war, when he was without means to pay them, they did not hesitate to serve him without present payment; and many who were captured . . . preferred to die rather than take the chance of life that was offered them on conditions of fighting against their old commander."[1]

Caesar the general, Caesar the politician and diplomatist of later years have been the subject of many a learned exposition by scholars who ignore or suppress the less worthy but essentially human traits in his character.

[1] Handford, S. A., *The Conquest of Gaul*, Penguin Books, 1951.

"His affairs with women", writes Suetonius, "are commonly described as numerous and extravagant; among those of noble birth whom he is said to have seduced were Servius Sulpicius's wife, Postumia; Aulus Gabinius's wife, Lollia; Marcus Crassus's wife, Tertulla; and even Gnaeus Pompey's wife, Mucia. . . ." His love-affairs in the provinces were recalled in a ribald rhyme sung by his soldiers as they marched into Rome behind their leader's chariot.

Home we bring our bald whoremonger;
Romans, lock your wives away!
All the bags of gold you lent him
Went his Gallic tarts to pay.[1]

Such a reputation probably did as much to win the affection of Caesar's troops as his brilliant generalship and proven personal courage. (Incidentally, if Roman women are to be judged by their surviving portraits, one hardly blames Caesar for seeking diversion elsewhere.)

Shortly after appointing Caesar as Governor of Cisalpine Gaul, with three Legions (infantry brigades of 5,000 men each), the Assembly (Parliament) of Rome extended his power to include Transalpine Gaul (southern France as far as the Pyrenees) and added a fourth Legion to his command. Moreover, they confirmed him in his appointment for five years, which was unusual. He faced a situation of extreme challenge and danger. The Germanic tribes were pushing across the Rhine into the plain of Alsace and between the Vosges and Jura Mountains. The Celtic Helvetii were preparing to move from Switzerland into central Gaul. Caesar defeated them both, and, thus encouraged, began to extend the limits of his province towards the north-west. The Belgic tribes who had settled beside the Seine, Meuse, Aisne and Sambre and Somme—a region famous in more recent wars— became alarmed and prepared to resist the Roman onset.

In a series of brilliant campaigns Caesar overcame these tribes and occupied their territory. Reaching the lower Loire, he built a fleet and succeeded in defeating the redoubtable Veneti, some of whom may have fled to Britain and occupied the hills of Hampshire and Dorset. In 55 B.C. he occupied the area between the

[1] Suetonius, *The Twelve Caesars*, translated by Robert Graves, Penguin Books, 1957.

Scheldt and the Somme, and, turning swiftly eastward, annihilated a large force of Germans who had crossed the Rhine. He
bridged the river and laid waste a large area on the east bank, to
teach the Germans a lesson. Rome's conquest of Gaul must be
accepted—and respected.

Thus in 55 B.C., Julius Caesar, soldier-adventurer in the full
pride of life, hero of many campaigns, with a triumphant army at
his back, gazed across the Channel to the mysterious island to
which many of his beaten enemies had fled, and which few Romans
had ever seen. His triumph was far from complete, though he had
reported to the Senate that all Gaul was subjugated. But though
there were still to be years of fighting ahead, a succession of
revolts to be quelled, Caesar felt justified in pressing his attack still
further. He would invade Britain. He had military reasons, of
course; the Gauls had been helped by the Britons, and some had
taken refuge among them, but there must have been other, more
powerful motives; personal pride, the desire to add one more
victory to those already won, and, perhaps, simple curiosity.

What lay on the far side of that steel-grey sea, and the rim of
white cliffs which sometimes gleamed on the horizon? He resolved to see for himself.

Before we follow Caesar across to Kent, let us look at the
island and its inhabitants. In some ways we know more than
Caesar could have known, but the facts which archaeological
research have revealed are, in the main, generalized, and impersonal. Like the ring-markings of a sawn tree-trunk (though less
regular) they show us the successive waves of invaders, Meso-
lithic, Neolithic, Bronze Age, Iron Age, who left their impression
on the island. Of these the Romans knew nothing, though they
may have wondered at such monuments as Stonehenge, Avebury,
and the great megaliths of Cornwall, raised some eighteen centuries before they arrived.

Most of the people with whom Caesar came into contact were
newcomers, kinsmen of the same Gaulish tribes whom he had
conquered in France and the Low Countries. For instance, in the
late second century B.C. tribes from Brittany settled in Cornwall,
building cliff-castles, huge stone, many-ramparted fortresses, and
villages of stone huts grouped around a courtyard. Later they

moved on to the Cotswolds, and may have exploited the iron of the Forest of Dean.

As the Romans moved into Gaul, streams of refugees crossed into Britain; the seafaring Veneti of southern Brittany may have been among them. The Veneti were notable shipbuilders. Caesar tells us that their ships were built of oak planks a foot thick, held together with iron bolts, with hulls so high out of the water that his galleys could not board them. These people were also redoubtable slingers, and it has been suggested that the multi-banked fortresses of Wessex and Dorset were built by the earlier inhabitants to protect themselves against the new form of warfare. From the existence of similar fortifications in Brittany, however, it would seem that the Veneti themselves made them.

Other immigrants built artificial islands in marshes, such as, for instance, the famous "lake-villages" at Glastonbury in Somerset. Some got as far north as Scotland; at Caithness one can still find examples of their dwellings; in the Orkneys they built stone "wheel-houses", and combined cattle-rearing with a little profitable piracy.

The tribes who gave most trouble to the invaders were the Belgae, people of Germanic origin who had settled in what are now Belgium and northern France, north of the Ardennes. They crossed over to Britain in large numbers and established themselves, not on the hills, as had their predecessors, but in the lower land, such as the Thames Valley and those of its tributaries.[1] They were numerous in Kent, Essex and Hertfordshire, and brought with them the new wheeled plough, which had a coulter and a mould-board and was drawn by teams of oxen. This implement enabled them to cultivate the heavier valley soils, which their predecessors had to leave untouched. They also used iron spades and axes.

Another powerful tribe whom Caesar had fought in Gaul were the Atrebates, who emigrated from the district around Arras. They settled in Berkshire and other areas south of the Thames. But the tribe which formed the main opposition to Caesar's landing were the Catuvellauni under their King Cassivelaunus, who

[1] Though they did occupy hill-fortresses on border-lands to protect themselves against the earlier settlers.

ruled from Wheathampstead over a large area which now comprises Hertfordshire and Essex.

It is important to remember that these newly-arrived immigrants had already had trade and cultural relations with Rome and the Mediterranean world.

Exports from Britain which reached the Roman world included wheat, hunting-dogs, and a species of freshwater pearl of which Caesar was particularly fond. In fact, the Roman satirists suggested that one of his reasons for invading Britain was to obtain such pearls for his mistresses.

Suetonius says:

> Fresh-water pearls seem to have been the lure that prompted his invasion of Britain; he would weigh them in the palm of his hand to judge their value. . . .

These pearls are still sometimes found in a large species of mussel. A few years ago one was found in—of all places—the Leg of Mutton Pond on Hampstead Heath, London.

How are we to imagine the appearance of Britain when Caesar landed? In the Home Counties we should hardly recognize the land we know. First, there were no roads—only prehistoric trackways which usually followed the ridges, avoiding the forests and marshes of the valleys. Such was the Icknield Way, which can still be traced in parts of the Chilterns, reaching the Thames Valley near Wallingford. The second difference we should notice was the presence of large forests where now there are fields. Much lowland which is now dry would be marshy, and there would be no towns or villages which we would recognize as such. But the population was increasing, and land-hunger forced some of the tribes to attack the forests and till the heavy soil of the valleys, e.g. of the Thames, Lea and Colne. But most of the country would have a wild, shaggy, uncared-for appearance; and wild life was abundant.

Occasionally, on some high ridgeway above the wooded valleys, we might meet a cavalcade of horsemen and charioteers; some Belgic nobleman and his entourage, the leaders magnificently equipped with shields, swords, and daggers of enamelled and inlaid bronze, wearing splendid golden ornaments, and with their famous hunting-dogs at their heels. Yet these splendidly-equipped warrior-leaders lived in settlements of extreme squalor. The lesser men would be dressed in skins or coarse woven cloths, but they would know that the Romans were on the coast of Gaul, and may have had wind of the impending attack, for refugees from across the Channel were constantly arriving.

Further west, on the chalk hills of Sussex, Hampshire and Dorset, we find a landscape little different from that we see today; except that the uplands would be well-populated, and there would be banked enclosures and small farms where now there is only smooth turf. Still further west, Dartmoor and Exmoor probably looked very much the same, save for the lack of roads. Northwards, on the midland plain and in the folds of the Pennines, we would probably encounter, mixed with the newly arrived Celts, elements of the older, darker, Mediterranean people, some of whom would still be using stone tools, as their ancestors had done.

In a few areas there were important local industries; deep in the Forest of Dean the iron-smelters worked; in Somerset were lead-mines, and in Cornwall tin. Far away to the north, beyond the Solway and Tyne, were people of an older stock, to whom the blond Belgae were foreigners, and who knew little and cared nothing about the lands which lay to the south.

Two important elements were the same then as now; our grey northern sea, and our grey northern weather. "The climate", wrote Tacitus, "is objectionable, with frequent rains and mists. . . . Crops are slow to ripen, but quick to grow—both facts due to one and the same cause, the extreme moistness of the land and sky."

CHAPTER THREE

RECONNAISSANCE IN FORCE

W HEN future historians come to write the history of the
Second World War they will be overwhelmed by the
weight of material; billions of words, in war corres-
pondents' despatches, in memoirs, novels, sound-recordings,
films. Yet if every record perished save the *Memoirs* of Sir Winston
Churchill, our historian would still be able to follow the high
strategy of the war, nor would some of the human detail be
lacking. This, more or less, is the situation we encounter when
studying Caesar's invasions of Britain in 55 and 54 B.C. If any of
Caesar's companions kept a record, it has been lost. All that
survives is the section of Caesar's *War Commentaries* in which the
Commander-in-Chief set down his experiences in terse, soldierly
prose.

Since Caesar's account exists in several excellent translations,
it would be pointless to try to paraphrase them. Much of this
chapter, therefore, will consist of verbatim extracts in which the
great commander will speak for himself. The translation I have
chosen is that by Mr. John Warrington,[1] who has rendered it into
modern, idiomatic English which retains the lucidity of the Latin
original. He also abandons the convention under which Caesar
wrote in the third person, and allows the writer to speak directly
to the reader. He also gives units of money, weights and measure
their modern English equivalents, and where modern place-
names can be identified with their Latin origins he gives them; for
instance, *Avaricum* was Bourges, and the phrase *in finibus Haeduo-
rum* (in the territory of the Aedui) meant the district now called
Burgundy.

Before launching his first attack, Caesar took two precautions.
He sent an agent, a former Atrebatian ruler named Commius, to
make contact with the Atrebates who had settled in Britain, and
he sent one Caius Volusenus in a warship to reconnoitre the British

[1] Warrington, John, *Caesar's War Commentaries*. J. M. Dent, 1953.

46

coast and report. Meanwhile, he ordered the whole army into the district now called Artois, where the mainland is nearest the British coast, and concentrated in the same place all the ships he could lay hands on, including those which he had had built for the war against the Veneti. These ships would be of two main types, transports and war-vessels. It is difficult to imagine what they were like, because the few representations of Roman vessels which have come down to us were carved by sculptors who were not naval experts, and in any case belong to a period somewhat later than Caesar's. Some of his ships, which were built on the Gaulish coast for operations against the Veneti, were probably of somewhat stouter build than that of the typical Mediterannean war-galley. Caesar has an interesting passage in Book III describing the ships used by the Veneti of south Brittany:

> These vessels were relatively flat-bottomed, and could therefore ride the shallows or on an ebb-tide. With their unusually tall prows and sterns they could weather high seas in a gale of wind; and the hulls, made entirely of oak, were capable of standing up to any amount of rough handling. The cross-timbers consisted of beams a foot thick, fastened with iron-bolts as thick as a man's thumb, and iron chains instead of ropes were used to secure the anchors.
>
> Their sails were made of war hides or thinly-dressed leather, . . . probably due to a mistaken belief that canvas was unequal to the violence of Atlantic gales and unsuitable for manœuvering vessels of their burden. In an encounter with these ships our sole advantage was speed derived from the use of oars. . . . Their bulk rendered them safe against ramming, while their height placed them virtually beyond reach of our missiles and grappling-irons. Besides, when it began to blow hard and they were running before the wind, they were not only more seaworthy, but could heave-to in shallow water without fear of damage from reefs and jagged rocks; whereas all these factors constituted a serious danger to our shipping.

We can deduce from this passage (a) that the Roman ships had a deeper draught than those of their opponents; (b) that Roman hulls did not stand so high out of the water; (c) that they were less substantially built, and less seaworthy in northern waters, and (d) that they used oars (as Mediterranean shipping had done for centuries), whereas the Veneti vessels did not. This fact had an important bearing on the success of the first British landing, when the sound of the oars and the unfamiliar shape of the warships alarmed the Britons.

Incidentally, this reliance of the Gaulish seamen on their sails proved a disadvantage, for, as Caesar says, "our men had prepared one device that proved most useful—sharp-pointed hooks fixed into the ends of long poles, not unlike siege-hooks in appearance. These instruments gripped the halyards, which were drawn taut and then snapped by rowing hard ahead. As soon as the halyards were cut, the yard-arms naturally collapsed; and since the Gallic ships relied exclusively upon their rigging, they came to an immediate standstill when this was done."

The Romans, rarely innovators, were great adapters. In the Mediterranean, when forced to take to the sea, they copied Greek and Carthaginian vessels. I think it is reasonable to assume, therefore, that when they reached the Channel coast they adapted their naval warfare to the conditions prevailing in northern waters.

Volusenus returned five days later and made his report. He had not landed, but made a careful survey of harbours and landing-places. Caesar says, "a fleet of about eighty ships, which seemed adequate for the conveyance of two legions" (about 10,000 men) "were eventually commissioned and assembled, together with a number of warships commanded by the chiefs of staff, officers of general rank, and auxiliary commanders. At another port, some eight miles higher up the coast, were eighteen transports which had been prevented by adverse winds from joining the main fleet at *Portus Itius* (probably Boulogne); these were allotted to the cavalry. . . ."

The "warships" were presumably manned by marines, capable of fighting on sea or land, and probably equipped with *ballistae* and *catapultae*, powerful spring-guns worked by twisted cords, like the medieval cross-bow. The transports were purely troop-carriers, and would include numbers of captured Gaulish vessels, just as, when Hitler planned the invasion of Britain, he commandeered hundreds of barges. Did the presence of warships mean that Caesar anticipated naval resistance? It has always seemed strange to me that the Roman landing seems to have been

8. Model of a Roman legionary soldier, showing *pilum* (throwing spear), *gladius* (short sword), shield and body armour, in the Grosvenor Museum, Chester.

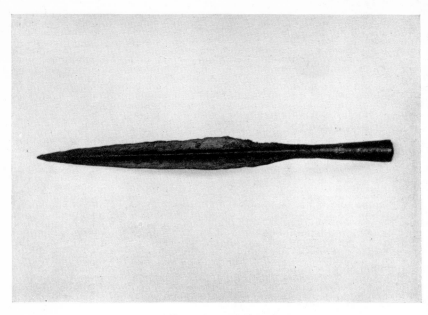

9. Roman spear-head.

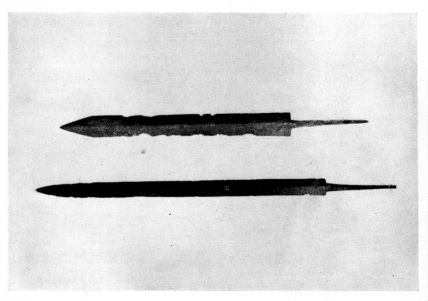

10. Two Roman short swords.

unopposed at sea, if many of the seafaring Veneti had fled to Britain and were established on the coast of Hampshire and Dorset. Perhaps they were too disorganized after the Roman victory; or, more likely, the Veneti, not being directly affected, made no attempt to help the Belgic tribes of the south-east, who were not seamen.

At any rate, when, at about 9 a.m., Caesar's eighty ships appeared off the cliffs of Dover, there were no enemy ships to intercept them. The tribesmen assembled on the cliff tops and eventually joined issue with the Romans on the beaches, in the action described at the beginning of this chapter.

When the Britons had been driven back, the Romans dug in and established their camp. Soon afterwards a delegation arrived from the Britons, led by Caesar's agent, Commius of the Atrebates. Commius had had a bad time; the Britons, refusing to accept him as a Roman ambassador, had thrown him into prison. They delivered up the Atrebatian chief unharmed, apologizing for their conduct, which they tried to excuse by blaming it on "the common people . . . they asked me to excuse this unprovoked attack on the grounds of their ignorance".

This is Caesar's account. One wonders how much truth there is in it. From Commius's conduct later, when he defied the Romans and, when captured, asked as a final privilege that "he should never again be asked to look on a Roman face", one strongly suspects that he had waited on the turn of events. If the Romans had been less successful, he might have appeared at their camp, not as a suppliant, but an enemy.

Four days after the landing the eighteen transports, carrying cavalry, arrived off the coast, but were driven back by contrary winds. A storm arose. There was a full moon and the tides were particularly high:

> The result was that the warships, which had been beached, became waterlogged; as for the transports riding at anchor, they were dashed one against another, and it was impossible to manœuvre them or to do anything whatever to assist. Several ships broke up, and the remainder lost their cables, anchors and rigging.

This misfortune gave the Britons fresh heart. Realizing that, if the Romans' ships were destroyed, they could not return, and

D

had insufficient food to maintain themselves in Britain, they rallied and attacked one of Caesar's Legions, the 7th, when it was reaping corn at some distance from the camp.

"Suddenly", writes Caesar, "the sentries on the gates reported an unusually large cloud [of dust?] in the direction in which the legion had gone. My suspicions were confirmed—the natives had hatched a new plot. . . . The battalions on guard duty were detailed to go with me to the scene of action, two others were ordered to relieve them and the rest to arm and follow on immediately. We had not been marching long before I noticed the 7th was in difficulties; they were only just managing to hold their ground with their units closely packed and under heavy fire."

Somewhere in the Kentish fields—we shall never know where—the man who was to become master of the Roman world spurred his horse, broke into the ranks of the attacking Britons, and routed them. The men of the 7th must have been greatly relieved to see their commander. What he said to them afterwards, whether of praise or blame, is not recorded. All we know is that, after several days of appalling weather, during which the Britons attacked the Roman camp, but were driven off, Caesar decided it was time to withdraw. Winter was approaching, and the campaigning season was over:

> Envoys came to sue for peace; they were met with a demand for twice as many hostages as before, and were ordered to bring them over to the Continent, because the equinox was close at hand and the ill condition of our ships made it inadvisable to postpone the voyage until winter. Taking advantage of fair weather, we set sail a little after midnight, and the whole fleet reached the mainland in safety.

Although his memoirs do not reveal it, Caesar must have felt extremely chagrined when he returned to Gaul in the autumn of 55 B.C. He had landed in Britain, but that was about all. No excuses concerning the late arrival of the cavalry, bad weather, and the lateness of the season could disguise the fact that he had failed. After his victories over the powerful tribes of Gaul, the inconclusive skirmishes with the Belgic tribes of south-eastern Britain would have seemed petty. His enemies in Rome, of whom there were many, must have been well aware of his discomfiture; his own troops, who, as he himself admitted, had no use for a failure, must also have looked to him to restore their shaken morale. But his main motive must, surely, have been personal. Total conquest could hardly have been in his mind, for Britain was an unimportant island off the coast of Gaul; and Gaul was still unsubdued, though occupied. Also, Britain was a thoroughly unattractive place, wet, misty, and dull, the home of barbarians distasteful to a civilized, Mediterranean man. Yet there it was—a challenge. Perhaps, if Caesar had been asked why he wished to return to Britain, he might have replied in the words of the explorer who was asked why he had to climb Everest: "Because it is there."

He returned to Italy—naturally—for the winter, but before leaving gave instructions that as many ships as possible be built for the next season's campaigns, and the old ones repaired. He had learned much about shipbuilding from his experiences.

"Detailed instructions were left for the dimensions and shape of these new vessels", he wrote. "To simplify loading and beaching, they were to be constructed with a somewhat lower freeboard than that commonly used in the Mediterranean, especially as I had noticed that, owing to the frequent ebb and flow of tides, the waves in the Channel are comparatively small. To allow for heavy cargoes, including numerous pack-animals, they were to be rather wider than those used in other waters; and all were to be fitted with sails as well as oars, an arrangement which was greatly facilitated by their low freeboard."

When Caesar returned to Gaul in the following year he found that the troops had worked so hard that about 600 ships of the new type had been built, including twenty-eight transports. He congratulated the officers and men responsible, and ordered the fleet to assemble at Portus Itius (Boulogne), from which the previous invasion had been launched. Meanwhile, he set out with four legions and 800 cavalry to the country of the Terveri, a territory bordering on the Rhine, where there were signs of trouble. Two rival leaders, Indutiomarus and Cingetorix, were intriguing for power. Caesar, after encouraging the pro-Roman Cingetorix and taking hostages from his anti-Roman rival, returned to the coast, where the fleet was now ready for departure. But once again he delayed this time to deal with another Gaulish king of doubtful allegiance, one Dumnorix the Aeduan (i.e. from

Burgundy). Caesar wished to keep Dumnorix with him, knowing him to be "a political intriguer, ambitious, bold and very influential with the Gauls".

Realizing that Caesar was determined to take him to Britain, the Gaul protested that he was unused to sailing and feared the sea; also that he had religious duties which must keep him at home. Finding the Roman still inflexibly determined, Dumnorix waited for the moment Caesar was ready to embark, then fled from the camp with a few horsemen and made for home. Once again Caesar postponed his departure, and sent a strong force of cavalry with orders to bring back Dumnorix alive, if possible; but if he resisted, to kill him. The Gaul did resist, and was killed. Caesar then sailed.

His caution in this matter was typical as his daring at other times; both were part of his greatness. A lesser man, faced with an impatient fleet and army, and lured by the prospect of conquest, would have ignored these threats in his rear. But not Caesar. Britain might be a tempting prize, but it was not worth the risk of another Gaulish rising.

Shortly before sunset on July 6th, 54 B.C., he again sailed out of Boulogne Harbour, this time in command of 800 ships, ten times the number which took part in the operation of the previous year. He took with him five legions and 2,000 cavalry. The nominal strength of a legion was 6,000 men, but was usually less. But even assuming that each legion numbered not more than 4,500 Caesar's total force, with the cavalry and seamen, horses and pack-animals was a mighty one. Probably not less than 30,000 human souls were afloat on the Channel during that short summer night. At first there was a light south-westerly breeze, but at midnight it ceased, and the tide took the invaders well off their course. When dawn broke the distant coast of Britain was receding on the port quarter. Caesar waited for the tide to turn, and then gave orders to row towards the distant shore.

One can imagine the shouted words of command sounding across the heaving water, as the 800 ships, war-vessels and transports loaded to the gunwales with men, equipment and animals, slowly turned; then came the slow, rhythmic threshing of thousands of oars and the staccato grunts of the sweating oarsmen, keeping time with their strokes.

To many of the ardent young officers who crowded the decks it must have been the supreme experience of their lives; most would be literate, yet not one has left us any written record of the event. Only the words of the Commander-in-Chief have survived to tell the story:

> The soldiers worked splendidly and by continuous rowing they enabled the heavily-laden transports to keep up with the war-ships. The whole fleet reached Britain about noon, but the enemy was nowhere to be seen. We therefore disembarked and chose a site for the camp.

He does not tell us where, although the landing-place was probably made between Sandown Castle and Sandwich. While the camp was being made, scouts went out and brought in a few prisoners, who told the Romans that "a large native force had originally concentrated on the beaches, but had withdrawn and hidden themselves . . . when they saw the numbers of our fleet". This hiding place is believed to have been at Bigbury Woods.

Just after midnight, leaving ten battalions and 300 cavalry to guard the fleet, under Quintus Atrius, the main force began to move inland, and after twelve miles made contact with the Britons near the Great Stour, not far from what is now Canterbury. "They came down", writes Caesar "with cavalry and war-chariots and, by attacking from higher ground, tried to bar our passage of the river. Repulsed by our cavalry, they retired on the woods, where they had a strongly fortified position of great natural strength."[1]

The rest of Caesar's regrettably brief account is concerned first with the misfortune which struck his fleet, when a heavy storm rose and severely damaged it, and his brief encounter with the Catuvellauni tribe, under their leader, Cassivelaunus. One longs to know what Cassivelaunus was like. Caesar tells us nothing about him, save that his territory was seventy-five miles from the sea, north of the Thames, and that "until then he had been almost continually at war with the other tribes, but owing to the general alarm inspired by our arrival they had unanimously agreed to confer upon him the supreme command".

[1] These earthworks can still be seen, about one and a half miles west of Canterbury.

Even more than a description by Caesar one would like to have an account of the invasion by Cassivelaunus himself. For, reading between the Roman leader's carefully composed lines, it becomes clear that the British chieftain was a skilful and far-seeing general, who exploited the Romans' weaknesses to the full, and made adroit use of the superior mobility of his own forces.

This is what appears to have happened. The 7th Legion attacked and took the Briton's fortified camp above the Great Stour, a job to which they were well suited, having taken many such strong-points in Gaul. The method used was to pile up lumber against the fortifications, working under cover of their interlocked shields (the famous Roman *testudo*—"tortoise"), and then storm the position, driving the defenders from the woods with the loss of a few men. Caesar called off the pursuit, as the ground was unfamiliar, and he wished to use the remaining hours to complete the entrenchment of his base camp.

Next day, infantry were sent to overtake the fugitives and had actually succeeded in making contact when grave news reached them. During a heavy storm overnight nearly all the war-vessels had either been wrecked or driven ashore: "The anchors and cables had parted, seamen and pilots had been helpless, and heavy damage had been suffered as a result of collision." Not for the first or last time Britain's weather had come to the aid of its defenders.

Forty ships had been completely destroyed, and others badly damaged. Caesar called out skilled workmen from the legions, and sent for others from Gaul. A messenger was sent to Labienus, who had been left at Boulogne, to build as many new ships as he could with the forces at his disposal.

Meanwhile, at terrible cost in labour, the ships were hauled ashore, beached, and surrounded by a line of fortifications. The work was done in ten days, with men working night and day.

Caesar returned inland, and for the first time encountered Cassivelaunus. Somewhere, we cannot be sure where, the Romans were met by a large British force which engaged them in a fierce running fight, in which charioteers and light horsemen continually harried the slow-moving Romans, skirmished, disappeared into the woods, and returned again. When the legions tried to dig in, the Britons returned and caught them off their guard:

They rushed unexpectedly from the woods, attacked the out-posts which were stationed in front of the camp, and some heavy fighting ensued . . . the troops were unnerved by these strange tactics, and the enemy with amazing dash broke through the gap and retreated to safety. . . . Throughout this peculiar engagement, which took place in full view of the camp, it was evident that our troops were too heavily armed; they could not follow up when their opponents gave ground, and they dared not abandon their regular formation.

This was a form of guerrilla warfare, which reminds one of Lawrence's lightning camel-raids on the Turkish columns and bases during the First World War. Behind it all we can detect the keen eyes of Cassivelaunus watching from the woods and high places as the heavy Roman columns marched on over the hills of Kent and down into the marshy valley of the Thames, where London now stands. He must have known that he could not hope to defeat Caesar in a pitched battle on chosen ground, so, probably sending home his foot-soldiers, he contented him-self with harrying their advance with his swift chariots and cavalry, cutting off their advance parties, disturbing them when they tried to pitch camp, never giving them rest.

Caesar has left a vivid account of the British charioteers' tactics:

They began by driving all over the field, hurling javelins; and the terror inspired by the horses and the noise of the wheels is usually enough to throw the enemy ranks into disorder. Then they work their way between their own cavalry units, where the warriors jump down and fight on foot. Meanwhile, the drivers retire a short distance from the fighting and station the cars in such a way that their masters, if outnumbered, have an easy means of retreat to their own lines. In action, therefore, they combine the mobility of cavalry with the staying power of foot-soldiers.

The areas in which they could use such tactics must, however, have been in fairly open ground. Cassivelaunus's chief hope was to destroy Caesar's base camp and cut him off from his fleet and sources of supply. What Caesar's feelings were at this moment we can only imagine. If he had ever hoped to subjugate and occupy the island he must now have abandoned the idea. The damage to his fleet must have been a severe blow, and on the far

side of the Channel Gaul seethed with rebellion. All he could
hope to do in the meantime was to make a demonstration of
Roman power, secure the submission of the tribes which had
opposed him, and return. So he led his armies towards the
Catuvellaunian stronghold. Its location, and the route thereto, he
learned from the Trinovantes, with whom Cassivelaunus had
been at war.

One Trinovantian prince named Mandubracius had travelled
to Gaul and put himself under Caesar's protection, because
(according to Caesar's account) Cassivelaunus had assassinated
the young man's father. I think we should regard such stories
with reservation; they sound suspiciously like the excuses which
later conquerors have used to justify aggression. However, it
seems certain that, on arrival in Britain, the Romans made contact with the Trinovantes, who were left unharmed. Noting this,
five other tribes from southern and eastern Britain sent delega-
tions to Caesar's camp and submitted. "They told me", he writes,
"we were not far from Cassivelaunus's stronghold, which was
strategically placed among woods and marshland, and that large
numbers of men and cattle were gathered there."

Factories, tarmac roads, railway yards, and a million smoking
chimneys now cover the sweep of land down which Caesar and
his army marched to the Thames. Even the place where he
crossed is unknown.

"The river can be forded only at one point", he writes, "and
even there the crossing was difficult. Large native forces appeared
in battle order on the far bank, which was also defended by a line
of pointed stakes; and some deserters in our custody revealed
that more of these obstacles were planted underwater in the river-
bed. The cavalry were sent over first, the infantry being ordered
to follow soon afterwards; but the legionaries dashed through
with such speed (though only their heads were above water)
that they were over as soon as the mounted troops. The Britons,
overpowered by this combined attack, fled from the bank."

Several places have been suggested as the point where the
legions crossed. It may have been near Westminster Bridge or
Chelsea; current archaeological opinion favours Brentford, where
Roman and British objects have been found. As a North Lon-
doner, I would like to think that Caesar forded the Thames at

Westminster, and then crossed my own Hampstead Heath to reach Edgware, Elstree, St. Albans and Wheathampstead. This was the line of the later Roman Watling Street. On the other hand, if he did cross at Brentford he probably followed the Colne Valley, past what are now Denham, Rickmansworth, Watford, and so to St. Albans. By whichever route, he eventually came to the Catuvellaunian stronghold, which he describes as having "superb natural defences, which had been improved by strong fortifications". The legions attacked from two sides, and after a brief resistance the enemy retired, escaping via the other side of the fortress. The Romans took plenty of cattle, but few men.

We cannot be sure where this place was, but, in 1937, Sir Mortimer Wheeler excavated remains of a hill-fort near the village of Wheathampstead in Hertfordshire. He found a ditch, 100 feet wide and 30 feet deep, which had surrounded a 100-acre enclosure, within which was a substantial amount of Belgic pottery *without any Roman admixture*. Now, at nearby Verulamium, which later became the Belgic capital, Roman influence begins round about 20 B.C. Wheathampstead seems to have been abandoned earlier than this date, and may be the Catuvellaunian stronghold which Caesar attacked. It fits his description, and no other Hertfordshire hill-fort has yielded such a large amount of pre-Roman Belgic pottery.

On the other hand, there are over a score of Belgic hill-forts in the area which have either not been dug at all, or only "scratched"; for instance, there is one at Ravensbrough, near Hexton, another at Sharpenhoe, a third at Walbury Dells, near Bishop's Stortford, and others. All are built along the northern escarpment, where the ground suddenly changes from Home Counties chalk to Midland clay, looking north towards what was then still unconquered territory.

Meanwhile, unless a more likely site turns up, Wheathampstead will continue to do duty for the camp of Cassivelaunus, and appears as such in current textbooks.

The capture of Wheathampstead was virtually the end of Caesar's expedition. He re-crossed the Thames, marched back to the coast and found that, in his absence, certain Kentish tribes had made a heavy attack on the camp, but were defeated, leaving many dead and several prisoners, including a chieftain, one

Lugotrix. Hearing of the failure of this enterprise, which he probably instigated, Cassivelaunus came to terms with Caesar:

> Acting through Commius, he sent a delegation to discuss terms of surrender. . . . I demanded hostages, fixed the annual tribute payable by Britain into the Roman treasury, and strictly forbade Cassivelaunus to interfere with Mandubracius and the Trinovantes. After receiving these hostages, we returned to the coast.

The newly-built ships which Labienus had been ordered to build were delayed by bad weather. Only a few reached Britain. It was now September, and the equinox was approaching. Caesar decided to delay no longer, but put to sea with his damaged, overloaded fleet on a calm, moonlit night:

> We weighed anchor at 9 p.m. and the whole fleet reached land safely at dawn.

That was the last which Caesar has to tell us about Britain and the last which Britain was to see of the Romans for nearly 100 years. Cassivelaunus, chief of a minor Celtic tribe, lived on in his forest stronghold, sired sons, and resumed his war with the Trinovantes. Caesar, the world-shaker, pursued the path of power, through Gaul, the civil war, the defeat of Pompey, the bed of Cleopatra, the victory over Labienus at Munda; until in 44 B.C. the daggers of Brutus and his fellow-conspirators ended the life of one who had "held the world in awe".

In Britain he left a fading memory, and the decaying ramparts of his base camp near Worth. In time they, too, disappeared. Today, children play on the shingle where his galleys grounded, their cries mingling with the gulls' scream and the timeless thunder of the surf.

CHAPTER FOUR

THE ROMAN ARMY

NINETY-SEVEN years passed before the Romans again set foot in Britain—years of revolutionary change, both in Rome and Britain. In Rome the power-struggles between rival generals, such as Caesar and Pompey, eventually destroyed the old Roman Republic, replacing it by the personal rule of the Emperors. When Caesar raided the island its population consisted mainly of Iron Age Britons with a relatively small number of Belgae concentrated mainly in Hertfordshire and along the Kent coast. By A.D. 43, when the Romans returned, the Belgae had established an empire with a ruling aristocracy which had extended its power over the whole of south-east England, and had penetrated westward, probably as far as the Bristol Channel, and northward as far as the Wash. After Caesar's raid, although the conqueror had penetrated only a short distance into Britain, the Romans regarded their conquest as in being. Commius, who had been the enemy of Rome, became her ally—a clever piece of diplomacy on the part of Augustus, Caesar's successor, who thus made use of the party opposed to Cassivelaunus. For a time the Britons paid tribute to Rome, but later discontinued it.

Caesar's brief visit, though relatively unimportant in the history of Britain, does at least provide us with a vivid first-hand account of how such an operation was mounted, which is why I have quoted from it at some length. When we come to study the Great Invasion—and the occupation of Britain by the Romans—written records are sparse and unsatisfactory, depending mainly on two sources: Tacitus, who had first-hand information through his father-in-law, Agricola; and Cassius Dio, a Greek historian who was born more than a century after the second Roman invasion.

There are yawning gaps in this story, which archaeologists and epigraphists have tried to fill, the first from a detailed examination of Roman sites in Britain, the second from surviving inscriptions. But the gaps are still there, and will be respected by the present writer.

However, before we try to piece together the scanty evidence relating to the Claudian invasion of A.D. 43, it may be worth while to summarize such information as we have concerning the Roman Army. Here again we encounter difficulties, since, apart from the records of campaigns, e.g. in Arrian and Josephus, much of our knowledge of Roman military organization is derived from much later sources, from Ammianus Marcellinus (c. 330-400), who wrote when the Roman Empire was in decline, and from Vegetius (A.D. 383-450), who was even later. He wrote a manual of military tactics, *de re militari*, which was a compilation of the works of earlier writers. It is important to understand that both these authors lived some *three hundred years* after the events which this book seeks to describe. Imagine a contemporary historian writing a learned treatise on the tactics of Cromwell. That is how Vegetius and Ammianus stand in relation to the armies which Aulus Plautius led into Britain.

However, there is an important difference. Admittedly Ammianus and Vegetius wrote during the sunset of Roman power, but, in its tactical formations, weapons, equipment, and organization, the Roman Army of A.D. 350 was much nearer to the Roman Army of A.D. 43 than, say, the 1st Paratroop Brigade is to Cromwell's Ironsides. In addition, both writers, and especially Vegetius, were drawing heavily on earlier authorities, whose works have since vanished. Both were soldiers, which is an advantage from our point of view. In an age when Roman power was disintegrating under the impact of barbarian invaders, they tried to revive it by recalling the organization, strategy, tactics and equipment of those earlier armies which had won for Rome the mastery of the world.

In addition to these sources, which were available to eighteenth- and nineteenth-century writers, we can draw upon the researches of archaeologists who have dug and examined sites all over Europe, interpreting them in the light of current knowledge. There are hundreds of Roman military camps which have revealed the type of weapons and equipment the Roman Army used. There are sculptures, and numerous inscriptions through which we can trace the careers of Roman officers. There are the military diplomas, which were awarded to Roman soldiers when they had completed their term of service, and which awarded them Roman citizenship. Perhaps the most fascinating of all are the Roman military documents, including lists of recruits, medical reports, duty rosters and even soldiers' letters home which turned up at Oxyrhyncus in Egypt. All these provide valuable evidence, but one must be on one's guard. Scholars such as Mr. Eric Birley, who have devoted a lifetime to the subject, do not necessarily accept the confident assumptions which one finds in some textbooks. The statements made in this chapter must, therefore, be regarded as tentative, and subject to modification. They are based mainly on the information and advice of Mr. Birley himself, Professor Graham Webster, Dr. John Morris of University College, London, and Mr. G. R. Watson, Lecturer of Classics at the University of Nottingham. The conclusions are my own, and not necessarily those of any of these gentlemen.[1] I have also quoted some interesting facts given by the late Mr. Jack Lindsay in his book, *The Romans were Here*.

The backbone of the Roman Army was the infantry soldier:

> . . . the iron legionary, who, with shield fitted close to his left shoulder, and sword-hilt sunk low, cut his way through the thickest hedge of pikes.[2]

The Roman legion, 6,000 or more men (on paper, though less in fact), was solid, slow-moving, heavily armed, irresistible. It corresponded, in many ways, with a modern infantry brigade. Like a modern regiment, it had its own name, e.g. "Trajan's Own Loyals", its history, traditions, and battle honours. It consisted of nine ordinary cohorts, 500 strong. It had a double-sized Number One Cohort which included the best fighting troops and the H.Q. personnel. In each cohort were six "centuries", or companies, each with eight men under an officer called a centurion (company commander). Like his modern counterpart, he wore service dress, carried a cane, and wore shoes. The other ranks wore boots; the slang name for them was *caligatae*—"the booted ones", or, as we would say, "footsloggers".

The principal arms of the legionary were the long, slender

[1] Some of this material has been published already in my book, *Seeing Roman Britain*, Evans Brothers, 1957.

[2] Oman, Sir Charles, *The Art of War in the Middle Ages*.

throwing-spear, the *pilum*, and the short Spanish sword, the *gladius*, for close in-fighting. He wore a metal helmet and carried a semi-cylindrical shield. The uniform consisted of a tunic, over which he wore a cuirass, which varied in form; the soldiers depicted on Trajan's Column—one of the best visual sources of information—wear breast- and back-plates reinforced by iron hoops.

Centurions, of which a number of representations exist on British tombstones, wore a finer dress with a double kilt, metal shoulder pieces, ornamented belt and flowing cloak.

The tunic was worn under the cuirass to prevent the metal entering the flesh if it was penetrated. It is difficult to tell, from Trajan's column, whether the legionaries of this period wore leather, or leather with metal inserts. But by the second century A.D. they had adapted the *lorica segmentata*, consisting of metal strips, arranged horizontally across the body and vertically across the shoulders (see Professor Webster's brilliant reconstruction of a legionary's equipment facing p. 48). But in the first century, the time of the Great Invasion, this type of armour was not used; in fact there was probably considerable variety in the military dress. Standardization came later, under the Flavian Emperors. A good illustration of 1st century equipment is the picture of the centurion Facilis, at Colchester (p. 80). This is the only representation of a 1st century centurion found in Britain. He has a leather corslet with metal shoulder-pieces, greaves on his legs, wears a cloak and carries a staff. Compare this with illustration 8 and the difference will be obvious.

On Trajan's Column (there is a fine facsimile of it in the Victoria and Albert Museum) you can study the legionaries on the march. In one scene they are shown crossing the Danube, marching at ease, without helmets, and carrying their campaigning kit: trenching-tools, mess-tins, cooking-pots, and kit-bags. On another relief found at *Mogontiacum* the men are in action, fully-armed with helmets, swords, and shields, and carrying their throwing-spears, which they flung before a charge. Crests are not shown; apparently they were only fixed to the helmet for ceremonial parades.

Actual examples of this equipment can be studied at many museums in Britain—for instance, at the British Museum, at

Corbridge (*Corstopitum*), which was a supply base for the troops
on Hadrian's Wall, and in the National Museum of Antiquities at
Edinburgh, which contains a wonderful collection of tools and
military equipment found at Newsteads by Mr. Curle: helmets,
swords, spears, pioneers' axes and picks, cavalry harness, and
smiths' tools. There is another fine display at the Hunterian
Museum in Glasgow. Northern England and Scotland—the
Roman military zone—are the best places in which to study the
Roman Army.

To return to the legions; the Roman infantry soldier had to be
more than a fighting man; he had to be capable of making roads,
building forts and bridges, and the legionary ranks contained
many craftsmen, such as carpenters and smiths. Heavy equipment
was carried on the backs of pack-animals, though, in suitable
country, commandeered wagons were sometimes used.

From the time of Caesar onwards a legion usually included an
artillery formation using *catapultae* and *ballistae*, powerful spring-
guns operated by twisted cords under tension. They could fire
small projectiles over a considerable distance, and could put down
a barrage before the infantry moved in.

In addition, each legion had its contingent of "admin. bods"—
orderlies, clerks to handle the paper-work, etc.—and a medical
staff to look after the sick and wounded:

> In the hospital at *Carnuntum* on the Danube the entry hall led into
> the reception-room, with the operating theatre beyond. Around
> were sixty little rooms, suggesting the sixty centuries of a legion.
> At Novaesium there were small rooms for N.C.Os., and the
> operating theatre had a raised hearth for heating and cleansing
> instruments. At Housesteads, the fort of a military cohort or
> auxiliaries, there was a small hospital with rooms opening off
> corridors. Fendoch, another auxiliary fort, had a corridor hospital
> with wards on either side.[1]

There were also the *auxilia*—auxiliary troops, drawn from many
parts of the Empire—Spaniards, Hungarians, Germans, Syrians,
Greeks, Egyptians, Gauls, and (after the Conquest) Britons.
Many of these were mounted troops, and were usually equipped
with their own native arms. The Syrians, for instance, carried
their deadly composite bow; there were slingers from the

[1] Lindsay, J., *The Romans were Here*, Frederick Muller Ltd., 1956.

Balearic Isles, and other troops. These auxiliaries were of inferior status to the legionaries, and their pay was less. They were organized in cohorts, which might be 1,000 men or 500, divided like the legions, into centuries. They were rarely based in their home countries; for instance, one finds, among the auxiliaries serving on Hadrian's Wall, men from Spain, Germany, Africa, and even as far as Syria. Similarly, troops recruited in Britain manned forts along the Rhine and the Danube. Although these units retained the name of the district from which they were originally recruited, in time their ranks were filled from the area in which they were based.

Cavalry units were organized in *turmae* (squadrons) and *alae*—"wings"—suggesting one of their original functions, which was to act as a screen, protecting the flanks of the infantry. They were also very useful in pursuit, when the enemy's resistance had been broken. Later they were used independently. Archers were also used in Britain and elsewhere. At Housesteads in Northumberland there is a fine tombstone of a Syrian bowman wearing a tunic and cloak, quiver slung over his back, and carrying his bow in the left hand and an axe in the right.

In war the auxiliaries fought in front, the legions being held as an iron reserve in case of need. In peace the auxiliaries manned the frontier forts, along the Rhine, the Danube, in Syria, and later along Hadrian's Wall in Britain. The legions occupied permanent bases behind the frontier, ready to go to any threatened point if the frontier-line was broken. They also came up from their depots to serve on detachments in the frontier forts.

The legion, as a military formation, goes far back into republican days, and was at first recruited from men of Roman blood. Originally they formed a citizen army, which, after defending the homeland, would go back to its farms. Later, when Roman citizenship was extended to the whole of Italy, legionaries were drawn from a much wider field, but were still mainly men of Italian birth. Later still, as the frontiers were extended far beyond Italy, legions were sometimes recruited from among the conquered peoples, e.g. Caesar, during his long campaign in Gaul, obtained some of his best troops from among the Gauls, not only in northern Italy, but in southern France. But the essential difference, apart from those of organization, pay and equipment, was

11. Bust of the Emperor Claudius.

12. Visor of Roman para[
helmet found at Newstea[
Scotland.

13. Decorated Roman helmet
found at Newsteads, Scotland.

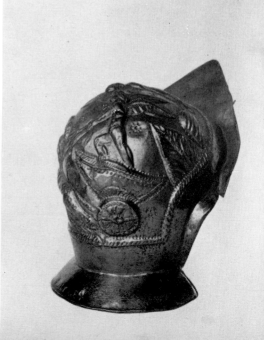

that the legionaries were Roman citizens; the auxiliaries were not, although they were usually granted full Roman citizenship when they had completed their twenty-five years' service.

This was one of the main inducements to join the Roman Army, the first fully professional, regularly paid military force in the world. These men joined voluntarily, because the Army offered them regular pay, a good life, and a career. They signed on usually in their 'teens. At the end of twenty-five years they retired, with a substantial gratuity, and, above all, they were given Roman citizenship, which carried with it many privileges.

Although these facts may not appear to have an immediate bearing on the Roman invasion of Britain, I think they are important, because they help to break the false stereotype of "Roman soldier", a swarthy Italian in helmet and cuirass, marching across Britain, and show us the man beneath the armour: the human being, Italian, Gaul, German, Syrian, Greek; how he fitted into the Roman system, and what he got out of it.

What were the rewards of an army career? And what was meant by "Roman citizenship"? Perhaps the best way to explain this is by quoting from the Military Diplomas, of which some 200 exist, found in many parts of the Empire. (See illustration 38 opposite p. 141). They are pocket-sized certificates of bronze, testifying that the holders had completed their military service, had become Roman citizens, and saying why. There is one from Britain, dating from A.D. 110, but backdated to 106:

> The Emperor Trajan Germanicus Dacius, Chief Priest, Tribunician Power for the 14th time, six times Imperator, Consul for the fifth time. To the infantrymen and cavalrymen who are serving in the double battalion of Britons, *Ulpia Torquata* which is in Dacia under Terentius Scaurianus.

(This means that a British unit serving in what is now Roumania had distinguished itself, and had been granted, *en bloc*, Roman citizenship.)

> . . . whose names are written here, served loyally and faithfully in the Dacian War, discharged before the time expired. I grant them Roman citizenship. Dated the 11th of August, at Darmathithae, in the Consulship of Minicius Natalis and Licinius Silvanus. To the infantryman Marcus Ulpius Novantico, son of Adcobrovatis Novantico, of *Ratae*. . . . [Our italics.]

E

Ratae was Leicester, in the English Midlands. This man, serving in A.D. 106, probably enlisted in about A.D. 85, about a
generation after the original conquest. Leicester was then
scarcely thirty years old. The man's name was Novantico. For all
we know, he may have been a ploughboy. The kind of recruits
one could collect from Leicester in the eighties would be the
toughest and most serviceable young men. Twenty years later,
Novantico comes back, now Marcus Ulpius Novantico, and a
Roman citizen, with a good enough gratuity to buy himself a
fair-sized farm. He is a veteran, and in a small town such as
Ratae must have been, he would be one of the comparatively
few Roman citizens around the place; quite capable of becoming
the Lord Mayor in a few years, and founding a noble family.
Incidentally this document, which is a legal one, proves that
Leicester was even then a municipality.

It was this kind of opportunity which provided one of the
main inducements to join the Roman Army. There must have been
many thousands of Novanticos in the army which followed
Aulus Plautius when he landed in Britain. They were not serfs
following a hereditary chieftain to whom they were bound by
blood or feudal ties. They were professional soldiers to whom
military service was a career, with a reasonable hope of security
at the end of it. Their loyalty was not to their tribe or province,
but to their regiment, to their commander and comrades:

> The Oath to the Emperor was the basis on which the legion's
> loyalty and sense of solidarity was built. The Silver Eagle was the
> emblem of this emotion, of the legion's closely guarded group-
> life. It was dutifully cared-for and had its yearly birthday cele-
> brated with ceremonial pomp. In battle it was the rallying-point,
> and to lose it was a disgrace.[1]

A clear example of this loyalty to the regiment, and to its
symbol, the Eagle, is shown in the action of the standard-bearer
of the 10th Legion, who waded ashore, carrying the Eagle, when
his companions were temporarily unnerved by the sight of the
waiting Britons. The Eagle meant to a legion what its regimental
colours mean to a modern army regiment.

Let us now look at the chain of command, starting with the
officers. The senior ranks of the Roman Army were filled by

[1] Lindsay, J., *op. cit.*

men to whom military command was only a part of their duties and responsibilities. In the days of the Roman Empire there was not the distinction which exists today between civilian and military life. There was what we might call the "senatorial career", which included both civil and military command. Perhaps this can best be explained by quoting from the career of a typical Roman official of high rank, Platorius Nepos, who was Governor of Britain in the time of Trajan and Hadrian. In fact it was he who supervised the building of the Wall, which we shall discuss later. Here we will study his career purely from the standpoint of a Roman officer of the type selected to command the army of invasion.

Like hundreds of other high Roman officials, Platorius Nepos had his career inscribed on stone.[1] From this we learn that he was born in Aquilea, which is now Venice. Here is the record of his career, starting from his ultimate office, and descending to his first:

> Consul, Augur, Legate of the Province of Britain, Legate of the Province of Lower Germany, Legate of the Province of Thrace, Legate of the 1st Adiutrix Legion, *Quaestor* of the Province of Macedonia, Candidate of the late Emperor Trajan, Curator of the Cassian, Clodian, Camillian and New Trajan roads, Tribune of the 22nd Primagenia Legion (*Pia Fidelis*) Praetor, Tribune of the Plebs, *Triumvir Capitalis*, Patron of the City of Aquilea.

We will start with the junior offices and work up to the senior. First, *triumvir capitalis*; that meant that, about the age of eighteen or twenty, he was one of a board of three who were nominally in charge of the police who arrested people on capital charges. At the age of about twenty-one or twenty-two the Triumvir went as Military Tribune to the 22nd Primagenia Legion, which was stationed on the Rhine. A Military Tribune was rather like the A.D.C. to a General in a modern army. In action they sometimes commanded quite large bodies of men, but, in between they could, if they wished, lead a pretty easy and pleasant life. Tacitus, for instance, complained that they normally indulged in riotous living, and cadged all the leave they could! Pliny, about A.D. 80, who was a Military Tribune, had to audit the accounts of attached

[1] Or on memorial inscriptions raised by the municipalities of the towns in which they were born.

units. The job was probably not unlike that of an A.D.C. or
Liaison Officer at Formation Headquarters. A keen young man
could learn soldiering that way, and many did, e.g. Julius Caesar.
But it was just as easy to be smooth and polite about the mess,
handing out the wine, auditing accounts, and being generally
useful and entertaining. The youth's manners and behaviour
would be tested, as well as his military ability, and reports were
sent back by his Commanding Officer to the personnel office in
Rome.

Platorius Nepos came back to Rome at about the age of twenty-
five, was elected *Quaestor,* and sent to the province of Macedonia,
for a year in charge of the not very complicated finance of that
province. After his quaestorship, Nepos became Tribune of the
Plebs. In the days of the Republic this official had been the
champion of the poor against the rich patricians, but now it was
simply an honorary office with no responsibilities. If Nepos had
not been Tribune of the Plebs, he might have been an *aedile,* i.e.
an officer responsible for seeing that shopkeepers did not intrude
on the public pavements, that temples were kept in good order,
and so on. This minor civil office would help him to gain administrative experience; and that, of course, was the idea. These
young men were being trained, not only to command armies, but
eventually to administer large provinces.

Next, he was Curator of a group of roads in Italy, seeing that
sums levied for their maintenance did not stick in someone's
pocket. Then, at the age of thirty, he became *praetor*; he judged
important cases and acted as the State legal officer. A year or two
later he went to command the 1st Adiutrix Legion. He would then
be between thirty-three and thirty-five, and I think we can say
that, at any given moment in the early Empire, the majority of
divisional commanders would be men under forty; that is a main
reason for the Roman Army's efficiency. General officers were
still young and vigorous. They would have had experience as
junior staff officers, perhaps some fifteen years before, and with a
good deal of civilian administrative experience, but with no
other military background.

After his legions, a staff officer might have gone on to become
proconsul of one of the comfortable, wealthy provinces in the
Mediterranean area, such as Aquitania or Transalpine Gaul.

14. Relief from Trajan's Column. Troops crossing a river.

15. Trajan's Column. Roman legionaries in action.

16. Maiden Castle: *Above:* Skeleton of a defender slain by the Romans found buried near the eastern entrance.

17. *Below:* Vertebrae of a slain defender of Maiden Castle showing Roman ballistae bolt embedded in the bone.

Nepos did not. He went on to become a Legate of Augustus (i.e. the Emperor) in Thrace (roughly, modern Bulgaria). Theoretically the Emperor was the *proconsul* of a very large area, including all provinces in which there were operational troops. In fact, these areas were governed by Legates, acting for him.

In A.D. 119 Platorius became *Consul.* The Consulship marked the turning-point between the early and later career. The Legions were commanded by men who were not yet *Consuls.* So were the provinces, such as Thrace, which had few troops in them, or a few provinces, like lower Pannonia, which had only one division. In these the Commander of the Legion was also the Governor. There was a considerable number of posts available for men who were not yet *Consuls,* but the only posts available for ex-Consuls were one or two very senior civilian appointments, senior Army commands, and two very senior pro-Consulates. Nepos went first to command an army of two divisions, and then to take charge of Britain, in which there were three. Thus he held one of the two major appointments in the Roman Army, Britain and Syria. He might possibly have risen even higher, and become pro-Consul of one of the rich Asian provinces, but for some reason he fell into disgrace; we do not know why. But his career is a fairly representative example, showing the ladder of appointments up which the Roman governing class climbed to high rank. It was, as Dr. Morris says, "a useful way of picking out the best from a pretty average group of men, and training them to govern the civilized world".

I have chosen Platorius Nepos's career, not because it was unusual, but because it was typical. In subsequent chapters there will be references to such titles as "Military Tribune", "Quaestor", "Praetor". "Legate of the Legion" and so on. By themselves, such names mean nothing to the non-specialist. But they have considerable relevance if the reader recognizes that "Military Tribune" means, roughly, A.D.C., that "quaestor" means financial officer, "Praetor" Judge, and "Legate" the C.O. of a division, always bearing in mind that there are no exact parallels between the Roman Army and the armies of today. But at least they enable us to recognize the *relative* importance of these various ranks. For instance, we can understand that when Petillius Cerialis commanded the 9th Legion which was mangled by Boudicca he was then a major-general serving under Suetonius Paulinus, the Governor and Commander-in-Chief.

Years later Petillius Cerialis returned to Britain, this time as Governor. One of his subordinates, an able young officer named Gaius Julius Agricola, was in command of the 20th Legion, holding the same rank—major-general—which Petillius had held during the Boudiccan revolt. A dozen years later, Agricola, having served in other provinces and holding ranks of intermediate importance, returned to Britain as Governor and Commander-in-Chief.

So much for the officers. Now we will look more closely at the other ranks and their non-commissioned officers. Largely through Roman documents which have survived in Egypt, where the dry climate has preserved them, we can learn how a recruit joined the Army, the method of his selection (which included a medical examination), his barrack duties, how much he was paid and what proportion was deducted, and even the kind of letters he wrote home. This information, supplemented by what Vegetius and Ammianus say about training and campaigning, tells us a great deal about the ordinary Roman soldier. I am indebted to Mr. G. R. Watson and Dr. Morris for the translations.[1]

"Whoever is going to levy recruits", wrote Vegetius, "must look at the face, the eyes, the whole shape of the man, to see whether he will make a good fighter. So a young man who would be thought suitable for warfare should have shining eyes, an erect carriage, a broad chest, muscular shoulders, strong arms, long fingers, a modest belly, feet and calves sinewy . . . ", etc.

Sometimes a young man of good family who wished to join a legion would carry a letter of introduction. Here is such a letter addressed to one of the military tribunes (there were six to a legion) from his orderly:

> To Julius Domitius, tribune of the Legion, from Aurelius Arceleus, his orderly, greetings.
>
> I've already recommended my friend Theon to you, and now again I beg you, Sir, to keep him before your eyes, as though he were me; he is the sort of fellow you ought to like, for he has left his family and affairs to follow me and has looked after me in

[1] And to the British Broadcasting Corporation for permission to reproduce some of the material broadcast in my documentary programme, "The Roman Army".

every way. So I beg you to accept this introduction to you so that he can tell you everything about our business. Keep this letter before your eyes, Sir, and imagine I am talking to you.

The prospective recruit then had to undergo an examination, known as a *probatio,* which included a medical check. Here is a document, also from Egypt, which seems to be the discharge certificate of a failed applicant:

> Copy of a certificate of discharge in the 12th year of the Emperor Tiberius Claudius Caesar Augustus Germanicus, on the 28th day of the month of Pharmouthae. This man was discharged by Gnaius Virgilius Capito, the Army Commander.
>
> Tryphon, son of Dionysus, weaver, with weak sight owing to a cataract.
>
> On the list of those from Oxyrhyncus. The examination was conducted at Alexandria.

Tryphon, who failed to pass the M.O., was an Egyptian, presumably of Greek stock, judging from his name and that of his father. Eye diseases are common among the poor of Egypt today, and no doubt they were then.

Recruits who passed the test were posted to a unit. Another document, dated the sixth year of the Emperor Trajan, A.D. 103, details the men recruited for the third cohort of the Itureians. It is addressed from the Prefect of Egypt to the Commanding Officer of the cohort.

> From Gaius Minicius Italus . . .
> My dear Calcianus,
> Please give orders that the . . . recruits approved by me be included in the rolls of the cohort with effect from the 19th February. Their names and marks of recognition I have appended to this document.
> Gaius Veturius Gemellus, 21 years, no mark of recognition.
> Gaius Longinus Priscus, 22 years, scar on the left eyebrow.
> Gaius Julius Maximus, 25 years, no mark of recognition.
> Gaius Julius Saturninus, 23 years, scar on the left hand.
> Yours faithfully,
> GAIUS MINICIUS ITALUS,
> *Prefect of Egypt.*

Rigorous training followed. Here is an extract from a Roman

Army training manual which will strike a familiar chord to modern soldiers who have been on battle-courses:

> Single stakes, six feet high, are fixed to the ground. The recruit attacks them as if they were an enemy, with a wickerwork shield and a wooden sword. He attacks as though against the head and face, against the flank, the knee and the legs; withdraws, comes up from the side, slinks up as though it were a real enemy, threatens him with his wooden sword, using all the strength and skill needed in real battle.

The same writer on the use of the sword in battle:

> Especially they must learn to thrust, rather than slash, for the Romans easily beat those who fight by slashing, and despise them. A slash-cut rarely kills, however powerfully delivered, because the vitals are protected by the enemy's weapon, and also by his bones. A thrust, going in two inches, however, can be mortal. You must penetrate the vitals to kill a man. Moreover, when a man is slashing, the right arm and side are left bare. When thrusting, however, the body is covered and the enemy is wounded before he realizes what has happened. So this method of fighting is specially used by the Romans.

Vegetius, on the subject of marching, or, as he calls it "the military pace":

> In the beginning of their preparation, therefore, the recruits must be taught the military pace, for there is no point which must be watched more carefully on the march or in the field than the preservation of their marching ranks by all the men. This result is impossible to achieve unless by continual practice they learn to march rapidly and in equal time. For an army that is split and disarranged by stragglers is always most seriously imperilled by the enemy. Accordingly in the summer months, at any rate, a march of twenty Roman miles must be completed in five hours at the military pace. When the full pace, which is more rapid, is employed, a distance of twenty-four Roman miles should be achieved in the same period.

Eleven Roman miles are roughly equivalent to ten English miles. The "rapid pace" was therefore about four-and-a-half miles per hour. On the excellent military roads built by the Romans wherever they conquered, great distances could be covered in a very short time by fit and well-trained infantry.

Apart from weapon-drill, route marches and manœuvres were worked out, with suitable stopping-places for food and rest. During these exercises the troops practised open-order fighting and learned the formations required to defeat ambushes or sudden attacks. Physical training formed a vital part of the training. "Athletes train to achieve perfection", wrote Vegetius. "How much more should you!" Jumping, swimming, tree-felling, carrying heavy packs all helped to keep the men in condition.

> In Britain, when local recruits were taken into the army, practice camps where the raw lads were trained to dig and entrench, existed north of Haltwhistle, by Cawthorn (Yorks) and on Llandrindod Common.[1]

There is a fine example at Woden Law.

Food was extremely simple. Corn was the main item, with soup, bread, vegetables, and lard. Meat was rarely eaten. In fact, Tacitus tells us that during the Siege of Tigranocerta the soldiers only ate flesh-food when threatened by starvation. They carried mess-tins and cooking-pots, and no doubt certain men in each unit would be detailed to do the cooking. The main drink of the other ranks was vinegar-and-water. Later wine was occasionally drunk, but in the main the statement that "the Roman Army marched on vinegar" is a true one. Incidentally, this fact will explain that when the Roman centurion offered Jesus Christ a sponge soaked in vinegar, he was performing a charitable act. It was his own standard drink.

Pitching camp for the night was an elaborate, orderly and disciplined operation. "When the Roman Army camps for the night", Vegetius wrote, "it builds a defended city". This was hardly an exaggeration. At the halt at the end of a long day's march, every man knew his job. Where necessary, the land was cleared of obstructions (which is why the troops carried scythes and sharpening-stones); then they threw up a rectangle of turf banks, with entrances at each of the four sides and guard-points at the corners. Sentries were set, and the leather tents (of which fragments were found at Newstead) were set up in symmetrical rows, with quarters for the commander and his staff. Good

---

[1] Lindsay, J., *op. cit.*

sanitary provision was made, with latrines and cesspits. Meanwhile, detachments were sent out to forage for food, carrying
small hand-sickles to cut corn where it was obtainable.

Examples of these "marching-camps" have been found in
several parts of England, e.g. in Yorkshire, where they mark the
path of Cerialis's advance.

The permanent forts built along the frontiers and at strategic
points were an elaboration of the temporary camps. They were
almost invariably of rectangular plan, with rounded corners, like
a playing-card. Two main streets, the *via praetoria* and the *via
principia*, led from the entrances and crossed in the middle
and near the junction was a large building called the *principium*, or
headquarters building of the garrison. At Caerleon in Monmouthshire, it had a paved courtyard in front, surrounded by a
colonnaded walk, beyond which were ranges of small rooms, the
armoury and arsenal of the legion. Further west was a small aisled
hall, and then more rooms, offices, staff-rooms and the regimental
chapel and strong-rooms (including the bank). In this block the
commanding officer would have his office and staff; there would
be Army clerks, and files of documents (including leave passes?)
—everything the modern British Army calls "bumf". The C.O.
had a spacious private house, sometimes with a garden. The
men were quartered in long, stone-built barrack blocks, each
housing a single company (century) of men with their centurion,
who had more roomy quarters at one end. At Caerleon the
barracks were divided up into twelve double rooms for the private
soldiers, each consisting of a small outer room, where the men
kept their arms and equipment when off duty, and a larger
living-room behind it.

These forts were built to a common basic plan, though with
local variations; that is why it is sometimes possible to deduce
the purpose of a building even when only part of it has been
excavated—by noting its position in relation to other known
buildings and comparing it with similar structures in other
legionary forts. For instance, there was one at Neuss in the
Rhineland which bears some resemblance to the Caerleon structure. Caerleon, of course, was a big legionary fortress; the
auxiliary forts were smaller and less complex, but similar in
design.

"But where was the N.A.A.F.I.?" asked a frivolous ex-Service friend when I pointed out the resemblance between a Roman legion and a British regiment. He was surprised when I told him that Roman soldiers in barracks *did* have the equivalent of a N.A.A.F.I. Outside the walls of nearly all forts you will usually find a bath-building. A good example can be seen at Chesters (*Cilurnum*), just behind Hadrian's Wall on the North Tyne. These were not mere ablution-rooms. A Roman bath was very like what we call a "Turkish bath", a place for relaxation after a hard day's work. It had a series of rooms heated to varying temperatures, from lukewarm to very hot. You stripped, sweated the dirt out of your system; then, after a cold plunge and a brisk rub-down, relaxed with your friends or gambled your pay (i.e. whatever was left after you had banked a proportion with the Army Savings Bank) at the Roman equivalent of "crown and anchor". The bath was a kind of club, and every Roman settlement of any size had one:

> Gossip and gambling took place in the fore-rooms. . . . In leisure hours the soldiers played games, gambled, wrote letters, drank, hunted and carried out regular sports. We hear of the fight of a Gallic auxiliary and a legionary; and the Batavians excelled at swimming.[1]

However, it would be false to paint too rosy a picture. Roman soldiers grumbled just as much as their modern successors, and often with good cause. For instance, Tacitus puts into the mouths of certain mutineers under Tiberius the following words:

> Why do we go on obeying a handful of centurions, and a still smaller pack of tribunes, as if we were slaves? What better time to have the guts to demand redress, by prayer of swords, when a new emperor is scarcely settled on his throne? . . . A soldier's life is heavy and unrewarded, that we know, body and soul bought for ten coppers a day. And out of that he must buy clothes, tent equipment, weapons, blunt the callousness of centurions and pay for exemption from duties. It's nothing but blows and wounds, cruel winter and fatiguing summer, disastrous war and useless peacetime.[2]

This, however, refers to a time of disturbance and unrest,

---

[1] Lindsay, J., *op. cit.*   [2] *Ibid.*

when a "barrack lawyer", would have full scope for his talents. For most of the time I suspect that the legionary soldier was fairly content.

But there is one passage from this quotation which is borne out by a document discovered in Alexandria, in Egypt. It is a Roman soldier's pay-book, dating from A.D. 83-4. From this it is clear that the compulsory deductions, for uniform, food, bedding, etc. were considerable.

In the first century A.D. a private soldier's pay was 225 denarii per annum, paid in three instalments, but the Emperor Domitian (A.D. 81-96) raised this to 300 denarii a year. The pay could be supplemented by loot and by Imperial bounties. In Egypt, however, the troops seem to have been paid in drachmae, the local currency, and received 248 drachmae for each pay-period. But there were a number of compulsory stoppages, as follows:

		Drachmae
Bedding	. .	10
Food	. . .	80
Boots and straps	.	12
Annual Camp Dinner		20 (in the first pay-period only)
Burial Club	. .	4 (in the second period only)
Clothing	. .	60 (in the first period, 146 in the third)

Out of 248 drachmae due to him in the first pay-period, our soldier got only 66. In the second he received 142. This was the balance he withdrew, leaving the balance in the Army Savings Bank to accumulate.

Among these entries, some will be familiar to present-day soldiers, others not. The "Annual Camp Dinner" strikes an obvious chord. The "Burial Club" has its modern parallels in civilian life—a kind of life insurance to pay for one's funeral. Others will seem a bit hard.

Vegetius explains why the troops were expected to deposit part of their pay with the Bank:

> . . . from the bonuses which were issued to the troops a half-share was retained with the Colours and preserved there for the men themselves, to prevent its being wasted by the Other Ranks through extravagance or the purchase of useless articles. . . .

18. Vespasian: Commander of the 2nd Augusta Legion under Aulus Plautius (A.D. 43): Emperor A.D. 71-9.

19. Part of the ramparts of Maiden Castle, Dorset, the great Iron Age fortress attacked by Vespasian and the 2nd Augusta Legion.

"Useless articles" . . . those who have served in Egypt will know what *that* means. Was there a Muski Bazaar in A.D. 84? And were the Egyptians already selling those appalling carpets with a hand-woven reproduction of the Pyramids?[1]

Vegetius continues in his solemn way:

> For the majority of men, and in particular those who are poor, are in the habit of spending all that they are able to acquire. This putting aside of money, however, is in the first place shown to the men themselves to be advantageous; for since they are maintained at the public expense, their personal savings are increased with every bonus by their half-share.

The Roman Army had non-commissioned officers, some of which have approximate equivalents in a modern force. Starting with the lowest ranking soldier, they ran as follows:

Miles gregarius: Private. Also bore the slang-name *caligatae*—"the booted".

Immunes: The *immunes* are immune from ordinary fatigues, a privilege gained through undertaking special responsibility. Compare *gefreiter* ("freed man") in the German Army.

Tesserarius, Optio, Signifer: Roughly equivalent to sergeants. The *Signifer* was the standard-bearer. But he also had administrative duties rather like those of a modern Company Quartermaster Sergeant. He was roughly equivalent to a warrant-officer. He was also responsible for the Army pay-chest and banked the money deposited by the troops in the Army Savings Bank.

Aquilifer: Carried the Eagle, the regimental emblem.

Beneficiarius: An orderly officer on attached duties, whose rank depended on that of the officer on whose staff he was serving.

Cornicularius: Officer in charge of the Headquarters Staff. It is not possible to equate his rank with other ranks.

---

[1] This may not be as fantastic as it sounds. For instance, Luxor and the Valley of the Kings' Tombs was a popular tourist attraction in the Graeco-Roman period. Witness this scribble by a Ptolemaic soldier of about 300 B.C.: "I, Philastrios the Alexandrian, who have come to Thebes, and seen . . . the work of these tombs of astounding horror, have had a delightful day." Nearby are pencilled comments on the tombs left by members of the Eighth Army 2,000 years later.

Centurion: Company commander, in charge of a century. Some
rose from the ranks, but the greater number were commissioned directly. The responsibilities of Centurions differed
widely. The Chief Centurion or *primus pilus* were equivalent
to a full colonel, whereas the junior centurions were more
like lieutenants.

The centurions were the backbone of the Roman Army.
Newly-fledged platoon commanders in modern armies sometimes
feel that their platoon sergeants, professional soldiers, could well
do without them. The same, no doubt, was true of the Roman
centurions and the aristocratic young sprigs from Rome who
came to a legion as military tribunes. For, whereas the military
tribunes came in for a short spell of service, the centurions, or
most of them, had been in the Army all their lives; to them the
Army was a profession and a career. Several Roman generals
have paid tribute to their centurions, e.g. Julius Caesar in his
Gallic War.

Of the millions who served in the Roman Army, a mere hand-
ful has left us a record. There are the smooth, impersonal records
of the historians, Caesar, Tacitus, Dio Cassius, Suetonius. But
there are no Roman *Memoirs of an Infantryman*; no Roman Sassoon
or Brooke or Baring has left us any single clue by which we could
assess the quality of the Roman fighting-man, or lift the veil on
his private emotions. Apart from "official history" all we have
are the ruined forts, the roads, bits of armour and equipment, and,
from Egypt, a few precious documents of a type which one can
find in modern Britain on 100 barrack-room notice-boards.
Take, as an example, the document reproduced on the opposite
page.

That duty roster dates from the reign of the Emperor Domitian,
about 1,800 years ago. Note particularly the names of the various
centurions, Helius, Decrius, Serenus, etc. Apart from the Latin
names and a few archaisms, this roster might well be contemporary. On October 3rd Gaius Julius Valens is ditching. On October
8th Gaius Amelius Valens is on duty in the Armoury. On the
same day Publius Clodius Secundus is cleaning his Company
Officer's shoes, whereas on the previous day he was on sentry-
duty at the camp gate. From the 9th to the 10th Gaius Domitius

NAME	1	2	3	4	5	6	7	8	9	10
G(aius) Domitius (C)e(ler)									Leave by permission of Prefect	
G(aius) Aemilius Vale(ns)	Uniform of Helius						?	Armoury	Bath-house fatigue	Bath-house fatigue
G(aius) Julius Valens	Sand	?	Ditch-ing	Boots	Armoury		Bath-house fatigue	Batman	Duty in century	Bath-house fatigue
L(ucius) Julius Oc(ta)via(nus)	Sand				Duty in century	Bath-house fatigue	H.Q. guard	Street duty	Duty in century	?
P(ublius) Clodius (S)ecun(dus)	Camp-market duty?		Duty in century				Gate guard	Cen-turion's boots	Helius' shoes	Helius' shoes
M(arcus) Arrius Niger					Barrack fatigue	Barrack fatigue	Barrack fatigue	Barrack fatigue	Barrack fatigue	Barrack fatigue
L(ucius) Sextiliu(s) G(e)rm(a)n(us)	Gate guard	Regi-mental colours	Bath-house fatigue	?	Duty in the Century of Decrius					
G(aius) Julius F....	?	Windows ?			Duty in the Century of Serenus					
Q(uintus) Cassius Ru(f)us	The island	Camp-market duty?								
G(aius) Julius Long(u)s Sipo						In the century of Helius				Duty in the century

Celer is on leave (by permission of the Camp Prefect), whereas on the same two days Publius Clodius Secundus is looking after Helius's shoes.

But look at the duties of Marcus Arrius Niger. Whereas his comrades are engaged in a variety of duties, there appears, opposite Marcus's name, the same monotonous entry every day: "Barrack Fatigue". One wonders what Marcus had been up to! Modern soldiers who have been "put on a charge" should sympathize with him.

The aim of the Roman system of military training, says Vegetius, was to make warfare "not a dread, but a delight". A million "horse-laughs" would, no doubt, have greeted this remark if the troops could have heard it. Most soldiers are inveterate cynics—at least on the surface—and yet, to any professional soldier, as distinct from the "citizen armies" of which one hears so much nowadays, the Roman system, developed and perfected 2,000 years ago, seems a fair one. It was thorough and efficient. It made warfare tolerable; even, at times, enjoyable. It cared for the material welfare of its troops, gave them security, regular pay and a chance of promotion. It instilled into them a pride in their regiment, and reverence for its traditions; an intense, local loyalty more appreciable than a vague allegiance to a State, a class or a political dogma. There was no drab "people's militia" in the Roman Army.

The Roman senior officers probably contained a higher proportion of able generals than most modern armies, if only because such men were given their divisions before their arteries had hardened. As to the N.C.Os. and other ranks, they may have grumbled, but at least they had a personal stake in the system they had sworn to defend. It gave its citizens—Italians, Gauls, Britons, Africans, Jews—equality under the law, and a sense of overall unity. One could travel from the Tyne to the Euphrates without a passport, without crossing a frontier, without ever feeling that one was a foreigner. The Romans seem to have had no marked sense of racial superiority. How could they, being themselves drawn from many races? Having subdued the barbarians, they then set about turning them into good Romans. A Palmyrenian from the Syrian desert, one Barates, married a British girl and settled in Northumberland, where their tombstones can

20. Memorial stone of Facilius (Roman Centurion) found at Colchester.

21. Emblem of the 20th Legion.

22. Tablet with the emblem of the 2nd Augusta Legion, found at
Benwell, Northumberland.

still be seen. Both were Romans, with Latin as a common tongue.

Now, having seen how the Imperial Army was recruited, trained and led, we will follow it into Britain.

For some of the information in this chapter I am indebted to Professor Webster's excellent booklet "The Roman Army" published by the Grosvenor Museum, Chester.

F

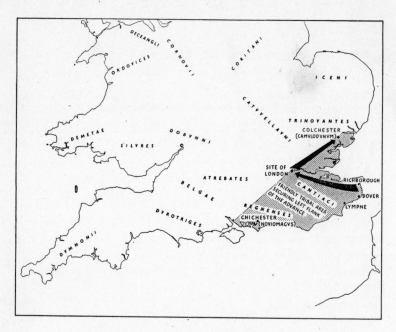

Initial advance of Aulus Plautius, A.D. 43.

CHAPTER FIVE

THE GREAT INVASION

WHEN Julius Caesar raided Britain in 55 and 54 B.C., his main motive was to "teach the natives a lesson" by a show of Roman strength. Permanent occupation was not contemplated. Several decades later the Greek geographer, Strabo, sums up a rather chilly account of Britain with the words "the island does not call for a garrison. It would take at least a legion and some cavalry to exact tribute there, and the total cost of the army would be as much as the revenue collected."

When, in A.D. 43, the Emperor Claudius despatched four legions to Britain, the Romans were bent on permanent conquest. What had happened to make them change their opinion? Suetonius, whose contempt for the clownish Emperor Claudius shows clearly in his biography, remarks:

> Claudius's sole campaign was of no great importance. The Senate had already voted him triumphal regalia, but he thought it beneath his dignity to accept these, and decided that Britain was the country where a real triumph could be most readily earned. Its conquest had not been attempted since Caesar's day; and the Britons were now threatening vengeance because the Senate refused to extradite certain deserters who had landed in Gaul during Caligula's reign.[1]

This writer also says that Claudius "fought no battles and suffered no casualties", but that "his triumph was a very splendid one, and among those whom he invited to witness it were his provincial governors, and several exiles as well". In fact, Suetonius makes the Claudian invasion sound like the gesture of a fatuous ass, who, by emulating the warlike achievements of his ancestors, hoped to convince his subjects that he was not the fool they assumed him to be. Yet Claudius was not a fool, and there

[1] Suetonius, *The Twelve Caesars*, translated by Robert Graves, Penguin Books, 1957.

must have been deeper motives, for even under inept and half-lunatic Emperors there were cool and able brains directing the Roman military and political machine.

The real reasons for the invasion were probably (*a*) that increasing trade relations with Britain had revealed the potential wealth of the island; (*b*) that south-eastern Britain was no longer the home of separate, independent tribes but had become a powerful kingdom; (*c*) that the English Channel was not a good frontier; Britain could harbour refugee Gaulish malcontents, and provide a base for an attack on the Roman mainland.

Fifty years after Caesar's departure the Catuvellauni, of Hertfordshire, overcame and absorbed the Trinovantes of Essex and part of Kent. About A.D. 10 the Catuvellaunian King, Cunobelinus, established himself at *Camulodunum* (Colchester) on the River Colne. The name means "the fortress of Camulos", a Celtic war-god, whom the Catuvellauni had brought to Britain from Gaul. From this place Cunobelinus—Shakespeare's Cymbeline—ruled an area which included the Chilterns, the lower Thames Valley, Essex and a substantial part of Kent. The capital was not a town in the modern sense, but an area of about twelve square miles protected by huge dykes, and containing scattered clusters of huts. Coins struck by Cunobelinus are of Roman type, and many of them show an ear of corn, the natural product of Essex.

Strabo, in his *Geography*, mentions as products of Britain, "corn, cattle, gold, silver and iron . . . also hides, slaves, and clever hunting-dogs".

"Minerals are not found in the territory of Cunobelinus", writes Professor Richmond. "He must have drawn his silver from Derbyshire or Somersetshire and his gold from further west. But other items in the list could all have figured among the exports of his kingdom, and we get a picture of how the imports of such a Celtic prince were balanced. The subject Trinovantes would produce the corn, the middle Thames and the Chilterns the cattle, the forests the hides and pelts, the aristocratic kennels the hunting dogs. The slaves form a darker picture, recalling the fact that no neighbours of a thriving native kingdom were exempt from slave-raiding and head-hunting."[1]

[1] Richmond, I., *Roman Britain*, Penguin Books, 1955.

In return Cunobelinus imported wine, silver table-ware,
bronze-plated furniture, fine pottery, ivory, jewellery and glass.
In a rich grave at Lexden, near Colchester, archaeologists found
examples of these splendid objects, including a bronze table and
statuettes, silver-studded chain-mail and an iron-bound litter.
They may have belonged to Cunobelinus himself, though there
is no proof of this.

We must now consider the other tribal areas into which Britain
was divided. A King called Verica had ruled in what are now
southern Surrey and Sussex, until driven out by Cunobelinus just
before the Claudian invasion. This exiled monarch then went to
Rome and implored Claudius to help restore him to his kingdom
—providing another plausible excuse for invasion. Verica was of
the same family as Commius, Caesar's agent of nearly a century
earlier.

Further west still were the Dumnonii of Devon and Cornwall;
north of them lay the territory of the Dobunni, in what are now
Somerset and part of Gloucestershire. In East Anglia lived the
powerful Iceni, who later produced the warrior-Queen Boudicca;
in Leicestershire and Lincolnshire were the Coritani, and further
north still the Parisi of Yorkshire and the mighty Brigantian
tribe, who occupied an area which included Lancashire, part of
Yorkshire, Westmorland, Cumberland and County Durham.
Beyond the Severn, the mountains of Wales protected the Silures,
the Deceangli, and the Ordovices. As for the lands beyond the
Tyne and Solway, they were unknown territory, which the
Romans were not to see for another generation.

The picture we have to keep in mind is, first, a confederation of
tribes living in south-eastern Britain, owing allegiance to Cunobelinus and his sons. This confederation met the shock of the
first Roman attack. But beyond them, to the west and north,
were other tribes who at first stood aloof, taking no part in the
initial resistance. When the Romans entered their territory they
fought them, or submitted, according to the inclination of their
rulers. Some tribes, such as the Iceni of Norfolk, at first accepted
Roman rule and then rebelled. Others fought and afterwards submitted. Some, like the followers of Queen Cartimandua of the
Brigantes, allied themselves with the Romans against their
own kinsmen. There was no standard pattern; resistance was

piecemeal, loyalties local and personal, never national. There was no "British nation".

Let us glance at the Roman Empire in A.D. 43. After Caesar's conquest of Gaul, successive Roman generals had fought to establish an eastern frontier along the Rhine. The fierce German tribes, the Chatti, the Cherusci, the Chauci, lurking in their dark northern forests between the Rhine and the Elbe, were impossible to conquer. Even Roman discipline sometimes collapsed under the pressure of the Teuton warriors, who, in the words of Tacitus, had "wild, blue eyes, reddish hair and huge frames that excel only in violent effort"; men accustomed to forests and marshes where the slow, heavily-armed legionaries were at a disadvantage. Three legions, under Varus, were hacked to pieces in the Teutoburg Forest by German forces under Arminius; their whitened bones were found six years later when Germanicus re-crossed the Rhine to avenge Varus. After a generation of bitter fighting, the most that the Romans could do was to hold the Germans back beyond the Rhine by a chain of frontier forts, some of which can be seen today.

Of the four legions selected for the invasion of Britain, three were stationed on the Rhine, and the fourth was in Pannonia (Hungary), on the Danube; all guarded the north-eastern frontiers of the Empire. They were (1) the 2nd Augusta, stationed at Strasbourg (*Argentorate*); (2) the 14th Gemina from Mainz (*Mogontiacum*); (3) the 20th Valeria from Cologne (*Novaesium*) and the 9th Hispana from Pannonia. There may also have been a detachment of the 8th Legion. The total legionary force probably numbered about 25,000 men; with it came auxiliaries who brought the total force to about 50,000.

We must imagine these seasoned troops living in fairly comfortable, permanent forts of the type described in Chapter IV. Behind them lay civilized Gaul and in front, beyond the wide rivers, the trackless forests of Germany in which so many of their comrades had perished. Then, in the year A.D. 43, along came Narcissus, a freed slave, a close friend and adviser of the Emperor, to tell them that the divine Emperor had ordered them to sail to Britain.

They were a long way from Rome. To them the Emperor would be only a name; their loyalty would be to their com-

manders. So their reception of Narcissus was compounded of
suspicion, resentment and contempt (for the man had been a
slave). When he mounted the rostrum to relay his master's
orders a wave of anger and derision hit him. For Britain, to the
legionaries, lay beyond the borders of the known world, far out
in the great river of Ocean, beyond which, if one sailed far
enough, one's ships would topple over into a bottomless abyss.
In the words of Dio Cassius:

> The soldiers were indignant at the thought of carrying on a cam-
> paign outside the limits of the known world, and would not yield
> him obedience until Narcissus, who had been sent out by Claudius,
> mounted the tribunal of Paultius and attempted to address them.
> Then they became much angrier at this and would not allow
> Narcissus to say a word. . . .

There was an ancient festival in Rome called the *Saturnalia*
(our Christmas festivities are descended from it) in which slaves
were allowed, for a brief time, to dress in the robes of their
masters and assume their functions. The sight of Narcissus on the
rostrum appealed to the humorous instincts of some wag in the
crowd. He yelled, *"Io Saturnalia!"* The troops roared with
laughter. The tension broke. Narcissus managed to get a hearing,
and succeeded in commanding the troops' attention. What might
have become a mutiny dissolved in laughter. When the legionaries
were dismissed to their quarters, they found themselves packing
their kit and preparing to embark for Britain.

"They were sent over in three divisions", writes Dio Cassius,
"in order that they should not be hindered in landing—as might
happen with a single force."

From the fact that the four legions came from stations on the
Rhine it is almost certain that they sailed down the river into the
North Sea and then cruised southward along the coast of Belgium
and northern France until they reached the Pas de Calais, where
they would steer westward. Dio Cassius gives us no clue. He
merely says:

> . . . in their voyage across the first [division] became discouraged
> because they were driven back in their course, and then plucked
> up courage because a flash of light [a meteor?] rising in the east
> shot across to the west, the direction in which they were sailing.

So they put in to the island and found none to oppose them.

The splitting-up of the invading force into three divisions may have been due to the widely-dispersed bases from which the legions came. The 9th Hispana had the longest journey, for their base was beside the Danube, in Hungary. They would have had to march some 400 miles overland to reach the Rhine, after which they would have had to cover an even greater distance to reach the coast. The 2nd Augusta, at Strasbourg, would have to move about 400 miles down the river before reaching the sea; the 14th Gemina, from Mainz, were about 300 miles from the coast, and the 20th Valeria, from Cologne, were nearest, about 200 miles from the mouth of the Rhine.[1]

North-west of Cologne the twentieth century has wiped out most of the landmarks the Romans would have recognized. Dusseldorf, Duisburg, Essen, with their chimneys, steel-works and marshalling yards have obliterated everything save the ancient river. Westward, beyond the German frontier, where the divided river rolls sluggishly through the plains of Holland, elements remain of that sombre, waterlogged landscape which the Romans knew, the land of the strong-swimming Batavi; though today there are cornfields where once were only bird-haunted marshes and lakes. Finally, among the desolate creeks of the Dutch coast, near Dordrecht, or Beveland, or Walcheren, where the flat land seems to float on the flat sea, the laden galleys began to heave to the Channel swell; the tiller tugged at the helmsman's arm; the gulls screamed above the slanting decks, and salt spray broke over the bows, drenching the crouching, cursing soldiers. Ahead lay Ocean, the "limit of the world". Ahead lay Britain.

A few miles from Sandwich, on a flat knoll some eighty feet above the flat meadowland which stretches to the sea-coast, lies Richborough, scheduled as an "Ancient Monument". From the clipped turf surrounded by neat Office of Works fencing rise the three surviving flint walls of the old Roman fortress, though these date from a period some three centuries after the Claudian invasion. Within that enclosure archaeologists have revealed ditches which can definitely be dated to the time of Claudius.

[1] All this is assuming that the invading force *did* sail down the Rhine, and did not march overland to Boulogne.

The occupation of the site during the reign of Claudius and the presence of a defensive earthwork of that date had already been proved by our previous excavations [writes Mr. J. P. Bushe-Fox], but the significance of this work had not been established. This earthwork has now been shown to consist of a mound with two defence ditches on its west side, stretching north and south from a central entrance. . . . This earthwork . . . was built against attack from the west and not from the east. Its date can definitely be assigned to the reign of Claudius and its purpose was undoubtedly to cover the disembarkation of his legionaries and their war material at the time of his invasion of Britain in A.D. 43, while after the army had advanced inland it doubtless served for supplies and the ships drawn up on shore.[1]

This careful, cautious, matter-of-fact report of scant interest to the layman is of great significance to the historian. For it pinpoints one of the places at which the invading forces landed. Dio Cassius tells us that the legions sailed in three divisions, and it has been assumed that they landed at three points on the Kent coast, i.e. Dover, Lympne, and Richborough. At each of these places there are harbours, and at each Roman remains have been found.

Haverfield says: "We may presume that they landed at the three ports of Richborough, Dover and Lympne."[2] Collingwood says, "the first phase of the conquest opened with the landing of the expeditionary force, in three divisions, perhaps at the three ports of Richborough, Dover and Lympne".[3] Professor Richmond says, ". . . the forces had landed at three different points, presumed to be the natural harbours of Dover (*Dubrae*) and Lympne (*Lemanae*) as well as the main landing-point in Thanet. Room for deployment was thus secured."[4] This supposition may well be true, and, as an amateur, I would not presume to question it. However, the words "perhaps" and "presumed" suggest that the authorities are not certain, and the fact that Dio Cassius merely states that the Romans *sailed* in three divisions, not that they landed at three places, leaves the whole matter open to speculation.

[1] *Fourth Report on the Excavations of the Roman Fort at Richborough, Kent,* by J. P. Bushe-Fox, C.B.E., M.A., F.S.A., Society of Antiquaries, 1949.

[2] Haverfield, S., *The Roman Occupation of Britain,* Clarendon Press, 1924.

[3] Collingwood, R. C., *Roman Britain,* Clarendon Press, 1932.

[4] Richmond, I., *Roman Britain, op. cit.*

There is unmistakable evidence of a Claudian camp at Richborough (*Rutupiae*) at which place the Romans raised a great
marble monument (the foundations of which still exist) which may
have been intended to commemorate the landing. Is it not possible
therefore that the entire force concentrated here before marching
into the interior?

In addition to the names of the four legions which took part,
we have those of a few officers. Aulus Plautius led the combined
force; Cassius Dio describes him as "a senator[1] of great re-
nown". We also know the name of one legionary commander
(*legatus*, roughly equivalent in rank to a major-general) because
he happened to be Vespasian, who later became Emperor. His
brother, Sabinus, served under him in the 2nd Augustan Legion.
Dio Cassius also mentions an officer named Gnaeus Hosidius
Geta, who was decorated for his gallantry in the Battle of the
Medway, and Rubrius Pollio, a Prefect of the Praetorian Guard,[2]
who also distinguished himself, and was honoured by Claudius
for his service in the "British War". These are the only names
which Dio gives us. Suetonius only mentions Claudius's part in
the operation, and that very briefly. Tacitus, in his *Annals*,
probably gave a much longer account, but the section of his book
describing the first six years of Claudius's reign is missing.
These writers are our only documentary sources for the first
stage of the invasion. For the rest we have to rely on judicious
speculation, aided by such scanty archaeological clues as can be
gathered.

Every writer on Roman Britain is faced with the same meagre
facts, which are usually given without comment. One or two
authors have seized upon the sparseness and vagueness of the
Roman reports to construct revolutionary theories of their own,
which run counter to the views of most historians. But in the
main, the method I propose to adopt is to give (*a*) evidence,
documentary and archaeological; (*b*) the interpretations of this
evidence by competent authorities, and (*c*) where there are gaps
in our knowledge (abysses is perhaps a better word!) admit them,
but attempt to show how they might be filled. The method of the

---

[1] Senate, the deliberative assembly of the Roman people.
[2] Imperial household troops, roughly equivalent to our Guards Brigade.
Claudius probably brought over a contingent, with a detachment of the 8th Legion.

detective, who has to piece together a complete story from a few random clues, is very like that of the archaeologist.

Now let us return to *Dio's Roman History*. He tells that the landing was unopposed, and that the Romans at first had great difficulty in making contact with the Britons. Moreover, "when they [the Britons] did assemble, they would not come to close quarters . . . but took refuge in the swamps and the forests, hoping to wear out the invaders by fruitless effort, so that, just as in the days of Julius Caesar, they should sail back with nothing accomplished".

> Plautius, accordingly, had a deal of trouble in searching them out; but when at last he did find them, he first defeated Caratacus and then Togodumnus, the sons of Cunobelinus, who was dead. . . . After the flight of these kings he gained by capitulation a part of the Bodunni, who were ruled by a tribe of the Catuvellauni; and leaving a garrison there, he advanced farther and came to a river.[1]

The obvious landing-place for a large invading force sailing from the nearest point on the French coast would be the coast of Kent, where Caesar had landed nearly a century earlier. It gave an approach to the Thames Valley basin, north of which, the Romans knew, lay the enemy capital of Camulodunum. We know from archaeological evidence at Richborough that there was a Claudian camp there, as well as a very large monument which might have been built to commemorate the successful invasion of Britain. There were also Roman ports at Dover (Dubrae) and Lympne (Lemanae). We know that the invading force sailed in three divisions, and they probably landed at these three places. Moreover, as Collingwood says:

> If we may assume, and there is some reason for assuming it, that the main Roman roads of Britain were made largely during the campaigns of conquest, we may infer from the map of Roman roads in Kent, that the entire force concentrated at Canterbury before moving westward forcing the passage of the Medway. . . .[2]

No name is given by Dio to the river which Aulus Plautius crossed, but if the Romans did land on the Kent coast and were

---

[1] *Dio's Roman History*, translated by Ernest Cary, Ph.D., Loeb Classical Edition, Heinemann, 1924.

[2] Collingwood, R. G., *Roman Britain, op. cit.*

marching towards the Thames, the Medway was the first large
river which they would encounter. But so far no archaeological
evidence has turned up to indicate where the Romans made their
hotly-opposed crossing. For quite a lively battle took place at the
river, as we learn from Dio:

> The barbarians thought that the Romans would not be able to
> cross it without a bridge, and consequently bivouacked in rather
> careless fashion on the opposite bank; but he [Plautius] sent
> across a detachment of *Batavi* who were accustomed to swim
> easily in full armour across the most turbulent streams. These fell
> unexpectedly on the enemy, but instead of shooting at any of the
> men they confined themselves to wounding the horses that drew
> their chariots; and in the confusion that followed not even the
> enemy's mounted warriors could save themselves.

Notice the intelligent way Plautius used his auxiliary troops.
The Batavi, who lived in what is now Holland, were much better
at swimming rivers than the legionaries, so he sent them first.
Among the officers who watched this operation was a vigorous
young man of thirty-four. The intelligent brow was hidden under
a plumed helmet, but nothing could conceal the strong nose and
the heavy, thrusting jaw. Long cloak hanging from his shoulders,
muscular arms folded across his steel cuirass, he looked what he
was, a tough legionary commander who had seen some service.
He had served as a colonel in Thrace, and later, when Claudius
became Emperor, was sent to Germany to take command of the
2nd Augustan Legion. Now, with what in modern terms would
be the rank of major-general, he was leading his legion into
Britain. Thus, on the muddy banks of a British river, somewhere
near Rochester, we catch a glimpse of an infantry officer who was
later to rule the Roman world, Vespasian.[1]

Plautius, seeing the confusion of the Britons on the further
bank, spoke quickly to Vespasian, who, with his brother,
immediately led a detachment of his legionaries further along the
bank, then swam or waded across the river to take the Britons
in the flank.

> So they, too [writes Dio] got across the river in some way and
> killed many of the foe, taking them by surprise. The survivors,

[1] For these physical details, see the portrait on his coins.

however, did not take to flight, but on the next day, joined issue with them again. The struggle was indecisive until Gnaeus Hosidius Geta, after narrowly missing being captured, finally managed to defeat the barbarians so soundly that he received the *ornamenta triumphalia*.[1]

After their defeat, the Britons "retired to the Thames at a point near where it empties into the ocean and at floodtime forms a lake".[2] It has been a 2-day battle followed by a planned withdrawal by the British. Caratacus knew what he was doing.

So far, all is fairly straightforward, if one accepts Kent as the landing-place; the majority of historians of Roman Britain interpret Dio's account as I have done. Yet one must admit that the Greek writer's story, which was written long after the event, does contain some obscure passages. For instance, he implies that Aulus Plautius defeated Caratacus and Togodumnus *before* advancing to the first river, which we assume to have been the Medway. Then, he tells us "after the flight of these kings he gained the capitulation of the Bodunni . . . and leaving a garrison there, he advanced further and came to a river".

Now, assuming that Dio had his facts correct, where did this first battle take place? Or was the first brush with the enemy actually at the Medway, and the second at the Thames? Again, who were the Bodunni? No tribe of this name is mentioned by any other Roman or Greek historian. Had Dio, perhaps, transposed the "d" and the "b" in the word Dobunni, a well-known Celtic tribe which lived in what is now Gloucestershire? But if it was indeed the Dobunni who capitulated to Plautius in the first stage of the invasion, what were they doing in Kent? Unless—terrible heresy—the landing was not in Kent at all?

There is nothing new in this suggestion. William Camden (1551-1623), the father of British archaeology, identified Dio's "Bodunni" with the Dobunni more than three centuries ago. But if he was right, some very awkward questions arise. How amusing it would be if in, say, some Egyptian rubbish-pit, the missing part of Tacitus's *Annals* turned up, with an account of the invasion which blew all the accepted theories sky high![3]

[1] *Dio's Roman History, op. cit.*   [2] *Ibid.*

[3] Another huge earthwork, just north of Chichester, has attracted some attention. It has not been dug, and may well be Belgic or even medieval. If, however, it proved to be Claudian, it might cause a drastic revision of existing theories.

For those who enjoy mysteries, here are two puzzling bits of archaeological data which may or may not have some relevance to the invasion. There are two hill-forts, the well-known "sugar-loaf" hill called "the Caburn" near Lewes in Sussex, and another at Ightham, south of Maidstone, Kent, both of which were burned by attackers during this period. Burned brushwood was found piled against the gates, and from pottery found on the site the excavators deduced that the forts could have been stormed round about A.D. 40. But precise dating is impossible; no pottery will tell you if the event occurred in A.D. 41 or 43, so that the attackers could have been (*a*) the forces of Cunobelinus at war with Verica in about A.D. 41 or (*b*) the Romans smoking out Caratacus in A.D. 43. We know that after the death of Togodumnus, his brother, Caratacus, retreated westward and continued to give the Romans trouble for a further nine years; but more of him later.

We will assume that Aulus Plautius advanced through Kent to the Thames Valley, as Caesar had done. "The Britons", Dio tells us, "easily crossed because they knew where the firm ground and the easy passages were to be found; but the Romans in attempting to follow them were not so successful. However, the Batavi swam across again and some others got over by a bridge a little way upstream, after which they assailed the barbarians from several sides at once and cut down many of them."

This mention of a bridge is also puzzling, for if, as Dio says, the crossing was made "where the river empties into the ocean", i.e. east of Tilbury, the river was far too wide to be bridged. But Dio's story is extremely vague, written by a man who had never seen Britain and who, in any case, was using earlier and probably corrupt accounts. Looking at the map, my guess is that the Romans approached the Thames from the direction of Chatham and Gillingham, and reached it somewhere near Gravesend. The Thames would not be as it is today. There would be wide marshes and mud-flats; the river had not been dredged to accommodate big ships.

Somewhere near Woolwich, or perhaps even further west, where London now stands, the 40,000 men of Plautius's force, infantrymen, horsemen, pack-animals and possibly wagons, struggled and skidded down the muddy slopes, and cut their way through the forest of reeds. Caratacus crossed the mud-flats with his men by a route they knew. The Romans attempted to follow and got into trouble, though some of their cavalry got across. But the Romans were familiar with great rivers. They had crossed the Rhine to fight the Chauci and the Chatti under Germanicus. Caesar had bridged the Rhine 100 years earlier. Dio mentions a bridge, which some historians assume to have been a British structure. It seems to the present writer that the Romans could have built it themselves probably from commandeered boats.

On the north bank were more treacherous marshes (presumably the Lea Marshes), which the Britons knew well. "In pursuing the remainder" (of the Britons), writes Dio, "they got into swamps from which it was difficult to make their way out, and so lost a number of men."

Up to this point the two principal enemy leaders had been Togodumnus and Caratacus. Then Togodumnus was killed, perhaps in contesting the crossing of the Thames, and the British tribesmen, "so far from yielding, united all the more firmly to avenge his death. Because of this fact and because of the difficulties he had encountered, Plautius became afraid and, instead of advancing further, proceeded to guard what he had already won, and sent for Claudius."[1]

Here we meet another difficulty. Dio Cassius implies that Plautius had met with such stiff resistance that he decided to call a halt and appeal to Claudius for help. But Suetonius has a very different story to tell. According to him, Claudius, the least military of emperors, regarded the British expedition as a heaven-sent opportunity to acquire a little easy glory, which might compensate for his obvious deficiencies. Suetonius makes the divine Emperor look a fool. For example, he mentions that "if ever he [Claudius] arrived a little late in the dining hall, there was nothing for it but to tour the tables in search of a vacant couch; and when he took his usual after-dinner nap the company exercised their wits by putting slippers on his hands as he lay snoring, and then gave him a sudden blow with a whip or cane to wake him, so that he rubbed his eyes with them".[2] Claudius's mother called him a monster: "If ever she accused anyone of stupidity she would exclaim 'He is a bigger fool even than my son Claudius!' "

[1] Dio's Roman History, op. cit.   [2] Suetonius, The Twelve Caesars, op. cit.

On one occasion Claudius "staged, on the Campus Martius, the realistic storm and sack of a fortified town, with a tableau of a British king's surrender, at which he presided in his purple campaigning cloak". On another occasion, when presiding over some gladiatorial sports in the Roman arena, "when the gladiators shouted, 'Hail, Caesar, we salute you, who are about to die,' he answered sarcastically, 'Or not, as the case may be.' They took him up on this and refused to fight, insisting that his words amounted to a pardon. Claudius grew so angry that he was on the point of sending troops to massacre them all . . . however, he changed his mind, jumped from his throne and, hobbling ridiculously down to the lakeside, threatened and coaxed the gladiators into battle. . . ."[1]

His wife, the sophisticated, sensual Messalina, delighted to deceive her ridiculous husband. One can hardly blame her, since his personal habits, as described by Suetonius, included "an uncontrolled laugh, a horrible habit, under the stress of anger, of slobbering at the mouth and running at the nose, a stammer, and a persistent nervous tic—which grew so bad under emotional stress that his head would toss from side to side".[2]

It might well be asked, "What has this to do with the Roman invasion of Britain?" I suggest that it has considerable relevance. For while such men as Aulus Plautius, Vespasian and the rest were struggling through the mud of the Thames and warding off British spears, the head of the Roman state, the most powerful man in the world, lounged in his luxurious palace on the Palatine Hill or played the fool to the Roman mob in the arena. The riches of the world were at his command. Like his predecessors, Tiberius and Caligula, and his successor, Nero, he became corrupt and vicious. Yet he was still the Emperor, Commander-in-Chief of the army, no mere figurehead, but wielding an absolute power such as few men have since possessed. It is hardly surprising that eventually it unhinged his mind.

Now Claudius receives a messenger from an island on the outermost fringes of the Empire. Aulus Plautius, with four seasoned legions and their auxiliaries, is halted at the Thames. It was the Emperor's privilege and responsibility to lead his troops into the enemy capital and receive the surrender of the conquered.

[1] Suetonius, *The Twelve Caesars, op. cit.*   [2] *Ibid.*

23. Another type of Roman helmet.

24. Examples of *phalerae* (military decorations) worn on uniforms.

25. From a Roman smithy: axes and pliers found at Newsteads, Scotland.

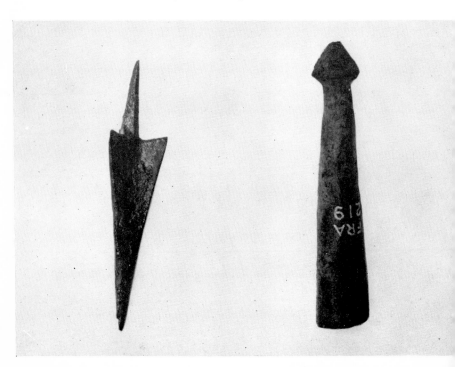

26. *Left:* Roman arrow head; *right:* Roman ballistae bolt.

So Claudius came. He bade farewell to Messalina and the court (one can imagine their mockery), put on his armour, gathered reinforcements from his household troops, a detachment of the 8th Legion and "extensive equipment, including elephants". He rode to Ostia, the port of Rome, and set sail for Marseilles. Suetonius says that he was "nearly wrecked off the Ligurian coast, and again near the Isle of Hyères, but made port safely".

"Thence", says Dio, "advancing partly by land and partly along the rivers, he came to the ocean and crossed over to Britain, where he joined the legions that were waiting for him near the Thames."

It would not be an easy journey even today; from Rome to Ostia, westward along the Riviera coast to Marseilles, up the Rhone Valley to Lyons or beyond; north-westward through Burgundy to the Seine Valley, across the plains of Picardy and Artois to Boulogne, where the ships were waiting to take him and his followers to Kent. Then the landing, perhaps at Richborough; a few hours' sleep, and to horse again for the last sixty miles over the North Downs, or through the forested lowlands; past what are now Canterbury, Faversham, Chatham and Gillingham, until the broad, marshy valley of the Thames lay below. Finally, Claudius would see the huge tented camp surrounded by its earthworks, the huddle of ships on the hither bank of the broad river. He would smell the salt air blowing in from the estuary, see the gleam of the standards as his senior officers rode out to meet him, and hear above the blare of welcoming trumpets, the swelling shout of "*Imperator....Imperator....Imperator....*"

For Claudius it must have been a great moment.

"Taking over command of these [troops]", writes Dio, "he crossed the stream and, engaging the barbarians, he defeated them in battle and captured *Camulodunum*, the capital of Cunobelinus. Thereupon he won over numerous tribes, in some cases by capitulation, in others by force, and was saluted as *imperator* several times, contrary to precedent; for no one man may receive this title more than once for one and the same war."

The Emperor stayed in Britain only sixteen days. He received the submission of the conquered tribes, then, after bidding Plautius subjugate the rest of the country, hurried back to Rome to celebrate his triumph. The Senate awarded him the title of Britannicus, and two triumphal arches were erected, one in Rome and another in Gaul. Messalina also received her share of the glory. She was granted the privilege of occupying a front seat at the Circus, and of using the *carpentum*, a covered carriage, the use of which, inside the walls of Rome, was allowed only as a special mark of distinction.

And Claudius had a large commemorative inscription carved, which can still be seen in the Palazzo Barberini in Rome. A translation reads:

> *To Tiberius Caesar Augustus Germanicus, the son of Drucus; Pontifex Maximus; in the eleventh year of his Tribunician power; his fifth consulate and the twenty-first occasion of his being saluted Imperator; Father of the State and the People of Rome—because, without any mishap he received in unconditional surrender eleven conquered British kings, and for the first time reduced trans-Oceanic barbarians under the power of the Roman people.*

DAMNONII

VOTADINI

NOVANTAE

SELGOVAE

BRIGANTES

PARISI

DECEANGLI

CORNOVII

ORDOVICES

CORITANI

ICENI

SITE OF LINCOLN
(LINDVM)

9TH. LEGION

DEMETAE

SILVRES

DOBVNNI

GLOUCESTER
(GLEVVM)

20TH. & 14TH. LEGIONS?

CATVVELLAVN

TRINOVANTES

COLCHESTER
(CAMVLODVNVM)

SITE OF BATH

ATREBATES

CHARTERHOUSE
(LEAD MINES)

BELGAE

SITE OF
LONDON

RICHBOROUGH

CANTIACI

DOVER

LYMPNE

DVROTRIGES

2ND. AUGUSTAN LEGION

REGNENSES

CHICHESTER
(NOVIOMAGVS)

SITE OF
EXETER
(ISCA)

DVMNONII

ISLE OF WIGHT

ADVANCE UNDER AULUS PLAUTIUS 43-47 A.D.

BORDER CAMPAIGNS OF OSTORIUS SCAPULA 49-50 A.D.

CHAPTER SIX

VESPASIAN AND THE SECOND LEGION

CAMULODUNUM, the Catuvellaunian capital, stood near
modern Colchester. Some of the mighty earth-banks
which surrounded it can still be seen, especially at Lexden.
But Roman Colchester, the later *colonia*, on which the present
town stands, was built at a little distance from the old Belgic
settlement.

"Left to himself", writes Mr. M. R. Hull, "Plautius would now
wish to push his front line well inland from the capital and establish winter quarters for his legions. We know little or nothing of
the disposition of his forces, and it is unlikely that anything like
the whole expeditionary force was present at the capture of
Camulodunum. The most part of the troops present at the
capture would at once press on to extend their hold on the
country, but it may be regarded as certain that some of them
wintered here for the first season, and probably for some years
afterwards. We have not been able to find military camps at
Colchester, but the fine tombstone of Longinus, a *duplicarius*
[junior officer] of the First Thracian Cavalry, who died here on
service, is of very early date, and implies that his unit was stationed
here. It may be seen in the Museum."[1] There is also the tombstone
of Facilis already described.

This passage, written by one of our most able archaeologists,
typifies the caution with which a conscientious scholar must
approach the task of describing the Roman invasion. Up to the
capture of Camulodunum, one has some sparse documentary
evidence, eked out by archaeological research. There follows an
awkward gap. Dio Cassius ignores Britain and goes on to describe
events in Rome and elsewhere. Tacitus tells us nothing of this
period; neither does Suetonius, except for a few lines in his
biography of Vespasian, which we will consider later. In the
meantime, what happened? We are left only with informed

[1] M. R. Hull, M.A., F.S.A., *Roman Colchester*, Colchester Town Council, 1952.

speculation. Plautius "would now wish to push his front line inland" . . . "it is unlikely that the whole expeditionary force was present" . . . "it may be regarded as certain that some of them wintered here" . . . and so on.

All this may well be true but we have no proof. It is curious that, up to now, no remains of a large legionary camp have been discovered at or near Colchester. On the other hand, there is a mysterious road pointing at the Abbey Field south of the town. Does it lead to a Roman naval base on the coast, or could it mean that there was, at some period, a legionary camp on the Abbey Field? As the latter is still in the possession of the War Department, we are unlikely to know for some time.

There are no records of any significant military fortifications of any sort in the lowland zone of Britain, i.e. south of the Fosse Way. They begin and become numerous beyond the Fosse. Therefore, with one exception, that of the 2nd Augustan Legion, it is extremely difficult to state with precision where the four legions were during the early years of the occupation. The standard theory, which is given in all textbooks, is that the 2nd Augusta campaigned in the west, the 9th pushed north towards Lincoln, while the 14th Gemina and the 20th Valeria Victrix took a north-westerly route, towards the Welsh marches and Chester. This theory may well be true, but (again apart from the 2nd Augusta) it rests on the slenderest of evidence. It can be summed up in a page.

Tombstones of soldiers of the 9th Legion have been found at Lincoln, dating from the early period. Between 1945 and 1953 the Lincoln Archaeological Research Committee unearthed the foundations of the legionary fortress on the hill-top north of the river gap, near the later *colonia*.[1] Professor Graham Webster suggests that the 9th was at Lincoln round about A.D. 48, remaining there until 71, when it moved to York.

Tombstones of soliders of the 14th Gemina have been found at Uriconium (Wroxeter) near Shrewsbury. There is also one to an officer of the 20th, a *beneficiarius* but he was not at the time attached to his unit. But no trace of their legionary fortress has

---

[1] A town built for retired veterans of the Roman Army. Beside the one at Lincoln, there were *coloniae* at Colchester, Gloucester, and elsewhere. But these were towns: not military camps.

been discovered, and the fact that they were buried at Wroxeter does not necessarily prove that they were stationed there. But Wroxeter was near the Welsh border and a likely spot from which to keep watch on the Welsh hill-tribes. The 20th was at Chester in A.D. 70 or thereabouts. It *may* have been stationed at or near Uriconium before moving on to Chester.

With the 2nd Augusta we are on much firmer ground. First, there is a vital scrap of documentary evidence from Suetonius, who, in his biography of Vespasian, says that the Emperor, in his early career, "proceeded to Britain, where he fought thirty battles, subjugated two warlike tribes, captured more than twenty strongholds, besides the entire Isle of Wight (*Vectis*)". Tiles stamped with the name of the 2nd Augusta have been found at Seaton in Devon, at Sea Mills near Bristol, and in Gloucester. The legions, when building permanent quarters, used to stamp certain of their roof tiles with their legions name and number, and these tiles provide useful evidence, though, as they were not dated, they have no chronological value. But "pigs" of lead bearing the legionary stamp have been found in lead-mines at Charterhouse in Somerset, and these can definitely be dated to A.D. 49, only six years after the conquest.

These few facts—and one dramatic piece of archaeological evidence which will be described later—are all we have with which to bridge the gap between A.D. 43 and A.D. 50, when Tacitus takes up the story. So we are forced to speculate. How did the Romans stand after the fall of Camulodunum? They had captured the capital of the late King. One of his sons had been killed. The other, Caratacus, who had controlled the western part of the kingdom, was in retreat.

The petty kingdom of Verica in Sussex had become a client-state. Its King, Cogidumnus, on whom Cunobelinus had made war, gladly accepted Roman protection, and was awarded, by Claudius, the unique title of *Rex et Legatus Augusti*, which made him the Emperor's representative while still retaining his royal title. We know this from an inscription found at Chichester (Noviomagus), Cogidumnus's capital; it is now set in the wall of Chichester Town Hall. The collaboration of Cogidumnus must have been of great values to the invaders, as it safeguarded their left flank and provided them with a base from which to

launch their attack on Wiltshire and Dorset. They also received
the submission of Prasutagus. King of the powerful Iceni tribe
of East Anglia, which gave them so much trouble later.

What would be the Roman's basic strategy? Among archaeologists there are two main lines of thought. One is that, over a
period of four years, the legions advanced slowly, at the rate of
about twenty miles a month, until they reached the Humber-
Severn line, where they halted. The other, which to me appears
more plausible, is that they rapidly followed up their advantage
by occupying the whole of Cunobelinus's kingdom, disarming the
inhabitants, fortifying the frontier, and consolidating what had
been won.

To the writer, as distinct from the professional archaeologist,
the depressing aspect of the Claudian invasion of Britain is the
absence of *personalities*. With Caesar it is different. His may only
have been a raid, but at least one knows what the man looked like
and what he thought. Most of the other men concerned in the
Great Invasion are mere names. We know Claudius, of course,
from the pages of Tacitus and Suetonius, but he was a fleeting
visitor. No one knows what the commander, Aulus Plautius,
was like and, among his opponents, only Caratacus emerges as a
person, because Tacitus described his last battle, and admired his
dignified behaviour when he was taken captive to Rome. But we
do know something about the commander of the 2nd Augusta,
who led the attack on the west, because through a trick of Fate
he later became Emperor, and therefore rated a biography by
Suetonius.

Therefore, since what men are is usually more interesting than
what they do, let us try to visualize Vespasian as he prepares to
lead his brigade into Wiltshire, Dorset and Devon.

We already know the big, jowly face with its powerful nose
and bruiser's chin. The thin irregular line of the mouth, in-
drawn, self-controlled, matches the shrewd eyes under the knit
brows. Not a relaxed face; not the face of a sensualist, such as
Claudius or Caligula, but that of a soldier and man of action;
strong, but not brutal, firm, yet capable of tolerance, even of
gentleness.

The Roman wits made great play with that look of concentration. "Vespasian", writes Suetonius, "was strong, well-formed,

but always wore a strained expression on his face; so that once, when he asked a well-known wit who always used to make jokes about people, 'Why not make one about me?' the answer came, 'I will when you have at last finished relieving yourself.' "

The character, as drawn by Suetonius, matches the portrait. He came of an obscure *bourgeois* family; his father was a tax-collector in Asia who later became a banker. Vespasian's early career was conventional; military service in Thrace, a *quaestorship* in Crete and North Africa; marriage to Flavia Domitilla, who bore him three children. Later, when Claudius became Emperor, Vespasian was given command of a legion in Germany, one of the four ordered to Britain. We glimpse him for a moment at the crossing of the Medway, and later we hear from Suetonius that he fought thirty battles, subdued two powerful tribes and captured twenty *oppida* (stronghold). That is all the historians tell us about Vespasian the legionary commander, although Sir Mortimer Wheeler, has uncovered one of the forts which Vespasian stormed, and shown us how the operation was carried out. But in his study of Vespasian the Emperor, Suetonius gives us some interesting facets of his character. Unlike Tiberius, Gaius, Claudius, Nero and their successors, Vespasian was not a vicious tyrant, sensualist and pervert. Nor was he ashamed of his origins:

> He was from first to last modest and restrained in his conduct of affairs, and more inclined to parade, than to cast a veil over his humble origins. . . . He had anything but a craving for outward show; on the day of his triumph the painful crawl of the procession so wearied him that he said frankly; "What an old fool I was to demand a triumph, as though I owed this honour to my ancestors or had ever made it one of my own ambitions! It serves me right." . . . Vespasian showed great patience if his friends took liberties with him in conversation, or lawyers made innuendos in their speeches. . . . Thus he complained only once about Mucianus, a bumptious and immoral fellow who traded on his past services . . . and then in private and common acquaintance, his concluding words being, *"But, personally, I am content to be a male."*[1]

The same writer mentions that—

> . . . Vespasian was nearly always just as good-natured, cracking

[1] Our italics.

frequent jokes, and, though he had a low form of humour and often used obscene expressions, some of his sayings are still remembered. . . . Once a woman complained that she was desperately in love with him, and would not leave him alone until he consented to seduce her. "How shall I enter that item in your expense ledger?" asked his accountant later on learning that she had got 4,000 pieces out of him. "Oh," said Vespasian, "just put it down to 'love for Vespasian'."

"My researches show", adds Suetonius, "that no innocent party was ever punished during Vespasian's reign except behind his back or while he was absent from Rome, unless by deliberate defiance of his wishes or by misinforming him about the facts of the case." For a Roman Emperor, that was high praise. The two "very strong tribes" mentioned by Suetonius must have been the Durotriges and the Belgae, whose fortresses were in Dorset and Wiltshire.

We do not know which route the 2nd Augusta took when it marched into the west. A glance at the Ordnance Survey Map of Roman Britain suggests a possible line of advance from Noviomagus (Chichester) which, as we have seen, was the capital of Cogidumnus, who had made peace with the Romans. From this point it was a short step to the Isle of Wight, which Suetonius specifically states was conquered by Vespasian. Presumably the Navy provided transport and supplies, just as, at a much later date, the Roman fleet kept pace with Agricola's army as it marched up the east coast of Scotland. "Combined operations" are not new.

From the Southampton area several routes were available; northwards to Winchester (*Venta Belgarum*), the tribal centre of the Belgae, north-westward to Salisbury Plain and the Mendips, south-westward to the chalk downs of Dorset. Here Vespasian would meet a different kind of country, and a different type of people, from those he had encountered in Essex and Hertfordshire. He would meet Belgic tribesmen who owed no allegiance to Cunobelinus—defiant and warlike men whose grandfathers had been driven from Gaul by the Romans and who had taken over and fortified the hill-tops of Wessex. They were experts in sling-warfare, like the Veneti of southern Brittany, the same people who had nearly defeated Julius Caesar in a naval battle a century earlier.

As the heavy Roman infantry, sweating under the armour, advanced steadily along the river valleys, they would see on the skyline the frowning ramparts of Belgic forts. Forward parties of mounted auxiliaries, screening their advance, would capture prisoners and bring back intelligence to the commanders; they had seen this fort or that fort; they estimated its strength to be so many thousand men. Sometimes there would be skirmishes with the enemy; at other times the legion advanced unhindered, yet always wary of an ambush.

Always Vespasian and his staff would be looking for strong-points which would have to be neutralized in order to safeguard their army's further advance. Nowadays it is difficult to imagine such conditions in the placid, pastoral countryside of Wessex. Yet to the Romans the uplands of Dorset must have been very much what the North-West Frontier of India was to the British Army of fifty years ago.

They would see Badbury Rings, with its deep ditches and high embankments manned by slingers. Probably they stormed and took this fort. Advancing to what is now the site of Dorchester, they would see *Mai-dun*—a stupendous fortress surrounded by ramparts over 100 feet high, enclosing an area two-thirds of a mile long and one third of a mile wide.

> The amount of manpower represented by these colossal embank-ments overpowers the imagination. In this respect alone Maiden Castle can be compared with the Pyramids of Egypt.
>
> Ovoid in plan, the successive lines of ramparts follow the line of the hilltop, here and there bulging outwards in the form of buttresses, and at other places biting into the plateau in long, concave curves. So sweet are the lines that they remind one of the functional streamlining of a ship or an aircraft; the lovely sym-metry of the east entrance, with its massive "hornwork", is clearly the work of a fine intelligence, a Vauban of the Iron Age. Here the approach path divides, and then has to outflank a second mighty breastwork before it pierces the inner rampart in two places.[1]

There is no doubt that the legion which Vespasian com-manded stormed and took Maiden Castle. Yet there is not a scrap of documentary proof. Our knowledge of the bloody battle which

[1] Cottrell, Leonard, *Seeing Roman Britain*, Evans Brothers, 1956.

took place beneath the ramparts of the eastern gate between the Roman legionaries and the Belgic defenders rests entirely on the evidence of the spade. The "dig" conducted by Sir Mortimer Wheeler between 1934 and 1937 revealed a story both tragic and heroic, and gives us hope that, when time and money are available, other hill-forts in the West Country and elsewhere might yield equally drastic results.

I once asked an archaeologist friend how Sir Mortimer, faced with the vast enclosure of Maiden Castle, knew where to sink the spade. He replied, "Wheeler has what we call a 'green hunch'— an instinctive feeling for *terrain* backed by a lifetime of experience. As an ex-soldier who commanded fighting formations, he is able to put himself in the position of a Roman commander faced with the problem of reducing a hill-fort, and of asking himself, 'How would *I* attack it?' "

At Maiden Castle there are two entrances, one at the west, the other at the east end. The western entrance, the most formidable of the two approaches, is highly complex—a maze of passages running between high embankments from which the defenders could rain sling-stones on the attackers. The eastern entrance, though formidable enough, is not so strong. Sir Mortimer argued that if Vespasian had had to storm the fort, he would have tackled the eastern approach, and therefore decided to sink his first trial-trenches there. He was amply rewarded.

Removing the turf and digging down, he found that the gateways had been flanked by high walls of stone dry-built of limestone blocks. At strategic points there were "ammunition dumps" of sling-stones, selected beach-pebbles of convenient size. Over 20,000 were found at one place. Within the ramparts, hastily dug in the chalk, were scores of shallow graves, in which lay the bodies of slain men and women, some with sword-cuts in their bones, some pierced with the small, neat hole made by the deadly Roman *pilum* (throwing-spear). Inside the defence lines was a huddle of burned-out huts. And everywhere there were sling-stones and the iron ballista-bolts fired by the Roman *ballistae*— powerful spring-guns. An unfortunate Briton had one of these missiles embedded in his vertebrae, and it had entered *from the front*.

Though the dead were hurriedly buried, Sir Mortimer tells

108   THE GREAT INVASION

us that "from few graves were omitted those tributes of food and drink which were the proper perquisites of the dead. With their cups and food-vessels and trinkets, the bones, often two or more skeletons huddled into a single grave and many of the skulls deeply scored with sword-cuts, made a sad and dramatic showing —the earliest British war cemetery known to us."[1]

What had happened? From the evidence it is possible to recreate the event. After capturing the Isle of Wight, the 2nd Augusta Legion probably crossed the River Frome at Dorchester. Two miles away it saw the sevenfold ramparts of the Celtic fortress towering above what were probably cornfields, like those which exist today. Whether an attempt was made to storm the west gate we do not know, since it has not been excavated, but it seems more likely that Vespasian shifted his main offensive to the weaker eastern approach:

> First the regiment of artillery which usually accompanied a legion put down a barrage of ballista-arrows. . . . Following the barrage, the Roman infantry advanced up the slope, cutting its way from rampart to rampart until it reached the innermost bay, where some circular huts had recently been built. These they set alight, and under the rising clouds of smoke the gates were stormed and the position carried.[2]

It had been a bitter struggle; not a fight between two professional armies, but between a regular battle-formation on one side and, on the other, hordes of men, women, and children, fiercely defending their homes. One can only imagine the rain of sling-stones, rocks and missiles hurtling down on the legionaries as, with shields interlocked above their heads in the *testudo*, they fought their way along the deep trenches. On this occasion at least the Romans did not "fight like gentlemen". They lost their tempers. How otherwise can one explain the fact that, among the slain were women, old men and children? "That the townsfolk fought back and fought hard is shown by the fact that they died with wounds in their faces."

Though there is no proof, I would like to think it was Vespasian

[1] Wheeler, Sir Mortimer, *Maiden Castle*, Ministry of Works pamphlet, H.M. Stationery Office, 1951.
[2] Wheeler, *op. cit.*

himself who called the troops to heel and perhaps inflicted summary punishment on the offenders. From his humane record as Emperor, one cannot believe that he would have willingly countenanced atrocities. Whatever happened, the legions eventually withdrew, after "slighting" the defences, and the Britons were left to bury their dead, as Sir Mortimer has described. Those who wish to study this grim but fascinating story at close quarters should visit the Dorchester County Museum, where the objects found at Maiden Castle are displayed.

One other West Country hill-fort has revealed evidence of Roman occupation, Hod Hill, near Blandford. This also was stormed by the Romans. Ballista-bolts have been recently found embedded in the native huts. Afterwards the fort was garrisoned by the Romans for about 20 years. One corner of this irregularly-shaped fort contains the neat, symmetrical outlines of the Roman fort, clearly visible from the air. Hod Hill, guarding the approaches to Cranborne Chase, was garrisoned. According to Professor Richmond, the native farmers of this area were "consistently kept, for generations, at a uniformly low level of existence, like *fellahin*. Unconditional surrender here brought in its train not freedom, but misery and the legionary garrison was there to enforce its first organization".[1]

To date, only two Dorset hill-camps have yielded evidence of Roman attack. Suetonius mentions *twenty*. Where are the others? Given time, funds and competent archaeologists, there is every reason to hope that evidence might be discovered which would help us to fill in the blank years between A.D. 43 and 47. For this, and other reasons, I believe that Roman Britain offers opportunities to young archaeologists as great, if not greater, than those presented by, say, Egypt.

Where Vespasian went afterwards, where he fought his other battles, and how long he stayed in Britain, we do not know. We know that the 2nd Augusta penetrated into Devon, the land of the Dumnoni, who do not appear to have given trouble. A tile of the legion was found at Seaton, in Devonshire. We also know that in A.D. 49 the legion was helping to work the lead-mines at Charterhouse in the Mendips, that they built a fortress at *Glevum*

[1] Richmond, I., *Roman Britain, op. cit.*

(Gloucester), possibly to protect the *Dobunni* of Gloucestershire against the unsubdued Silures living beyond the west bank of the Severn. Eventually the legion took up its permanent headquarters at *Isca Silurum* (Caerleon) on the Usk, where it remained for centuries. But that comes much later in our story.

As for the remaining three legions, the 9th, the 14th and the 20th, we have hardly a clue to their movements during the period A.D. 43-7, though from their later dispositions we can hazard a guess that the 9th moved northward to the Humber, and the 14th and 20th towards the Welsh marches. Probably they had less opposition than the 2nd, because the Iceni tribe of East Anglia were at first friendly, and the Coritani of Leicestershire do not appear to have been hostile. The usual period of office for an Imperial Governor was four years, so one may assume that Aulus Plautius returned to Rome in A.D. 47. When his successor, Publius Ostorius Scapula, replaced him, the curtain lifts again, and, in the pages of Tacitus we hear that—

> In Britain the situation . . . was chaotic. Convinced that a new commander, with an unfamiliar army and with winter begun, would not fight them, hostile tribes had broken violently into the Roman province. But Ostorius knew that initial results are what produce alarm or confidence. So he marched his light auxiliary battalions rapidly ahead, and stamped out resistance. The enemy were dispersed and hard pressed. To prevent a rally, or a bitter, treacherous peace which would give neither general nor army any rest, Ostorius prepared to disarm all suspects and reduce the whole territory as far as the Trent and the Severn.[1]

[1] Tacitus, *The Annals of Imperial Rome*, translated by Michael Grant, Penguin Books.

CHAPTER SEVEN

CARATACUS: THE LAST STAND

To keep a sense of proportion, it may now be helpful to look at Rome, for it is vital to remember that, to the Imperial Court and the Senate, Britain was a remote and not very important island off the coast of Gaul which appeared to be more trouble than it was worth. In fact, it seems highly probable that at this stage Rome had no intention of conquering the entire country, but merely of holding the economically productive Midlands and south, leaving the north to the barbarians.

Claudius had enough trouble on his hands elsewhere. He had annexed Mauretania and Judea; he was engaged in a struggle in the east, in Parthia and Armenia. Meanwhile, unknown to the Emperor, Messalina had entered into a liaison with Gaius Silius, the best-looking young man in Rome, and compelled him to divorce his aristocratic wife. At the heart of the Empire there was intrigue, corruption, murder and depravity. On its outer fringes, in Germany, in Asia and in Britain, the legions, under good or bad commanders, fought and died to hold or extend the frontiers. One of these officers was Publius Ostorius Scapula, who, Tacitus tells us, advanced the frontier to a line from the Trent to the Severn. Troops were moved forward from the Fosse Way, which may have been the frontier drawn by Aulus Plautius.

At about this time—A.D. 48—Messalina's blatant infidelities reached a peak. She consorted openly with her lover, Silius:

> It was full autumn; and she was performing in her grounds a mimic grape-harvest. Presses were working, vats overflowing, surrounded by women, capreing in skins, like sacrificing or frenzied Maenads. She herself, hair streaming, brandished a Bacchic wand. Beside her stood Silius in ivy-wreath and buskins, rolling his head, while the disreputable chorus yelled around him.[1]

Far away in Britain the harassed Governor was defending the

---

[1] Tacitus, *Annals, op. cit.*

province of which Claudius was the nominal conqueror. Did the Emperor know or care? One doubts it. Perhaps he sometimes read his legate's despatches, and shuddered at the memory of the wet, barbarous island which he had briefly visited. Perhaps—for imagination must fill in the gaps where history is silent—some young military tribune rode into Ostorius's camp on the bleak Cotswolds with the latest news from Rome; how the Emperor had at last taken revenge on his wife; how Messalina lay moaning in her room while an officer stood over her with drawn sword. "Terrified", writes Tacitus, "she took a dagger and put it to her throat and then her breast—but could not do it. The officer ran her through. . . . Claudius was at table when news came that Messalina had died. . . ."

Some may object that this has nothing to do with the Roman invasion of Britain. I suggest that it has relevance. For the invasion was carried out by men to whom the power-struggles at the centre of the Empire were in some ways more terrifying than the barbarians who menaced its frontiers. All were caught in the web. However able, however distinguished their services to the State, the lives of these officers were at the mercy of the Emperor and his creatures. At any moment a man might be hauled back to Rome to answer some trumped-up charge laid by an informer, and then done to death. The Governor's son, Marcus Ostorius Scapula, won the Oak Leaf for saving a comrade's life while serving under his father in the British campaign. He was a man of huge physique, expert in weapons, and went on to carve out a remarkable military career. Yet his end was squalid; trapped in his own villa by the emissaries of Nero, against whom he had conspired, he was forced to commit suicide.

But that was nearly twenty years later. At the time we are considering—A.D. 49-50—Publius Ostorius Scapula was facing a series of uprisings. The first to rebel were members of the Iceni tribe, who had originally been the Romans' allies. According to Tacitus, the reason for the Icenian revolt was the Governor's decision to disarm "all suspects". The real reason was probably fear of Roman exploitation, for it was this same East Anglian tribe which, eleven years later, was goaded to fury by the rapacity of the Procurator and the licensed brutality of the Roman veterans.

27. Roman cavalryman's stirrups.

28. Camp cooking pot.

29. Reconstruction of Iron Age chariot found in the Isle of Anglesey.

30. The Fosse Way from Beacon Hill, Somerset. This road marks approximately the frontier under the governorship of Ostorius Scapula.

Shortly afterwards the Silures of south Wales began to harry the Dobunni of Gloucestershire, and the Romans had to fight hard along the Welsh border, and in Monmouthshire and Glamorgan.

One of the best ways of grasping the general pattern of the invasion is to study the Ordnance Survey Map of Roman Britain (3rd Edition) published in 1956. In this beautifully produced map, the product of the most up-to-date research, including aerial survey, the civil sites are shown in black, the military ones in red; a solid square within a square for a legionary fortress, a solid or open square for a fort (depending on its type) a tiny red square for a "fortlet" and a small open rectangle for a temporary marching-camp. Of course, the map is still not complete, because new sites are constantly being discovered, but the overall distribution of known military sites is significant. (The maps on the end-papers have been based on the excellent Ordnance Survey production.)

The first fact one notices is that, south and east of the Fosse Way, there is hardly any red on the map, save for the forts along the coast; but west of the Severn, in the mountains of south Wales, the map is peppered with forts, as are Lancashire, Yorkshire and the north. Of course, this does not mean that there were no military sites in the south-east, since some of the civil settlements may have begun life as Army camps. However, from what Tacitus and Dio Cassius tell us, it is clear that this part of Britain, up to the Severn-Trent line, was occupied without very much fighting.

If we look a little more closely at the map, we shall see that there *are* minor forts, not only on the Fosse Way itself (a little to the south-west of Lincoln at East Stoke and Castle Hill), but also along a line running roughly parallel with, and to the north-west of it. Some at least of these camps were definitely in use during the early years of the occupation. For instance, there is one at Metchley, in Staffordshire, in the grounds of the Queen Elizabeth Hospital; it was built about A.D. 46 and abandoned some seventy years later. There are others at Greensforge, near Kingswinford, at Dodderhill, near Droitwich, and at Stretton Mill, near Gailey. These were large enough to hold auxiliary units of between 500 and 1,000 men. South-west of Droitwich, at Grimley, is another small camp; another is at Tedstone Wafer, about ten miles to the west, and at Bromfield, in the hills of Shropshire, nor far from Leintwardine, is a small marching-camp.

This cluster of small forts looks towards Radnorshire and central Wales; beyond them to the north lies Uriconium, where tombstones of men of the 14th and 20th Legions have been found; it would seem reasonable to suppose that the camps were built by these legions and their auxiliaries during their north-westerly advance. Yet, so far, their legionary fortress has not been found, although at Kinvaston, near the place where the present Wolver-hampton-Stafford road crosses Watling Street, there is a large fort, of half-legionary size, of Neronian date, which may be associated with the Boudiccan revolt. When parts of it were observed from the air great hopes were raised, but subsequent excavations have been limited in scope and disappointing in that it did not reveal Claudian remains.

Now we will look at the eastern counties, in which the 9th Legion operated. There is a small camp at Great Chesterford, about ten miles south of Cambridge; one at Water Newton (*Durobrivae*) on the Great North Road, a few miles west of Peter-borough; one at Ixworth, near Bury St. Edmunds; and a little marching-camp at Wighton, near the later, much more powerful camp at Brancaster. These camps were in the land of the Iceni. Much further north, along the Trent, were the camps of *Margi-dunum* (Castle Hill) *Ad Pontem* (East Stoke), with Broxtowe, Littlechester and Pentrich further west.

So far none of these areas has yielded any clear-cut evidence of fighting between Romans and Britons, such as Wheeler found at Maiden Castle. There are a number of hill-forts in north Somerset and south Gloucestershire which appear to have been attacked and burned in the first half-century of the Christian era; but dating cannot be precise, and the general consensus of opinion among archaeologists is that this destruction was the work of the Belgae thrusting into the interior before the Romans came—"beating up the locals", as one irreverent scholar put it to me.

For connoisseurs of what has been deprecatingly called "lurid archaeology" a discovery made at Bredon Hill in Worcestershire may be of interest. Here stood an Iron Age hill-fort, "the wooden gates of which had collapsed in flames, together with a set of human heads on which there were many marks of violence—the heads, it must be, of traitors or captured enemies".[1] The fort had probably been destroyed by Belgic tribesmen moving west. Such evidence helps us to understand the kind of people the Romans were fighting in Britain. Among the legionaries would be some whose fathers had fought the terrible Cherusci in the forests of the Rhine, people remotely akin to some of the British tribesmen. Six years after the Germans had annihilated three legions under Varus, the Romans returned to the Teutoburgian Wood, scene of the massacre: ". . . On the open ground were whitening bones, scattered where the men had fled, heaped up where they had stood and fought back. Fragments of spears and horses' limbs lay there—also human heads, fastened to tree-trunks. In groves nearby were the outlandish altars at which the Germans had massacred the Roman colonels and senior company commanders. . . ."[2]

Worse atrocities were committed in Britain during the Boudiccan revolt in A.D. 61.

Therefore, although evidence of British resistance to Ostorius Scapula is confined to the formal phrases of Tacitus, one must not underestimate the savagery of the fighting which took place in A.D. 50 in East Anglia and Wales. First to rise were the Iceni and some neighbouring tribes, who, according to Tacitus, gave battle "at a place protected by a rustic earthwork" which some think was at Cherry Hinton, near Cambridge. But the Romans broke through the defences, imprisoning the tribesmen within their own barriers, and then destroyed them. It was during this battle that the Governor's son, Marcus Ostorius Scapula, won the Citizen's Oak Wreath for saving a comrade's life.

Now it was the turn of the Welsh hillmen. Four tribes are mentioned; the *Deceangli,* who occupied the northern part of the peninsula, including Flint and Denbigh; the *Ordovices,* whose territory was further south, along the Berwyn Mountains and in Montgomery; the *Demetae* of Pembroke and Carmarthen, and the redoubtable *Silures* of Glamorgan and Monmouth. Tacitus says that, after defeating the Iceni, Ostorius "struck back against the Deceangli, ravaging their territory and collecting extensive booty. The enemy did not venture on an open engagement, and when they tried to ambush the column, suffered for their trickery."

[1] Lindsay, J., *op. cit.*   [2] Tacitus, *Annals, op. cit.*

Presumably this action took place somewhere in the mountains of Denbigh or perhaps in Snowdonia, because the historian adds that "Ostorius had nearly reached the sea facing Ireland when a rising of the Brigantes recalled him".

The Brigantes were a large and very powerful tribe ruled by an hereditary monarchy. They occupied what are now Lancashire, West Yorkshire, and an area northwards as far as the Tyne-Solway line. Later they were to give the conquerors much trouble and they may well have risen in support of the Deceangli at this time. But the rebellion was abortive. "The Brigantes subsided", writes Tacitus; "their few peace-breakers were killed and the rest were pardoned."

It is now, as we approach one of the most dramatic battles of the early campaign, that one longs for the missing pages of Tacitus describing the first six years of Claudius's reign. Now for a brief moment, one individual steps out from the featureless ranks of fighting men—governors, consuls, legates—takes on the faint colouring of personality, becomes something more than a name. The man is Caratacus, son of Cunobelinus, brother of Togodumnus; the same British prince whom we last heard of retreating westward as the Romans crossed the Thames and moved triumphantly on Camulodunum. Under the name Caradoc, he has passed into Welsh legend and is commemorated in several Welsh place-names, e.g. Caer Caradoc (the Fortress of Caradoc) in Montgomery. When we meet him in the pages of Tacitus he is already the hero of many battles, a brave and resourceful foe and focus of British resistance to the invaders. No doubt the missing pages would have told us much more about this British chieftain, who, in A.D. 50, was leading the Silures of Monmouthshire against the Romans:

> The natural ferocity of the inhabitants was intensified by their belief in the prowess of Caratacus, whose many undefeated battles—and even many victories—had made him pre-eminent among British chieftains.[1]

So troublesome did the Silures become that Ostorius had to establish a legionary garrison at Glevum (Gloucester). Which legion was this? We know that the 2nd Augusta occupied Gloucester for a time, but Tacitus expressly states that in order to

[1] Tacitus, *Annals*, *op. cit.*

"facilitate the displacement of troops westward to man it [our italics] a
strong settlement of ex-soldiers was established on conquered
land at Camulodunum. Its mission was to protect the country
against revolt and familiarize the provincials with law-abiding
government. Next Ostorius invaded Silurian territory."

It seems, then, that elements from other units were transferred
to the Severn from Colchester, perhaps to reinforce the men of
the 2nd Augusta, who could have been moved up from Somerset.
Again we cannot be certain, but it seems highly probable.

Fighting in the Welsh mountains would be guerrilla warfare,
at which Caratacus, like his ancestor, Cassivelaunus, was adept.
Tacitus talks of the British chieftain's "superior cunning and
topographical knowledge" which compensated for his inferior
military strength. The only way the Romans could hope to subdue
the Silures was to control the river mouths, and then, advancing
along the valleys, build auxiliary forts at strategic points, linked
by a permanent system of military roads from which the whole
area could be policed. This, in fact, was the method which
Julius Frontinus adopted many years later, as can be seen in the
disposition of his forts on the Ordnance Survey Map of Roman
Britain. But in the time of Ostorius Scapula, harassed as that
Governor was by raids all along the frontier, and with the
northern tribes restless and unsubdued, such a policy may not
have been possible; at any rate, it was not adopted.

The result was that, though the Romans penetrated into
Silurian territory, Caratacus avoided battle and slipping out of
the net, joined forces with the Ordovices of Powys, whose
stronghold lay behind the Berwyn Mountains. "The interpreta-
tion of the situation by Caratacus", writes Richmond, "is clear
from the action which he took. A British victory might enable
him to keep the Roman forces out of Wales for longer; but a
defeat might result in an immediate closing of the route of escape
to the north."[1]

Caratacus had decided to fight a pitched battle on ground of
his own choosing. Students of old battlefields have often attempted to identify the site from Tacitus's vivid account; but
alas, there are quite a number of Welsh hill-forts, all of which fit
his description equally well.

[1] Richmond, I., *Roman Britain, op. cit.*

On one side, he says were steep hills and "overhanging cliffs", and where the slopes were gentler they were strengthened by artificial ramparts of stone. In front was a river without easy crossings. Difficult approaches and easy escape routes gave maximum advantage to the Britons and maximum difficulty to the Romans. The place could have been Criggion, in Montgomeryshire, where the Severn swirls below high cliffs, and the whole setting has a dramatic beauty which is both evocative and appropriate. But there is not a jot of archaeological evidence to support Criggion against any of the other suggested sites.

Tacitus, like other Roman historians, was fond of putting into the mouths of each opposing general an eve-of-battle oration appropriate to the occasion, and he gives one to Caratacus. We need not dismiss this as fiction. At the period when Tacitus wrote, history was conceived as a form of dramatic poetry, strongly influenced by the Greek epic. I see no reason to doubt that, as Caratacus hastened to one point and another among his followers, he *did* "stress that this was the day, this the battle, which would either win back their freedom or enslave them for ever", and that "every man swore by his tribal oath that no enemy weapons, no wounds, would make them yield".

After first sending reconnoitring parties to find the weakest points in the enemy defences, the Romans crossed the river at several points, then stormed the ramparts. In this first attack they were beaten back by a shower of missiles, suffering many casualties. A renewed assault, under the cover of locked shields, was more successful, the Romans demolishing the crude stone rampart and then driving the Britons back at the sword's point. "While light-armed auxiliaries attacked with javelins, the heavy regular infantry advanced in close formation. The British, unprotected by breastplates or helmets, were thrown into disorder."

Their flank turned by the auxiliaries, while the legionaries attacked their front, the British forces lost cohesion. Those who escaped Roman swords and javelins fled over the hill-tops.

Behind this terse description we can detect a familiar story: the triumph of disciplined troops over brave but impetuous levies. Waging skilful irregular warfare, Caratacus had held out for years, but, once engaged in a major pitched battle, had been outmanœuvred and outfought. But not captured; when the British prisoners were brought in to the Roman camp Caratacus was not among them. He was hurrying northward to Brigantia, hoping to continue the struggle in the Pennines.

However, he had fought his last battle. Queen Cartimandua of the Brigantes, with whom he sought sanctuary, handed him over to the Romans, with whom she was in allegiance. A chained captive, Caratacus was taken by Ostorius to Rome to celebrate his triumph. It was the ninth year of the war in Britain.

Although it was customary for victorious Roman generals to exhibit their distinguished captives to the Roman mob, Caratacus seems to have aroused more than usual interest. "The people", write Tacitus, "were curious to see the man who had defied their power for so many years". The Praetorian Guard, in their splendid parade dress, stood in arms before their camp. The Emperor Claudius, his wife, Agrippina (who had replaced Messalina), and the chief officers of state watched from their high places. Thousands of citizens crowded the Forum and lined the decorated streets along which the procession passed. Under the hot Italian sky, so different from that of his own northern land, Caratacus moved, erect and dignified, behind the marching ranks of legionaries, their standards gleaming in the sun.

First came the British King's petty vassals "and the decorations and neck-chains and spoils of his foreign wars". Then followed his brothers, wife and daughter. Finally, came Caratacus himself. On reaching the dais where Claudius sat, he addressed the Emperor in words which, though they may not have been those which Tacitus gives him, were probably as outspoken:

> Had my lineage and rank been accompanied by only moderate success, I should have come to this city as friend rather than prisoner, and you would not have disdained to ally yourself peacefully with one so nobly born, the ruler of so many nations. As it is, humiliation is my lot, glory yours. I had horses, men, arms, wealth. Are you surprised that I am sorry to lose them? If you want to rule the world, does it follow that everyone else welcomes enslavement?

Claudius's response was magnanimous. He pardoned Caratacus and his family, ordering their chains to be struck off. They then paid homage to Agrippina, who was "conspicuously seated on

another dais nearby". This fiercely ambitious woman, mother of
Nero, was asserting her partnership in the Empire her ancestors
had won.

One wonders what happened afterwards to Caratacus. We
know that he lived on in Italy with his wife and children. They
would not, in any case, be permitted to return to Britain. We
have only one more comment from the British King, of whom
Petrus Patricius writes:

> On wandering about the city once and beholding its magnitude
> and the splendour of the houses, he exclaimed; "Why do you,
> who have got so many and so fine possessions, covet our poor
> tents?

DAMNONII

VOTADINI

SELGOVAE

NOVANTAE

STANWICK

B R I G A N T E S

PARISI

DECEANGLI

CORNOVII

LINCOLN
(LINDVM)

ORDOVICES

CORITANI

WROXETER
(VIRICONIVM)

I C E N I

CATVVELLAVNI

TRINOVANTES

DEMETAE

DOBVNNI

COLCHESTER
(CAMVLODVNVM)

SILVRES

GLOUCESTER
(GLEVVM)

ST. ALBANS
(VERVLAMIVM)

BATH
(AQVAE SVLIS)

ATREBATES

LONDON
(LONDINIVM)

RICHBOROUGH

B E L G A E

CANTIACI

DOVER

LYMPNE

DVROTRIGES

REGNENSES

CHICHESTER
(NOVIOMAGVS)

EXETER
(ISCA)

D V M N O N I I

FIRST INTERVENTION IN BRIGANTIA – ABOUT 55 A.D.

SUETONIUS'S ADVANCE 61 A.D.

RAIDS INTO SILVRIAN TERRITORY

✕ BATTLES

CHAPTER EIGHT

RESISTANCE STIFFENS

THE ten years following the capture of Caratacus were among the most momentous in the history of the invasion. In fact, fourteen years after they landed in Britain, the Romans came perilously near to losing the island altogether. The steps leading to the near-catastrophe of A.D. 61 are fairly easy to follow, though again documentary evidence is sparse. Our main sources of information are again Tacitus and Dio Cassius, supplemented by archaeology.

The story falls broadly into four sections: (a) further fighting in South Wales against the Silures; (b) trouble in Brigantia, in which the Romans had to intervene in a civil struggle between Cartimandua and her consort, Venutius; (c) the invasion of North Wales and conquest of Anglesey, a Druid centre of resistance; (d) the revolt of the Iceni under Boudicca. Put as bluntly as that, it might appear that the whole country was constantly torn by warfare, but, of course, this was not so. The Army, based on its legionary forts at Gloucester, Lincoln and some yet undiscovered point, fought on the frontiers, foraging into Wales and at one stage intervening in Yorkshire. Behind that military screen the rest of the country had begun to adopt Roman civilization.

In Rome the same ten-year period saw the death of Claudius, murdered by his wife in A.D. 54, and the succession of Nero, her son by a previous husband. Claudius's own son, the boy Britannicus, whom Agrippina hated, was poisoned in full view of the Emperor's court in the following year. There was war with the Sarmatians on the lower Danube, and bitter struggles in Armenia and Parthia, on the eastern frontiers of the Empire. Seen against the wider perspective of a vast and wealthy Empire, the efforts of Ostorius Scapula and his successors to maintain their hold on an obscure and unattractive northern island seem unimportant.

It seems very doubtful if, at this period, Rome ever intended to annex the whole of Britain. The expected mineral wealth which had attracted the Romans failed to materialize. The struggle against the British tribes tied down four legions, and the failure of the Romans to make more rapid progress should be judged in relation to the Empire as a whole. Britain's importance was mainly strategic, not economic. Compared with the rich Roman provinces in Europe, Africa and Asia, on which Rome was fattening, Britain was "expendable". It is, I suggest, important to keep this always in mind, not only at this period, but during the whole of the occupation. For instance, when, at a later date the Emperor Domitian recalled Agricola just when he seemed at the point of bringing the whole island under total subjugation. Domitian's decision may, as Tacitus suggests, have been due to jealousy of Agricola's success; but it is more likely to have been due to the need to transfer troops to more vital areas, the loss of which would have been far more severe than that of Britain.

When Ostorius Scapula returned to Britain after his Roman triumph the Silures were active again. "Roman troops left to build forts under a divisional chief of staff were surrounded, and only saved from annihilation because neighbouring fortresses learned of their siege and speedily sent help. As it was, casualties included the chief of staff, eight company commanders [centurions] and the pick of the men." This could have taken place anywhere, along the Severn Valley, in the Forest of Dean, or further west. "Battle followed battle", Tacitus writes. "They were mostly guerrilla fights, in woods and marshes. Some were accidental—the result of chance meetings. Others were planned with calculated courage. The motives were hatred or plunder."

Ostorius was enraged. Recalling the punishment inflicted on the Sugumbri, he ordered that the Silures be utterly exterminated. But his efforts were inconclusive. Two auxiliary battalions, tempted by the opportunity of plunder, fell into a trap laid by the Silures, and were cut to pieces. Encouraged by this success, the hillmen then began to tempt other British tribes to rise against the Romans. At this point, overcome by exhaustion and the weight of his responsibilities, Ostorius suddenly died, perhaps of a stroke. Claudius despatched Aulus Didius Gallus in his place.

When he arrived in Britain, Didius Gallus was greeted with the sombre news that one of the legions, under Manilius Valens, had been severely mauled, and the Silures were plundering far and wide.

Now we will leave the western frontier for a while and look at southern and eastern Britain. Ten years have passed since the legions landed in Kent; they are now far to the north and west, stationed at Lincoln, possibly in the west, the Midlands and along the lower Severn. The west of England, from Hampshire to Cornwall, is quiet. The Home Counties, where Caesar fought Cassivelaunus and Aulus Plautius defeated Caratacus, are peaceful and well-ordered. From the newly-built ports of Dover, Richborough and Lympne, well-built roads converge on *Durovernum* (Canterbury) from which another fine road marches westward through Springhead and Crayford to the crossing of the Thames at *Londinium*. Here a port has sprung up near the point at which the Walbrook enters the Thames, and traders have established themselves beside the busy wharves. Further north, in the valley of the Colne, the former capital of Cunobelinus is being transformed. At some distance from the now deserted Belgic settlement, a Roman *colonia* is being built for retired veterans of the Roman army.

Unlike the normal Roman-British towns, such as *Calleva* in Hampshire, and *Venta Belgarum* (Winchester), they were not British cities, built under Roman guidance, but Roman settlements, the inhabitants of which were Roman ex-soldiers. Their purpose, as Tacitus states with reference to Camulodunum, was simple; to "protect the country against revolt and familiarize the provincials with law-abiding government". In fact the Roman veterans were apportioned land taken from the former British inhabitants and encouraged to settle there. The new Camulodunum had broad, straight streets, a forum or market-place on the Roman plan, and a large, magnificent temple of white marble dedicated to the deified Emperor Claudius; "a blatant stronghold of alien rule", says Tacitus; '... its observances were a pretext to make the natives appointed as its priests drain the whole country dry".

The Britons had not been town-dwellers. Now the Romans encouraged the British tribal leaders to build cities on the Roman plan; planned towns with a rectilinear pattern of streets, main drainage, adequate sanitation, piped water, baths, and centrally-heated houses. The Britons moved out of their hill-forts and forest strongholds, and under the supervision of Roman architects and surveyors, built such cities; *Verulamium* (St. Albans) took the place of the old Catuvellaunian stronghold of Wheathampstead. The Atrebates of Hampshire built a city at *Calleva* (Silchester), between modern Reading and Basingstoke. The Regnenses of Sussex built *Noviomagus* (Chichester); in the remote Cotswolds the Dobunni built *Corinium* (Cirencester) as a tribal centre and mart for their wool-trade.

At the time of which we are writing—between A.D. 51 and 61, these developments were only beginning, but the pattern was being sketched out; the heroic days of tribal warfare and tribal loyalty, of hard living and military virtue, were giving way to an ordered, civilized existence under Roman law. The rough trackways were being replaced by straight, well-engineered roads, with staging-posts at regular intervals. The Celtic tongues were still spoken by the common people, but their rulers were learning Latin; and, clumsily at first, then more assuredly, the conquered Britons began to absorb the Graeco-Roman culture of that far-off Mediterranean world.

If this presents too idealistic a picture, it had its darker side. Some of the richer Romans saw in the newly-conquered provinces an opportunity for financial gain. They lent money to the British chiefs at exorbitant rates of interest. Seneca, Nero's adviser and the most popular writer of his time (*c.* A.D. 5-65) was among these speculative moneylenders. Prasutagus, King of the Iceni, was among his later victims. There were corrupt officials, greedy tax-collectors, and brutal soldiers. The invaders were not all good; nor were they all bad; in fact the usual human mixture.

As one travelled north and west to the frontier, beyond the Severn and the Trent, the roads ended; there were no more towns and way-stations; only the lonely forts manned by hard-fighting auxiliaries from Spain and Africa and Asia: slingers from the Greek islands, bowmen from Syria, German spearmen from the forests of the Rhine; and in their great walled camps beside the Severn and the Trent the iron legionaries lounged in their barracks, or, mustering to the sound of the trumpet, marched into the unknown, roadless lands beyond the frontier, where every forest track or mountain pass might conceal an ambush, and even one's nominal allies among the Britons were not always to be trusted.

These British "allies" were a perpetual problem. From the

beginning of the invasion, the Roman policy combined armed conquest with diplomacy. They fought and defeated the sons of Cunobelinus, but came to terms with Cogidumnus, King of Verica, in Sussex, awarding him the status of "client-king" in return for free passage through his territory. They had to subdue the west, but in East Anglia sought and obtained an alliance with the rulers of the Iceni. The Welsh tribes accepted no compromise; they fought the Romans. But the Dobunni of Gloucestershire and the Coritani of the Midlands do not appear to have opposed the invaders; at least there is no record of conflict in this region. Further north still, on either side of the wild, inhospitable Pennines, lived the Brigantes, numerically the biggest tribe in Britain. "This great area", writes Richmond, "sundered by the Pennines and their spurs into numerous divisions, each large enough to maintain powerful war-bands, must always have owed its cohesion to mutual advantages and to local balances rather than to inflexible domination from a single centre . . . the ancient way of reinforcing such a suzerainty was by marriage alliances."[1]

At first the Romans had no wish to occupy this remote province; they wanted only to safeguard their northern frontier by alliance with a friendly state. At some period between A.D. 43 and 47, of which we have no record in Tacitus, the Brigantian kingdom seems to have become a Roman "client-state", but it was never a reliable one; there had been the abortive rising in A.D. 49, when Ostorius was fighting the Deceangli; it may have been for this reason that Queen Cartimandua was so anxious to demonstrate her loyalty by handing over Caratacus in A.D. 51.

Not long before A.D. 57, the Queen quarrelled with her consort, Venutius, from whom she had been divorced, and the tenuous cohesion of the Brigantian state, based on marriage alliance, broke up. Cartimandua promptly captured the relatives of Venutius, who retaliated by invading her territory. Venutius, being anti-Roman, constituted a threat to their security. With memories of Caratacus in mind, the Romans intervened in Brigantia on the side of Cartimandua. For the time being the fire was smothered, but not for long.

These hackneyed facts concerning Cartimandua and her consort, their quarrel and the Roman intervention, have been stated

[1] Richmond, I., *Roman Britain, op. cit.*

and restated in every text-book on Roman Britain. They are based on the well-known passage in Tacitus, in which he compresses the events of several years into one short paragraph. It reads, in Sir Mortimer Wheeler's translation:

> After the capture of Caratacus, Venutius of the Brigantes, as I have already mentioned, was pre-eminent in military skill. He had long been loyal to Rome and had been protected by our arms while he was united in marriage to the Queen Cartimandua. Subsequently a quarrel broke out between them, followed instantly by war, and he then assumed a hostile attitude towards us. At first, however, they simply fought against each other, and Cartimandua by cunning strategems captured the brothers and kinsfolk of Venutius. This enraged the enemy, who were stung with shame at the prospect of falling under the dominion of a woman. The flower of their youth, picked out for war, invaded her kingdom. This we had foreseen; some cohorts were sent to her aid and a sharp contest followed, which was at first doubtful, but had a satisfactory end. A legion under the command of Caesius Nasica fought with similar results. For Didius, burdened with years and covered with honours, was content with acting through his officers and merely holding back the enemy. These events, though occurring under two governors and occupying several years, I have closely connected lest, if related separately, they might be less easily remembered.[1]

But the undying fascination of Roman Britain surely lies in the possibility of re-interpreting the ancient records in the light of fresh archaeological knowledge. This knowledge has been considerably increased, in recent years, by Sir Mortimer's masterly excavation of Stanwick in Yorkshire on behalf of the Society of Antiquaries. It now seems that Stanwick, a lonely site not far from Scotch Corner, was Venutius's great stronghold, and the site of his last stand.

Later I shall refer in some detail to Stanwick and the discoveries made there. Meanwhile, let us consider Sir Mortimer's comments on the above-quoted passage of Tacitus.

> The general trend [he writes] is not in doubt. Prior to the surrender of Caratacus in A.D. 51, the Romans had secured the collaboration of the Brigantian royal house, with a guarantee of military aid in

[1] Wheeler, Sir M., *The Stanwick Fortifications*, Society of Antiquaries, 1954.

the event of tribal recalcitrance. What other inducements were offered is not recorded, but analogy suggests monetary grants and trading facilities, the latter of which may be reflected in the relative importance of imported pottery found at Stanwick. The words of Tacitus, "as I have already mentioned", may imply an earlier reference in one of the lost books to this compact; certainly it carries back the first appearance of Venutius into the early years of the Occupation. . . . After A.D. 51 Venutius definitely broke with his Queen and succeeded Caratacus as leader of the resistance movement. Roman cohorts intervened on behalf of Cartimandua with hard-won success. In the circumstance the subsequent reference to similar action by a legion (presumably the 9th from Lincoln) makes sense only if a later intervention is in question; but Tacitus is here again summary and obscure. The general impression is that in the fifties of the century Cartimandua was holding on precariously with Roman aid, and presumably therefore within easy reach of it, against a persistent anti-Roman faction led by her formidable husband, who may equally be presumed to have had his headquarters *beyond the immediate reach of intervention*. [Our italics.][1]

In other words, possibly at Stanwick, a long way from the legionary base at Lincoln, which the Romans were occupying in the early fifties.

Roman strategists must now have begun to see that the Trent-Severn line was no longer tenable as a permanent frontier. Sooner or later the invaders would have to occupy Brigantia itself. But Didius Gallus, already an elderly man, was incapable of initiating such action, even had he wished to do so. He was content, as Tacitus says, with "merely holding back the enemy".

His successor, Quintus Veranius, conducted a few minor campaigns, but died before he had completed his term of office. By this time Claudius, murdered by Agrippina, had been succeeded by her son, Nero. Veranius, in his testamentary last words, informed the Emperor that if he could have been spared for a further two years he would have "presented him with the whole province". Mr. Eric Birley, in his paper, "The Significance of Quintus Veranius",[2] does not accept Tacitus's summary dismissal of Veranius as an idle boaster. In an interesting and closely-

---

[1] Wheeler, Sir M., *The Stanwick Fortifications, op. cit.*
[2] *Durham University Journal*, June, 1952, pp. 88-92.

1. Another view of the Fosse Way from the air, looking north-east from High Cross, Leicestershire.

DIS
MANIBVS
C·IVLI·FA·BALPINI·CLASSICIANI
...PROCROVINC·BRITANN
IVLIAINDIFILIAPACATAINFELIX
VXOR

32. Memorial stone to Julius Classicianus, Procurator (Financial Officer) of Britain after the Boudiccan revolt. Found near the Roman Wall, Tower Hill, London.

33. Leather shoes worn by women, found at Roman fort at Newsteads.

argued paper, he points out that the early career of Veranius, which can be followed from inscriptions, marks him out as a man of unusual promise. His advancement had been rapid; he had been chosen by Tiberius for responsible employment at the earliest possible stage, and his selection, by Nero, for the governorship of Britain suggests that "If Nero, then, in A.D. 57, decided to send a new governor of the calibre of Veranius to Britain, his mind must already have been made up. It was to be held, not evacuated; and not merely held, but brought more completely under Roman control."

The actions of Veranius's successor, Gaius Suetonius Paulinus, certainly suggest that Nero had decided on a "forward policy". This energetic soldier and administrator galvanized the Roman army of occupation into vigorous action. His previous military career, when he had defeated the tribes of the Atlas Mountains by striking at their distant plainlands, had equipped him to deal with the troublesome mountain-dwellers of north Wales. No doubt this was why he was chosen for the task. He struck first at the Isle of Anglesey, which was thickly populated, "hospitable to refugees, and the seat of a large community of Druids, fanatically antagonistic to Rome" (Richmond). The Druids appear to have been the spiritual centre of British resistance; there were politically-minded priests, and it was probably this fact, more than horror at their barbarous religious practices, which prompted Suetonius to move against them in force.

We do not know how his forces were constituted; probably there were contingents of the 14th and 20th Legions, and their auxiliaries. Moving along the coastal corridor, with the dark mass of Snowdonia looming above them, the Romans advanced to the Menai Straits, where flat-bottomed boats ferried the infantry across to the island.

> Then came the cavalry; some utilized fords, but, in deeper water the men swam beside their horses. The enemy lined the shore in a dense armed mass. Among them were black-robed women with dishevelled hair like Furies, brandishing torches. Close by stood Druids, raising their hands to heaven and screaming dreadful curses.[1]

For a short time, we are told, the Roman soldiers were paralysed

[1] Tacitus, *Annals, op. cit.*

I

by fear and horror. "They stood still", says Tacitus "and presented themselves as a target." Not until their general and officers urged them on, telling them not to fear a horde of fanatical women, did they begin to move, holding aloft their standards, drawing swords and locking shields against the furious barrage of missiles. The tribesmen, urged to frenzy by their priests, fought with the anger of men whose holiest sanctuary was being violated. But in vain. The Romans "bore down their opponents, enveloping them in the flames of their own torches", burning, killing, destroying. The sacred groves were hacked down. The altars, drenched with the blood of sacrificed prisoners, were overturned and broken. The priests and their women were massacred.

Some years ago an Air Force Station was being built at a site called Valley or "Llyn Cerrig Bach", in Anglesey. During the course of levelling the ground, the bulldozers turned up a number of iron objects. Eventually an archaeologist, Mr. Cyril Fox, visited the site and found that one of the contractor's vehicles was using a heavy iron chain to haul stumps out of the ground. It turned out to be a Druid slave-chain with five neck-rings. A number of other Celtic objects were found, including chariots and bronze ornaments. From the remains of a chariot a fascinating model was made which is illustrated opposite page 113. The site was evidently a Druid cult-centre, perhaps the one which Suetonius attacked. The slave-chain may have bound some unfortunate victim, sacrificed to one of the Celtic gods who demanded human lives. There were several of these: Taranis, Teutates and Esus. According to the poet Lucan, victims sacrificed to Teutates were killed by holding their heads under water until they drowned; there is a first-century silver bowl with a relief showing this form of sacrifice. A method of divination was to stab the victim in the back and observe his convulsions. These dark horrors, and those perpetrated by Boudicca's followers against their own countrymen, should check any cynicism one may feel about the "civilizing mission" of the Romans.

And it is easy to be cynical, particularly as one watches the next and most dreadful phase of the invasion, when Roman rapacity and injustice provoked a storm of violence and hate which soaked south-eastern Britain in blood. It is a sombre story redeemed only by its ending.

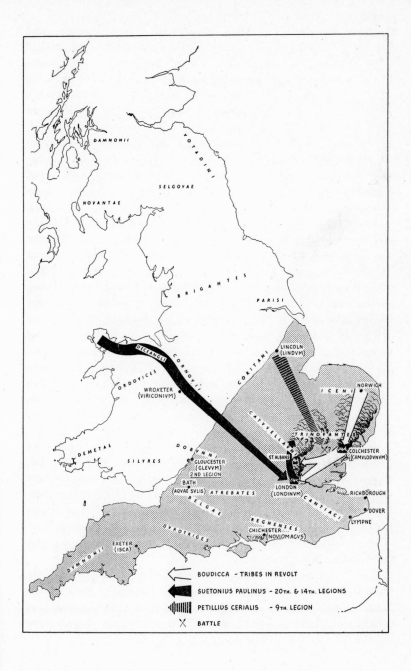

DAMNONII

VOTADINI

SELGOVAE

NOVANTAE

BRIGANTES

PARISI

DECEANGLI

CORNOVII

LINCOLN
(LINDVM)

CORITANI

ICENI

NORWICH

ORDOVICES

WROXETER
(VIRICONIVM)

CATVVELLAVNI

TRINOVANTE

COLCHESTER
(CAMVLODVNVM)

DEMETAE

SILVRES

DOBVNNI

GLOUCESTER
(GLEVVM)
2ND LEGION

ST ALBANS

BATH
(AQVAE SVLIS)

ATREBATES

LONDON
(LONDINVM)

CANTIACI

RICHBOROUGH

BELGAE

DOVER

DVROTRIGES

REGNENSES

CHICHESTER
(NOVIOMAGVS)

LYMPNE

EXETER
(ISCA)

DVMNONII

⟸ BOUDICCA — TRIBES IN REVOLT

◀ SUETONIUS PAULINUS — 20TH. & 14TH. LEGIONS

◀║║║║ PETILLIUS CERIALIS — 9TH. LEGION

✕ BATTLE

CHAPTER NINE

THE WRATH OF THE ICENI

W HEN Suetonius's forces were hacking down the sacred groves in Anglesey, messengers reached him with grave news. The Iceni had risen in arms, other tribes had joined them, and were marching on the unprotected cities of south-east Britain. It was a dangerous situation for the Romans. The 9th Legion was at Lincoln, the 2nd Augusta at Gloucester, and the Army, presumably units of the 14th and 20th Legions, was concentrated in the north-westerly tip of Wales, more than 200 miles from the scene of action. The accounts left by Tacitus and Dio Cassius are vivid, but these writers, absorbed in the epic drama of the situation, and writing years after the event, give us few details from which we can judge the military action.

The focus of resistance was the Iceni tribe, which had at first accepted Roman domination, though from time to time resisting it. Tacitus frankly admits that the cause of their resentment was exploitation, from which their neighbours, the Trinovantes, also suffered. When the Icenian King, Prasutagus, died, he made Nero co-heir to his realm with his own two daughters. By this device he hoped to preserve his kingdom and household; but in vain.

"Kingdom and household", writes Tacitus "were plundered like prizes of war, the one by Roman officers, the other by Roman slaves. As a beginning, his widow Boudicca was flogged and their daughters raped. The Icenian chiefs were deprived of their hereditary estates as if the Romans had been given the whole country. The King's own relatives were treated like slaves."[1]

It is important to remember that this bitter comment was written by a Roman.

The Trinovantes of Essex fared no better. We have already learned that, when the Silures attacked the Roman garrison on the Severn, units from Camulodunum (Colchester) were moved to Gloucester, their place being taken by retired veterans, who were

[1] Tacitus, *Annals, op. cit.*

34. *Above:* Part of the fortifications at Stanwick before excavation.

35. *Below:* The ditch and embankment of Stanwick as excavated. Note the rock bed and (*right*) part of the dry stone wall thrown down by the Romans when they "slighted" the defences.

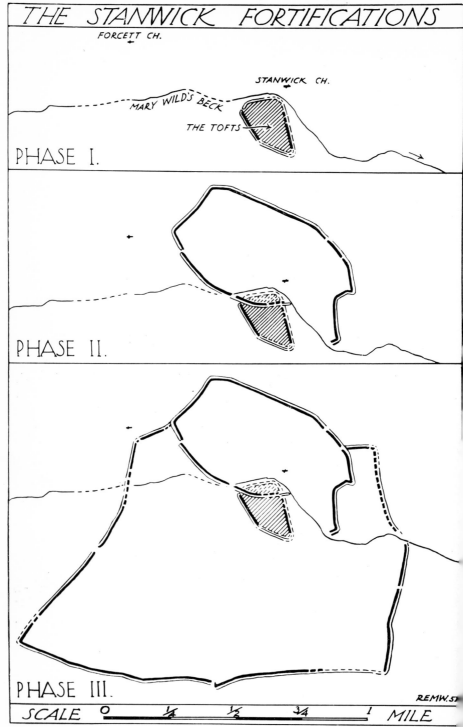

THE STANWICK FORTIFICATIONS

FORCETT CH.

STANWICK CH.

MARY WILD'S BECK

THE TOFTS

PHASE I.

PHASE II.

PHASE III.

REMW.51

SCALE 0 ¼ ½ ¾ 1 MILE

36. The Stanwick fortifications, showing three stages of development.

given land appropriated from the natives. These settlers "drove the Trinovantes from their homes and lands, and called them prisoners and slaves. The troops encouraged the settlers' outrages, since their own way of behaving was the same—and they looked to similar licence for themselves".

Looking at Colchester today—a pleasant little market town with multiple stores and cinemas—it is impossible to imagine it as the scene of one of the bloodiest episodes in the history of Britain. You approach it from London along the Roman road which was laid down not long after the invasion. At first this road passes through London's urban sprawl, and when at last it emerges beyond Romford, it is a broad, modern highway, flanked by large petrol stations, cafés advertising "dainty teas", and huge signs extolling the delights of Clacton and Southend. After passing through the little, unspoiled village of Lexden, near the site of Cunobelinus's capital, it approaches the modern town through an avenue of ancient limes. A signboard bears the proud inscription: "Colchester, Britain's oldest recorded town."

Colchester is an active, bustling, attractive place, thronged with cars, lorries and military vehicles. The High Street with its Town Hall, ancient inns and modern shops, is crossed at right-angles by another Roman street at the point called "Top of the Town". A narrow alleyway—in line with the main street—leads to the famous Balkerne Gate, which was one of the principal entrances to Camulodunum in Roman times. Turn right and descend the hill towards the Colne Valley and you will find substantial remains of the Roman city wall built in the late second century, long after the time of Boudicca. Retrace your steps, return along the main street and you will find, in a park on your left, the massive Norman castle, built in the twelfth century. It is now the Museum, and contains some of the finest Roman antiquities in Britain. But in the basement are the massive foundations of the Temple of Claudius, the actual building which Boudicca burned, and which Tacitus called "a blatant stronghold of alien rule". Mr. M. R. Hull writes of it:

> In the centre [of the Forum] stood the great temple of Claudius, built about A.D. 50 on such an elaborate scale that the Romans themselves ridiculed the ambition of the founder. It was of a well-known classical style, with a deep portico eight columns

wide and four deep. Colonnades ran along each side, but only half-engaged columns across the back. This plan is almost the same as that of the Temple of Mars Ultor in the Forum at Rome.

The great platform of this building still stands, hidden in the vaults under the Norman keep.

At the time of which we are writing, A.D. 61, the Temple would have been complete, rising high and white and resplendent on the hill above the Colne Valley, surrounded by the Forum or market-place, with its pillared Basilica or Town Hall, its shops and offices. From this wide, paved square ran straight, level streets paved and drained, bordered by well-built villas of stone with their baths and hypocausts. Nearby stood the temples of other alien gods and, on the outskirts of the city were the neatly-planned homes of the soldier-settlers, each with its plot of land filched from the Trinovantes.

It had no defensive walls; they were not considered necessary. "That was a matter which Roman commanders, thinking of amenities rather than needs, had neglected", comments Tacitus. Raw, new and unfamiliar, its white stone buildings violently outraging the green stillness of their familiar woods and meadows, the Trinovantian peasants must have hated Camulodunum; even their leaders, half-Romanized as they were, probably resented having to serve and maintain the temple of a foreign god.

The invaders had fouled their own nest. They had come, ostensibly, as bearers of a superior culture, yet their soldiers had behaved abominably, treating the natives like slaves. Greedy tax-collectors had exacted heavy tributes. The Procurator (imperial agent), Catus Decianus, was notoriously acquisitive, and was bleeding the inhabitants. "It was his rapacity", writes Tacitus, "which had driven the province to war."

Away to the north, in what is now Norfolk, the Iceni were also groaning under the Roman yoke. Seneca, one of several high Roman officials who had lent money to the British chieftains, now suddenly called in the loan which he had advanced to the Icenian King, Prasutagus. The King's daughter, Boudicca, a Queen of ancient lineage, had been flogged and her daughters violated. These are the incidents which Tacitus recalls; there must have been many others. The violent reaction of the British tribesmen could not have been provoked by a few isolated examples of injustice.

The Romans had been in Britain for fourteen years and, after the initial resistance, had been accepted. Probably, in the early years of the invasion, the inhabitants had received more generous treatment from the Army than from the civilians who followed in its wake. But now the legions were far away—on the Severn, the Trent, and in Wales.

The newly-created cities of Camulodunum, Verulamium (St. Albans) and Londinium lay open to attack. Most of the inhabitants of these towns were not Romans, but Britons who had accepted, and possibly profited by, Roman rule. We know from the experience of our own time what bitterness can be engendered against "collaborators"—those who, from self-interest or sheer necessity, have come to terms with an occupying force.

Even so, perhaps nothing would have happened if resentment had not found a focal point in a great leader, Boudicca. In Victorian times, under the name of Boadicea, which means "Victory" she became a romantic symbol of revolt; her bronze figure with streaming hair and defiant profile, still drives her scythed chariot outside the Houses of Parliament; the brave British Queen who defied the Romans.

"She was very tall", writes Dio Cassius, "in appearance terrifying, in the glance of her eye most fierce, and her voice was harsh; a great mass of the tawniest hair fell to her hips; around her neck she wore a large golden necklace; and she wore a tunic of divers colours over which a thick mantle was fastened with a brooch. This was her invariable attire."

These words have a ring of truth; though Dio lived long after Boudicca, he was probably drawing on descriptions by men who had seen her. It is a terrifying picture. The fierce warrior-Queen is the embodiment of a people's hate. Her red, streaming hair is a banner to the thousands who follow her war-chariot. Hers is no disciplined army, but a furious, plundering mob whose numbers swell as they press down through Suffolk on their way to unprotected Camulodunum.

"Don't fear the Romans!" she scoffs (in Dio's words). ". . . They protect themselves with helmets, breastplates and greaves. They provide themselves with walls and palisades and trenches.

Why do they adopt such methods of fighting? Because they are afraid! We prefer a rough-and-ready action. . . . Our tents are safer than their walls. Our shields protect us better than their suits of mail. . . . They can't stand hunger, thirst, cold or heat, as we can. They need shade and covering, kneaded bread and wine and oil . . . for us, on the other hand, any grass or root serves as bread, the juice of any plant as oil, water for wine, and any tree for a house. As for rivers, we swim them naked, whereas they don't get across them easily even with boats. . . . Let us show them that they are hares and foxes trying to rule over dogs and wolves!"

The Icenian centre, *Venta Icenorum,* was at Caistor St. Edmunds, near modern Norwich; its banks and ditches can still be seen. The Iceni may have moved along the line of the Roman road which still exists between Norwich and Needham Market, passing through the villages of Stratton St. Michael, Dickleburgh and Yaxley. Further south they would be joined by the Trinovantes of Essex. One hundred and twenty thousand tribesmen were on the march, burning and plundering the settlements and way-stations on their way to the Trinovantian capital.

Meanwhile, in Camulodunum, the inhabitants had appealed for help to Decianus Catus, the Procurator (financial officer), who, in the absence of Paulinus, was the highest Roman authority. He sent 200 men to supplement the tiny garrison. The town was panic-stricken. People said that "at night they heard, from the Senate House, foreign jargon mingled with laughter, and from the theatre outcries and lamentations, though no mortal man had uttered the words or the groans; houses were seen under the water in the river . . . and the ocean between the island and Britain once grew blood-red at flood-tide".[1]

Tacitus tells us what happened to Camulodunum:

> Misled by secret pro-rebels, who hampered their plans, they dispensed with rampart and trench. They omitted also to evacuate old people and women and thus leave only fighting men behind. Their precautions were appropriate to a time of unbroken peace.

In their shining new town above the Colne, without walls or even embankments to protect them, the inhabitants, Roman and British, watched fearfully while the massed tribesmen swarmed

---

[1] *Dio's Roman History,* translated by E. Cary, *op. cit.*

upon them, shouting their battle-cries. Among the defenders
would be Roman ex-soldiers, who doubtless did what they could
to hold back the enemy. But they were hopelessly outnumbered,
hampered by civilians and betrayed by Fifth Columnists. After a
two-day siege, the attackers broke in. Flames began to lick the
walls of the new houses of the settlers. Choked by rising clouds
of smoke, with the barbaric yells of the Britons in their ears, the
citizens retreated to the white temple of Claudius, the largest and
strongest building. In vain; it too was put to the flames, and the
last defenders were burned to death or butchered as they ran for
safety. The whole town was given up to loot and murder. "The
British did not take or sell prisoners", writes Tacitus. "They
could not wait to cut throats, hang, burn and crucify. . . ."

The tribesmen moved on, perhaps down the Roman road to
Caesaromagus (Chelmsford) and then into Hertfordshire. Their
track was marked by fire and slaughter. "By-passing forts and
garrisons, they made for where the loot was richest and the protection weakest." Verulamium (St. Albans), another newly-built
city, tribal capital of the Catuvellauni, fell to them; those of its
inhabitants who had not fled were massacred, their homes looted
and then burned to the ground. "Roman and provincial deaths",
writes Tacitus "at the places mentioned are estimated at 70,000."[1]

Archaeology confirms this grim story. In large areas of both
Colchester and St. Albans, a thick layer of soot and ashes marks
Boudicca's passing; a clear indication of which parts of these
cities were in existence in her time and which were built later.
There is a particularly fascinating piece of evidence at Camulodunum. Some years ago the authorities were re-laying a gas main
in the High Street and found Roman foundation walls jutting
out under the pavement from the modern buildings. Mr. M. R.
Hull, the archaeologist, was called to investigate. He found the
foundations of two Roman pottery shops which, from the familiar
layer of burned ash, had evidently been burned down by
Boudicca's forces. But the interesting point was that the party-
walls of the present buildings on the site—the Hippodrome
Cinema, Achille Serre's Dry Cleaners and a café, had been built
exactly on the footings of the Roman shops which existed before

[1] I have assumed that Verulamium fell before Londinium; but this is not certain.
L.C.

Boudicca burned them down—a remarkable continuity of property frontage.

A much grimmer instance—a vintage specimen of "lurid archaeology"—was found some thirty years ago on the site of *Margidunum* (East Bridgeford), just north of Nottingham. It is described and illustrated in the *Journal of Roman Studies*. The archaeologists found three skeletons: that of a man, aged about forty-five; with a Mediterranean skull; a woman, slightly younger, with a round British skull; and a boy of about fifteen, whose skull formation was of intermediate type. These skeletons had lain for some time, decomposing, before they were hastily buried, and beside them lay an unopened keg of oysters. (The wood of the keg had decayed, but its impression remained in the soil.) From the context of the grave the skeletons could be dated somewhere near the Boudiccan revolt.

The most plausible explanation of this find—though it causes some drama-hating scholars to avert their eyes—is that the bodies are those of a Roman soldier, his British wife and their son. They were just sitting down to enjoy their oysters—a favourite Roman delicacy—when along came the revolting British and spoiled the party. Later their friends returned, found the decomposing bodies, and buried them.

To return to Boudicca. From Verulamium the hordes of triumphant tribesmen began to move southward towards the Thames Valley and *Londinium*. We do not hear of London in Caesar's time, nor in that of Aulus Plautius, but by A.D. 61 it had become a flourishing port and mart. "This town", Tacitus says, "did not rank as a Roman settlement, but was an important centre for business-men and merchandise."

News of the revolt had reached Lincoln, where the 9th Legion was quartered. Taking some 2,000 men, mainly infantry, but with some cavalry, the young Legate of the 9th, Petillius Cerialis, hurried southward along the Irmine Street, then eastward, skirting the Fens, to intercept Boudicca's forces. But he could have had no idea of the scale of the rebellion. Against 120,000 men, what could 2,000 legionaries do? Somewhere—we do not know the place—Petillius's tiny force was surrounded and cut to pieces. Only the cavalry escaped with their commander. It must have seemed, at that moment, that the Romans were in danger of losing the whole island. Suetonius was still a long way off. Perhaps runners reached him with news of the 9th's defeat. We know he sent word to the commander of the 2nd Augusta, at Gloucester, to bring that legion to join him in the south. But the Legionary Commander was away and the Camp Prefect, Poenius Postumus, did not obey the summons. Perhaps he was afraid of a stab in the back from the warlike Silures. Whatever the reason, the 2nd did not march.

It would be wrong, I think, to imagine the whole of Boudicca's followers converging on London. More likely, they spread over south-eastern Britain in foraging and plundering bands, seeking out undefended settlements, killing Romans, and taking terrible revenge on all who had accepted Roman domination. As in our own times, "collaboration" became an excuse for working off private vengeance, a *carte blanche* for loot and murder. Into this disaffected area, from which all law and order had vanished, Suetonius now rode ahead of his forces, presumably elements of the 14th and 20th Legions with their auxiliaries. As they came down from the Midland plain, they would hear stories of British atrocities, and see with their own eyes the burned-out settlements, with the unburied corpses of the victims, some of whom had been hideously tortured. "They hung up naked the noblest and most distinguished women", writes Dio Cassius, "and then cut off their breasts and sewed them to their mouths, in order to make the victims appear to be eating them; afterwards they impaled the women on sharp skewers run lengthwise through the body. All this they did to the accompaniment of sacrifices, banquets and wanton behaviour, not only in all their other sacred places, but particularly in the grove of Andate."

But the main body of the army moved comparatively slowly. Polybius, though writing of the Roman Army some 200 years before Suetonius, allows us to watch the disciplined advance of a legion through hostile country:

> When the Commanding Officer had decided to halt the army for the night he sends out in advance a reconnaissance officer to chose a suitable spot for a camp. The spot chosen, ahead goes a small defence party, behind them surveyors. They have a standard drill. They measure the site, as laid down in the drill-books; they first stick up four big flags at the corners, to limit the area

of the camp. Then they plant smaller flags to mark the cross-streets, long ways and short ways and the subsidiary areas inside them.

The surveyors go along with their flags. Each unit in the Army knows exactly where in that camp its own street and quarter is. They march straight into the place, and each section or each group of ten men dumps off kit. They put down the tents, one or two men sit busy cooking the evening meal. The rest are detailed for various duties. A couple go out on guard duty outside the area, and a couple get busy digging a trench and throwing the earth up behind. By the time they have done that the two men of each section who have remained behind put up the tents for each section, and cook the evening meal.[1]

This is how the marching-camps were built, remains of which still exist in some parts of England. This is how the 14th and 20th Legions moved down from Anglesey, across bleak Cannock Chase, where now pit-heads and slag-heaps mar the skyline, crossing the Fosse Way at Vennonae (High Cross) where today the lorries thunder along the Holyhead Road, and down through Northamptonshire, past Towcester, Stony Stratford and Bletchley, and over the Dunstable downs—

twenty-four miles in eight hours, neither more nor less, head and spear up, shield on your back, cuirass-collar open one hand's breadth, and that's how you take the Eagles through Britain.[2]

Suetonius and his officers were moving at a faster pace. With their picked auxiliary cavalrymen, nerves alert for a hidden ambush, their scouts riding ahead and bringing back intelligence hour by hour, they cut through the hostile countryside and entered Londinium. The relieved citizens flung open their gates, and while the tired cavalrymen snatched a few hours' sleep Suetonius and his staff talked to the leading citizens. Terrifying stores were poured into their ears. The rebels had burned Camulodunum. Verulamium was in ashes. And now nothing stood between Boudicca and Londinium.

Suetonius, an experienced soldier, rapidly appraised the situation, and realized that his forces could not arrive in time to defend the city; in any case, his task was to save the province, not London, which was not a suitable place to give to Boudicca.

[1] Translated by J. Morris and M. R. Watson.
[2] Kipling, Rudyard, *Puck of Pook's Hill*.

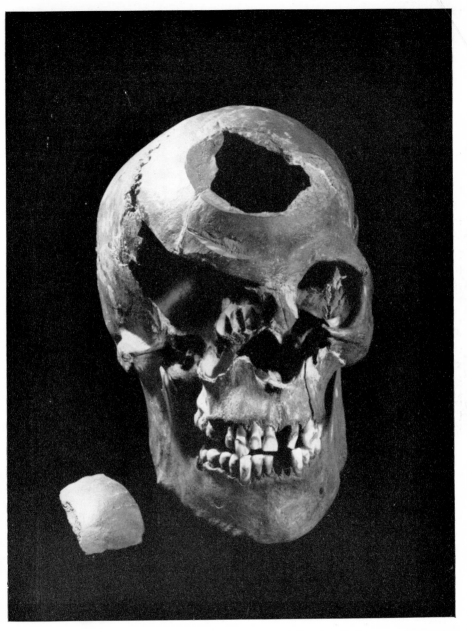

37. Mutilated skull (probably of prisoner) found in the ditch near the main gateway at Stanwick.

38. Roman Military Diploma awarded to auxiliary soldiers on termination of service. It granted them Roman citizenship.

"Eventually", writes Tacitus, "his numerical inferiority—and the price only too clearly paid by the rashness of the divisional commander [i.e. Petillius Cerialis] decided him to sacrifice the single city of Londinium to save the province as a whole. Unmoved by lamentations or appeals, Suetonius gave the signal for departure. The inhabitants were allowed to accompany him. But those who stayed because they were women, or old, or attached to the place were slaughtered by the enemy."

London has known many horrors in her eighteen centuries of existence—the Black Death, the Great Plague, the Great Fire and the fire-blitz of 1940. Those of us who have lived through the latest of these will find it hard to imagine anything worse. Death, anonymously delivered from the night sky, may seem the ultimate in terror, but one doubts if it was worse than the ordeal of the people of Londinium in A.D. 61.

At the time of the massacres which followed the partition of India and Pakistan, the poet Louis MacNeice, who saw them, remarked to the present writer: "They cured me of one illusion; that the ancient wars, fought with sword and spear, were more romantic than those fought with T.N.T." The people whom Suetonius left behind faced, behind their pathetic barricades, an enemy who outnumbered them a thousandfold; a merciless enemy, led by their implacable, red-haired Queen, in whom all feelings save those of greed, hate and vengeance had been banished. Where now the city typists hurry along Threadneedle Street, where the Bank of England stands, where the London Transport omnibuses roar along the Embankment, men and women, most of them British, were hacked, stabbed, and slashed to death, or burned alive in their homes, the ashes of which still lie in a thick layer, many feet beneath the steel-and-concrete office blocks.

The third chief city of Roman Britain had dissolved in flames before Suetonius had assembled his forces and, on carefully-chosen ground, turned to face the massed hordes of Boudicca. Again we have no idea where this battle took place. The Roman historians give us no clue to the site; and the archaeologists can only speculate. But both Dio Cassius and Tacitus have left vivid word-pictures.

"He [Suetonius] chose a position in a defile with a wood behind him," says Tacitus. "There could be no enemy, he knew, except in front, where there was open country without cover for ambushes. Suetonius drew up his regular troops in close order, with the light-armed auxiliaries at their flanks and the cavalry on the wings. On the British side, cavalry and infantry bands seethed over a wide area. Their numbers were unprecedented, and they had confidently brought their wives to see the victory, installing them in cars stationed at the edge of the battlefield."

The disproportion between the numbers of Britons and Romans is again emphasized by Dio. "Paulinus", he says, "could not extend his line the whole length of hers [Boudicca's] for, even if the men had been drawn up only one deep, they would not have reached far enough, so inferior were they in numbers; nor, on the other hand, did he dare join battle in a single compact force, for fear of being surrounded and cut to pieces. He therefore separated his army into three divisions, in order to fight at several points at one and the same time."

As in other wars of this kind, the original cause of the conflict had been washed away and almost forgotten in the tide of violence. Decianus Catus, whose rapacity had sparked off the revolt, had sneaked back to Gaul. The bodies of the Roman veterans whose arrogance and cruelty had roused the Trinovantes now lay rotting in the ashes of Camulodunum. What had originally been a justified rebellion against injustice and oppression had flamed into a blaze of indiscriminate terror, in which innocent and guilty alike were enveloped. Suetonius must have known that the fate of the island depended on the outcome of the battle. One does not envy him or his legions as they took their stand against the massed ranks of fanatical Britons, maddened by success. He must have been an extremely capable general, since his total force, according to Tacitus, was only 10,000 men. The 2nd Augusta had not moved from Gloucester, and the 9th had been severely mauled. Against the Romans stood a British force outnumbering them by at least ten to one.

In the speech to her troops which Dio puts into the mouth of Boudicca, she pours contempt upon the Romans . . . "men who bathe in warm water, eat artificial dainties, drink unmixed wine, annoint themselves with myrrh, sleep on soft couches with boys for bedfellows—boys past their prime at that—and are slaves to a lyre-player [Nero] and a poor one too. Wherefore may this

Mistress Domitia-Nero reign no longer over me or over you men; let the wench sing and lord it over Romans, for they surely deserve to be the slaves of such a woman after having submitted to her so long. . . ."

The same author makes Suetonius say to his men, "You have heard what outrages these damnable men have committed against us, nay more, you have even witnessed some of them. Choose, then whether you wish to suffer the same treatment yourselves, and to be driven out of Britain entirely. . . . Yet if the outcome should prove contrary to our hope . . . it would be better for us to fall fighting bravely than to be captured and impaled, to look upon our own entrails cut from our bodies, to be spitted on red-hot skewers, to perish by being melted in boiling water—in a word, to suffer as though we had been thrown to lawless and impious beasts. Let us therefore conquer them or die on the spot."

Tacitus gives to Suetonius a speech which is probably more in character; not a desperate warning of what will happen to the troops if they are captured, but an appeal to their military virtue:

> "Even when a force contains many divisions, few among them win battles—what special glory for your small numbers to win the renown of a whole army! Just keep in close order. Throw your javelins, and then carry on; use shield-bosses to fell them, swords to kill them. Do not think of plunder. When you have won, you will have everything." . . . The general's words were enthusiastically received; the old, battle-experienced soldiers longed to hurl their javelins. So Suetonius confidently gave the signal for battle.

It is difficult to follow the tactics of the Roman general in the fight which followed, as the accounts given both by Tacitus and Dio Cassius are conventional battle-pieces with plenty of colour, but few precise details of the action: "Light-armed troops exchanged missiles with light-armed, heavy armed were opposed to heavy-armed, cavalry clashed with cavalry, and against the chariots of the barbarians the Roman archers contended", etc. Tacitus says that the regular troops, keeping to the defile as a natural defence, launched their javelins at the approaching enemy. "Then, in wedge formations, they burst forward. So did the auxiliary infantry. The cavalry, too, with lances extended, demolished all serious resistance."

Tacitus probably knew more about warfare than Dio Cassius, but neither had seen the battle, and both were writing for a "literary" audience, not military historians. All we do know is that Suetonius's 10,000, fighting shoulder to shoulder in that narrow defile, flung back wave after wave of howling tribesmen, stood their ground, obeyed their commanders, kept their ranks, and gradually, throughout the long day, wore down their enemies. "But, finally, late in the day, the Romans prevailed; and they slew many in battle beside the wagons and the forest, and captured many alive", says Dio. And Tacitus adds: "The remaining Britons fled with difficulty, since the ring of wagons blocked the outlets. The Romans did not spare even the women. Baggage animals too, transfixed with weapons, added to the heaps of dead. It was a glorious victory, comparable with bygone triumphs. According to one report, almost 80,000 Britons fell. Our own casualties were about 400 dead and a slightly larger number of wounded. Boudicca poisoned herself."

Suetonius had prevented Britain from falling back into its aboriginal barbarism. All over the southern and eastern part of the country, fugitives from the battle were crawling home, broken and defeated. Away to the west, in his fortress beside the Severn, Poenius Postumus, Camp Prefect of the 2nd Augusta Legion, overcome with shame, stabbed himself to death.

"The whole army was now united", says Tacitus. "Suetonius kept it under canvas to finish the war. The Emperor raised its numbers by transferring from Germany 2,000 troops [to replace those of the 9th Legion lost in the battle with Boudicca], also eight auxiliary infantry battalions and 1,000 cavalry. These were stationed together in new winter quarters, and hostile or wavering tribes were ravaged with fire and sword."[1]

The familiar, hopeless pattern was beginning again: hate breeding hate; oppression breeding revolt; atrocity by the repressed answered by atrocity by the oppressor. And then a remarkable thing happened. Tacitus dismisses it in a few sneering lines in his *Annals*: "The newly arrived Imperial Agent, Gaius Julius Alpinus Classicianus, was on bad terms with Suetonius,

[1] Tacitus, *Annals, op. cit.*

39. Reconstruction of the legionary fortress at Caerleon. Military buildings are within the rectangle.

16. *Coerlears.* An imaginative reconstruction of a scene of the famous chemin de la . . .

and allowed his personal animosities to damage the national interests." Classicianus had been sent by Nero to replace the discredited Decianus Catus as Procurator. "He passed around", says Tacitus, "advice to wait for a new Governor who would be kind to those who surrendered, without an enemy's bitterness or a conqueror's arrogance. Classicianus also reported to Rome that there was no prospect of ending the war unless a successor was appointed to Suetonius, whose failures he attributed to perversity—and his successes to luck."

But Tacitus was a bitter man. Napoleon called him "a traducer of humanity", and one looks in vain in his works for any sympathy for human weakness. About Julius Classicianus little was known, apart from the comments of Tacitus, until a few years ago, when an inscription was discovered, near the Tower of London, giving a few details of his career and family background.

It reads: "In memory of Gaius Julius Alpinus Classiciani of the Fabian tribe, son of Gaius; Procurator of the Province of Britain. This monument was set up by his sorrowing wife, Julia Pacata, daughter of Julius Indus."

This inscription (a replica of which is fixed to the Roman wall on Tower Hill) revealed that Classicianus was the son-in-law of a Gaul. Julius Indus, his wife's father, came from Trèves, between the Moselle and the Ardennes. Classicianus remembered, when Gaul was conquered by Caesar, that the Romans had often been clement, and had delegated authority to the tribal chieftains and encouraged them to become Roman citizens. He himself had risen fairly high within the Roman system, and, in opposing Suetonius, may well have been trying to teach the new generation of Romans their own colonizing business. "Read your Virgil," he is alleged to have said. "Spare the conquered."

The second extraordinary fact is that Nero the cruel voluptuary, Nero the poisoner and incendiary, had sufficient intelligence to support a policy of moderation. He recalled Suetonius and sent a new, more sympathetic Governor to replace him. Instead of blind vengeance there was pardon; instead of reprisal there was reform. Grievances were redressed, old wounds healed. And Britain, which Rome had almost lost through the greed and folly of its officials, remained, for four centuries, a loyal province of the Empire.

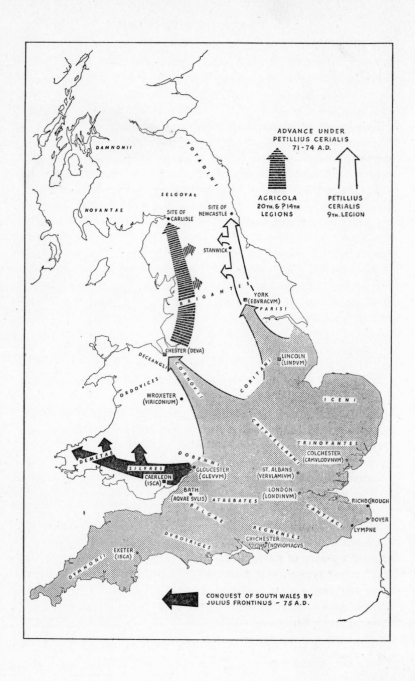

ADVANCE UNDER
PETILLIUS CERIALIS
71-74 A.D.

AGRICOLA
20TH. & ?14TH
LEGIONS

PETILLIUS
CERIALIS
9TH. LEGION

DAMNONII

NOVANTAE

SELGOVAE

VOTADINI

SITE OF CARLISLE

SITE OF NEWCASTLE

STANWICK

BRIGANTES

YORK (EBVRACVM)
PARISI

DECEANGLI

CHESTER (DEVA)

CORNOVII

LINCOLN (LINDVM)

ORDOVICES

WROXETER (VIRICONIUM)

CORITANI

ICENI

CATVVELLAVNI

DEMETAE

SILVRES

CAERLEON (ISCA)

DOBVNNI

GLOUCESTER (GLEVVM)

BATH (AQVAE SVLIS)

TRINOVANTES

COLCHESTER (CAMVLODVNVM)

ST. ALBANS (VERVLAMIVM)

LONDON (LONDINVM)

BELGAE

ATREBATES

CANTIACI

RICHBOROUGH

DOVER

LYMPNE

DVROTRIGES

REGNENSES

CHICHESTER (NOVIOMAGVS)

EXETER (ISCA)

DVMNONII

CONQUEST OF SOUTH WALES BY
JULIUS FRONTINUS - 75 A.D.

CHAPTER TEN

THE DRIVE TO THE NORTH

THE conciliatory Governor whom Nero sent over was G. Petronius Turpilianus (A.D. 61-3). We know nothing about him, and very little concerning his successor, M. Trebellius Maximus Pollio (A.D. 63-9), except that he had an unusually long term of office. Tacitus, in his usual sneering tone, says that Trebellius—

> was deficient in energy and without military experience, but he governed his province like a gentleman. The barbarians now learned, like any Romans, to condone seductive vices, while the intervention of our Civil Wars gave a reasonable excuse for inactivity.[1]

The same writer also tells us that there was a serious outbreak of mutiny among the Roman troops, who "accustomed to campaigns, ran riot in peace". Apparently Trebellius was so afraid of his army that he commanded only on sufferance:

> By a kind of tacit bargain the troops kept their licence, the general his life, and the mutiny stopped short of bloodshed.

His successor, Vettius Bolanus, also remained passive:

> There was the same paralysis in the face of the foe, the same indiscipline in the camp—only Bolanus was a decent man, with no sins to make him hated, and had won affection where he lacked authority.

Surely no man was damned with fainter praise than this. It must be remembered, however, that these extracts are from Tacitus's great biography of his father-in-law, Agricola. As an artist, the Roman historian understood the value of contrast; by implying that former Governors were apathetic, inefficient or cowardly, he could present his hero in a more shining light.

[1] Tacitus, *Agricola*, translated by H. Mattingly, Penguin Books (*Tacitus on Britain and Germany*), 1948.

One must hesitate to condemn the Governors who succeeded Suetonius on the evidence of Tacitus. He admires Suetonius, "who enjoyed two years of success, conquering tribes and establishing strong forts". He admires Petillius Cerialis, who implemented a new policy of conquest, though even he is outshone by Agricola.

The Governors who had to rule the island between A.D. 61 and 71 are dismissed with a few patronizing words, but their task must have been a hard one. They had inherited a legacy of hate, bloodshed, mutiny and repression. They had to hold the frontiers and allow the civilizing influence of Rome to have its effect in the conquered territory.

"The instrument of civilization used by Rome", writes Professor Richmond, "was the town and the many-sided attainments of amenity and social grace which successful civic organization involves. . . . The normal method of introducing the instrument in Celtic lands, where the most important political unit was the council of jealous tribal notables, was through the aristocratic families. These were encouraged to adopt Roman ways and to give their sons a Roman education, absorbing these things as the inward stamp of a new civilization whose outward habits and equipment possessed the magnetism of novelty and the prestige of success."[1]

Eighteen centuries later the British used similar methods in dealing with the native princes of India when the sons of maharajahs went up to Oxford or Cambridge to receive an English education. The Romans, unhindered by colour prejudice or feelings of racial superiority, went much further than the British, integrating the conquered provinces within the Roman system so completely that men of non-Roman blood could hold high command—sometimes even the highest. It is difficult to imagine an Indian as Commander-in-Chief of the British Army (and head of the State), yet one of the greatest Roman Emperors, Severus, was an African.

"The Empire", writes Collingwood, "was never, from its earliest days, homogeneous in race or blood; its homogeneity lay in its law and civilization."

Is this, perhaps, one of the reasons why the Roman Empire

[1] Richmond, I., *Roman Britain, op. cit.*

lasted so much longer than that of Britain? Such a question is not irrelevant to the story of the conquest. Although this book is concerned mainly with the military occupation of Britain, it is essential to keep in mind the peaceful transformation of the island which was going on behind the line of frontier forts. There the legions and their auxiliaries skirmished with the unsubdued tribes of the north and west; or, when they were not fighting, rested in their quarters. As with all fighting men in times of relative peace, their officers were probably hard put to keep them occupied. Drill, manœuvres, parades and inspections alternated with periods when the privates diced for their pay in the baths, or found consolation with the local women. The officers, when not similarly employed, would write letters home or listen eagerly to news of Rome from officers newly posted to Britain. They would hear, for instance, in A.D. 68, that Nero, after compassing the deaths of thousands, including his own mother, Agrippina, had himself been driven to suicide.

Beyond the frontiers, Britain was changing. London, St. Albans and Colchester were rebuilt, and new, straight roads scarred the countryside, as raw and alien as the railways of the nineteenth century. Elegant new towns were springing up in which the descendants of the chieftains who had defied Aulus Plautius lived in elegant comfort, wearing Roman dress and speaking Latin. Outside the towns were the country homes of the British nobility, luxurious villas with their dining-rooms, baths and central heating, remains of which still survive in many parts of southern Britain and the Midlands.

"And so", writes Tacitus acidly, "the Britons were gradually led on to the amenities that make vice agreeable—arcades, baths and sumptuous banquets. They spoke of such novelties as 'civilization', when really they were only a feature of enslavement."

All this took place in the peaceful south. To the north lived other tribes who, though they enjoyed trade and diplomatic relations with the Romans, were still independent. Among the rulers of such tribes some—like Queen Cartimandua—were pro-Roman; others were openly or secretly hostile.

Sometimes the Roman and anti-Roman factions quarrelled.

This happened in A.D. 69, the year after Nero's death, when the Roman world was torn by civil war, and the loyalty of the legions was divided. Roman historians later called 68-9 the Year of the Four Emperors, because four commanders were contesting for the vacant throne. Galba, who had revolted against Nero in Spain, adopted Piso Lincinianus, but both were defeated by Otho, former friend of Nero and "protector" of Poppaea Sabina, who became the Emperor's mistress and later his wife. After a quarrel with Nero over the lady, Otho was sent to govern Lusitania. Disappointed in his hope of being appointed Galba's successor, he had himself proclaimed Emperor and Galba killed. For a few months all the Roman possessions acknowledged Otho except the legions stationed in Germany. They supported their own commander, Vitellius, and defeated Otho's forces at Bedriacum. Otho then stabbed himself.

Vitellius had been the favourite of three Emperors. "Caligula admired his skill in chariot-driving, Claudius his skill at dice. Nero not only appreciated these talents, but was indebted to him for one particular service. At the festival, celebrated in his own honour, Nero was always anxious to compete in the lute-playing contest, but never dared do so without express invitation; so he used to leave his seat, while the whole theatre clamoured for him enthusiastically, and disappear until Vitellius, as President of the Games, came in pursuit and, on behalf of the audience, persuaded him to reconsider his decision."[1]

So writes Suetonius. If courtly qualities had been the main qualification for the purple, Vitellius should certainly have prevailed over Vespasian, who, according to the same author, used to fall asleep during Nero's interminable song-recitals. But fortunately for the Empire, the legions in Syria had other ideas. They wanted the rough-neck Vespasian who, with his son Titus, was then conducting the war against the Jews. The legions stationed on the Danube thought similarly, and proclaimed Vespasian Emperor in July A.D. 69. Under their general, Antonius Primus, supported by the eastern legions under Mucianus, they defeated the forces of Vitellius at Cremona. Vitellius met a horrible

---

[1] Suetonius, *Lives of the Caesars, op. cit.* Vitellius's father, Lucius, was even worse: "He begged Messalina to grant him the tremendous privilege of removing her shoes; whereupon he would nurse the right shoe inside his gown, and occasionally take it out to kiss it" (Suetonius).

death in Rome, when the soldiers dragged him, half-naked, with the noose round his neck, to the Forum. There they put him to the "torture of the little cuts"[1] and then killed him. When Vespasian entered Rome, Vitellius's mutilated body was rotting in the Tiber. Vespasian was proclaimed Imperator. Thus the tax-official's son who, twenty-six years earlier, had commanded the 2nd Augusta Legion in Britain, crossed the Medway and conquered the west for Aulus Plautius, now found himself ruler of the Roman world. He was then a man of sixty, with a powerful, jowly face marked, not by sensual excess, but a lifetime of hard responsibility.

"He missed no opportunity of tightening discipline", writes Suetonius. One day a young officer, reeking of scent, came to the Emperor to thank him for his promotion. Vespasian turned away in disgust and cancelled the officer's appointment. Afterwards he remarked, "I wouldn't have minded if he'd stank of garlic. . . ."

During this period of civil strife Venutius, former King of the Brigantes, whom Cartimandua had divorced, seized the opportunity of paying off old scores. Cartimandua had married her former husband's armour-bearer, Vellocatus, and now Venutius came out openly against the pro-Roman party. When he invaded Cartimandua's territory the legions had to intervene, rescuing the Queen with some difficulty. But Venutius remained in control of most of Brigantia.

Among the legions stationed in Britain only one, the 2nd Augusta—Vespasian's old regiment—came out openly in his favour. The 20th were at first against him and the 14th was withdrawn by the new Emperor, who replaced it by the 2nd Adiutrix; this was a new unit, recruited from the marines at Ravenna, who had been loyal to Vespasian and were awarded the title *Pia Fidelis* and the right to wear the Emperor's personal emblem. The 2nd Adiutrix was posted to Britain in A.D. 71 and quartered first at *Lindum* (Lincoln). At about the same time Vespasian sent to Britain as Governor Petillius Cerialis, his relative; the same Cerialis who, as the commander of the 9th Legion ten years earlier, had attempted to relieve Camulodunum when

[1] Perfected under the Emperor Caligula, who, when sentencing a man to death, used to say, "Make him feel that he is dying." The phrase became proverbial.

Paulinus was Governor. Now he returned to Britain as Commander-in-Chief.

With Petillius Cerialis begins a new stage in the conquest of the island. Under Nero the intention seems to have been only to occupy the south and Midlands, relying on the "client-kingdom" of Brigantia to secure peace and order in the north. But now the Brigantians had proved unreliable. Under their chieftain, Venutius, successor to Caratacus, they had a powerful army in the field which, unless destroyed, would be a thorn in the Romans' side. There was no alternative but to conquer and subdue the north; and this Petillius proceeded to do. The menace presented by the Brigantes must have been powerful, for, by all the rules of strategy, the Romans should first have secured their left flank by conquering Wales. But Petillius moved, not against the Ordovices or the Silures, but northwards into the Pennines.

Cerialis, somewhat naturally, chose his old legion, the 9th, as the spearhead of the attack on the north.

Tombstones have survived, set up by the survivors of soldiers of this famous legion, at Lincoln, York and elsewhere. Here is an early one from Lincoln (translated by A. R. Burn):

> To Gaius Saufeius, son of Gaius, of the Fabian tribe, from Heraclea, Soldier in Legion IX Hispana, who lived for forty years and served for twenty-two. He lies here.

Heraclea was probably in Macedonia, and Gaius Saufeius was therefore almost certainly a Greek.

From York comes an altar with the following dedication:

> To the holy god Silvanus, Lucius Celerinius Vitalis, Clerk in Legion IX Hispana, pays his vow gladly, willingly and duly. Let this gift be a possession for the faithful god. I must not touch it.[1]

Vitalis was an orderly-room clerk on the staff of the legionary commander. Silvanus is the familiar Italian spirit of the woods, a favourite god of Roman soldiers.

Lincoln had been a legionary fortress since about A.D. 48. Later, like Colchester, it became a *Colonia*, a settlement for retired soldiers, and the site of this has been known for many

---

[1] Translated by A. R. Burn, *The Romans in Britain*, Blackwell, 1932.

years. Not until quite recently, however, did Mr. Graham Webster discover the earlier legionary fortress.[1]

There was a timber palisade, with posts set at intervals of 5 feet in a palisade-trench. Outside was a rock-cut, V-shaped ditch 15 feet wide and 6 feet deep; inside was a compact earth and stone rampart with timber interval-towers. The area enclosed seems to have been about 42 acres, below the usual 50-60 acres normally provided for the accommodation of a legion. Was, then, the legion below strength? Or were special provisions made for its accommodation?

In A.D. 71 the 9th Legion was moved to York, and its place at Lincoln taken by the newly-arrived 2nd Adiutrix. This was clearly part of Petillius's forward policy. The land of the Parisi, on the Humber Estuary, was wedged between Brigantia and the former Roman frontier; it provided a bridgehead across which the Romans began to advance. "The steps of Cerialis", writes Professor Richmond, "can be traced, first at Borough-on-Humber . . . then at Malton, a second important Parisian centre, and finally at York." There the 9th built its fortress to dominate the Yorkshire plain, just as Caerleon was later built to command the plain of Glamorgan. And, as at Caerleon, on the Usk, there was a good waterway to the sea. From York, also, Petillius Cerialis was in touch with Chester, which in the early seventies became the headquarters of the 20th Legion, commanded by Gaius Julius Agricola, who had served in the same area ten years earlier under Paulinus. From these two bases the Brigantes could now be attacked on their eastern and western flanks.

Between York and Carlisle archaeologists have discovered three marching-camps, each big enough to hold a legion and some cavalry. These may have been built by the army of Cerialis on his march to the Solway.[2]

Those familiar with northern Britain may be curious to know if any site can be definitely associated with this phase of the invasion, as, for instance, Maiden Castle is with Vespasian and Colchester with Boudicca. Tacitus is not very helpful. He gives a few names of Roman commanders and their opponents, but

[1] See J.R.S. Report, Vol. 39.
[2] Cottrell, Leonard, *Seeing Roman Britain*, Evans Brothers, 1956.

hardly any place-names which can be identified. Here again we have to turn to the archaeologists for help, and again our chief helper is Sir Mortimer Wheeler.

In the introduction to his recently-published report "The Stanwick Fortifications" (No. XVII of the Research Committee of the Society of Antiquaries, 1954) he writes:

> The political and domestic feud between King Venutius of the Brigantes and his pro-Roman Queen, Cartimandua, came to a head about A.D. 51, whereafter Venutius remained a confirmed and active enemy of Rome. Cartimandua was twice or thrice rescued by Roman troops and her headquarters were therefore presumably within ready striking distance of the southern frontier of Brigantia; they may have been at the Almondbury hill-fort near Huddersfield. It may equally be supposed that Venutius now rallied the anti-Roman party beyond the immediate reach of Roman intervention, and *a site in northern Yorkshire would well fit the conditions as they affected him*. [Our italics.]

Users of the Great North Road will be familiar with the road junction at Scotch Corner, a few miles north of Catterick; here the road, which follows the Roman line, divides, one branch going north to Corbridge (*Corstopitum*), on Hadrian's Wall, the other north-westward to Carlisle (*Luguvalium*). A little beyond the junction, eight miles north of Richmond, in the North Riding of Yorkshire, are more than six miles of ramparts and ditch, a remarkable complex of enclosures. They stand in lonely country-side near the hamlet of Aldbrough St. John, and even as long ago as the sixteenth century aroused the curiosity of antiquaries.

> Betwixte thes to villages [wrote Leland] appere diverse hillettes cast up by hand, and many ditches, whereof sum be fillid with water, and sum of these dikes appeare about St. John's, that is paroch church to both the aforsaid villages [Aldbrough St. John and Caldwell]. Thes dikes and hilles were a campe of men of warre, except menne might think they were of ruines of sum old towne. The more likelyhood is that it was a campe for men of warre.

In more recent times local antiquaries have examined and planned the site; some correctly guessed its significance, as old Leland had done, but others thought the banks and ditches were medieval enclosures. Over 100 years ago a grave or graves found near the site (the exact spot is unknown) yielded over ninety objects belonging to the La Tène culture, including remains of chariots. They can be seen in the British Museum and may be, as Wheeler suggests "a northern counterpart of the rich content of the Lexden tumulus near Colchester, where also iron tyres were found".

Partly because of the remoteness of the site, partly because of its huge area, no scientific excavation on a large scale was carried out at Stanwick until 1951, when the Ministry of Works invited Sir Mortimer Wheeler to select and excavate a site in Britain under the provisions of the Ancient Monuments Act. "My response was never in doubt", he writes. He chose Stanwick.

CHAPTER ELEVEN

"A CAMPE FOR MEN OF WARRE"

To the present writer the excavation of a British camp—the
stripping of ancient turf, the spade sinking into damp
English clay—has a peculiar romance, even poetry, which
does not attach to digging in the stony soil of Greece, or in
Egyptian sand. Eighteen, nineteen centuries ago these quiet acres
swarmed with men: men digging, throwing up huge embankments, raising palisades, building gateways; men marching,
drilling, driving cattle. Then they march away. The naked earth
becomes green again, nettles choke the ditches, trees and shrubs
sprout from the embankments.

Centuries pass and other men come, building barns and
cottages, a church and a manor house, dividing the land by hawthorn hedges where small boys hunt for birds' nests, or play at
soldiers among the ramparts. Once in a while a solitary stranger
arrives, potters about among the long grass, asks a few questions,
and goes away. One such man writes, in his quiet study, "the
more likelyhood it was a campe for men of warre"; but he does
not know. No one knows, for the men who could have told him
have been dead for fifteen centuries, and left no record of their
passing. The seasons roll year after year, "the swallows to the
eaves returning". Then the railways come, and the ancient roads
which the Romans built become alive again; lorries thunder past
the sleeping camp.

Until a day comes when a new kind of visitor arrives, and stays;
young men and women with spades and picks, theodolites,
measuring rods, cameras and notebooks. Like detectives looking
for clues they dig, probe, examine, search and speculate. And to
them the old ramparts, neglected for so long, give up a few of
their secrets.

The word "clues" is used advisedly; the excavation of such
sites is a work of patient, skilled detection. For what can an
archaeologist hope to learn by excavating a complex of banks and

ditches? First, he has no written records to tell him what the place was; nor is he likely to find any after he has dug, save perhaps a few coins. Second, he is highly unlikely to discover any object of aesthetic or historic value; if any were left by the original builders, or the plunderers who came later, they will almost certainly have decayed in the damp soil. Wood and leather, for instance, rarely survive, except in ancient wells, where the water has preserved them. Iron tools and weapons corrode, pottery is fragmented, fabrics perish. Third, there will be no carved inscriptions, such as occasionally turn up on Roman sites, to give a precise date.

The archaeologist, it may be objected, is searching not for treasure, but information; yet what information of any value can be obtained under these conditions? These are the questions which a sceptical layman might fairly put to Sir Mortimer Wheeler before he began to excavate Stanwick. To obtain the full answers he must read the archaeologist's own report, written in that vivid, concise, factual style of which Wheeler is a master, and which—to this writer at least—is far more stirring than any amount of romantic speculation. Here I can only try to summarize.

An ancient camp, if scientifically excavated, can in fact tell the investigator a number of things. He may find fragments of pottery, uninscribed, undated, yet datable within a bracket of twenty or thirty years. A minute fragment of red Samian just under the turf may tell him when the camp was last occupied. Another fragment, lying, perhaps, deep down among the foundations of an embankment may tell him when it was begun. By measuring the thickness of a layer of mud, called "rapid silt", between the bottom of a trench and a scatter of building-stones above it, the investigator can sometimes estimate how soon after the trench was dug someone demolished its protective wall and flung the stones into the ditch-bottom.

Again, by careful surveying, measuring and selective digging, the archaeologist can trace the successive stages in the development of a camp: Which part was built first, and approximately when? When and how it was altered, enlarged, or abandoned? Armed with this information, he may then permit himself to speculate why these transformations were made. Then there are the gateways. Here, obviously, the traffic would pass, and if anyone dropped anything or threw it away it would more likely fall into the ditch near the gate than at any other place. *Ergo*, dig near a gateway, and, if you are very lucky you may even strike a layer of waterlogged soil with a few objects preserved. These may give a clue to date.

There is an ugly word, "typology", much used in archaeological circles. A hundred years ago and more, antiquaries were only interested in pots if they had an aesthetic value. But in the intervening century the science of "sequence dating", pioneered by Pitt-Rivers and developed by Petrie, has reached a high level of accuracy. By studying the development of pottery styles and types which changed as the years passed, archaeologists have reached a state at which they can pick up a bit of potsherd, refer to a catalogue and say, "Samian form 29" or "Camulodunum form 17." Though not giving as precise a date as, say, coins and inscriptions, pottery can tell the scholar a great deal, and enable him to fix an *approximate* date for the strata in which the sherd was found. The same is true, of course, of weapons, ornaments and other objects, but these are rare. Pottery, being valueless to the plunderer, remains, often in considerable quantities. The science of typology, like archaeology itself, is international.

This apparent digression may, perhaps, be excused by the specialists, because it was this technical knowledge and experience, common to all modern archaeologists, which enabled Wheeler to probe the secrets of Stanwick. But basic technique is one thing; how it is applied varies according to the archaeologist's genius—or lack of it.

The general appearance of the Stanwick enclosures can be studied in the plan opposite p. 133. There are three areas enclosed, or partially enclosed, by banks and ditches; Phase One, a relatively small, triangular space of some 17 acres near Stanwick Church; Phase Two, a larger enclosure, contiguous with this, covering 130 acres and almost surrounded by an earth rampart and ditch, with an entrance near its western corner. This enclosure is about three-quarters of a mile across at its widest point. But even this is insignificant compared with yet a third enclosure, Phase Three, an enormous southward extension of the first two. This measures about one and a quarter miles from north to south, and, at its widest point, is one and a half miles from east to west. It, too, is almost completely surrounded by a bank and deep ditch running for *three and a half miles* across the countryside, and enclosing an area of some 600 acres.

Who could have built it? What was it for? It was clearly a defended area, but in size far greater than most hill-forts. In any case it was *not* a true hill-fort, like Maiden Castle, though the line of banks and ditches followed the mild contours of the landscape. Wheeler and his enthusiastic young staff set to work. Obviously it was totally impracticable to excavate the whole vast complex. Instead, they dug at carefully selected points. They made a cutting through the bank and ditch of the small enclosure, known locally as "the Tofts", which means "site of a homestead" or "an eminence, knoll or hillock in a flat region".[1] They dug out a fairly large area, 3,500 square feet in extent, near the southern rampart of the same small enclosure. They dug a section across the defences of the second, middle-sized enclosure, where the rampart was 40 feet wide and survived to a height of just over 10 feet above the old ground-level and 22 feet from the ditch bottom; also at the foot of a knoll called Henah Hill, the highest point in the camp. They excavated at two points on the big, outer enclosure, sectioning the great bank and ditch some 100 yards from the place where they abutted on to the western corner of the middle-sized enclosure; they also dug at the southern gateway of the big enceinte, a gateway which, in Wheeler's words "constitutes a local salient in the centre of the southern defences, which here crown a gentle ridge, and but for trees, would line the horizon as seen from the summit of the Tofts".

From these excavations Wheeler was able to deduce that the Stanwick fortifications showed three main stages of development, which he called Phases One, Two, and Three.[2] From pottery found on the site he was able to assign approximate dates to these separate phases; dates which have considerable significance when considered in relation to the known history of the Roman invasion.

The reason for his deductions must be studied in Wheeler's own report, but, briefly, he reached the conclusion that Phase

[1] As defined by the *Oxford Dictionary*.

[2] There was a fourth phase, but this was probably Anglo-Saxon.

One, the small 17-acre enclosure, which included the Tofts hill-fort, was occupied by a native population with some South British elements within the twenty years following the Roman landing in A.D. 43. Phase Two, the larger, middle-sized enclosure, with its two miles of defences, pierced by a strong gateway, seems to have been built between A.D. 50-60. The extension appears to have been made in order to include water supply from the Mary Wild beck. Structurally, Phase Two was radically different from Phase One.

At a slightly later date came Phase Three, the building of the largest enclosure, precisely similar in character to Phase Two but of immensely greater size. A curious fact about this structure was that the entrance, which broke the three and a half mile line of embankments on the southern side, was never completed. "It was", says Wheeler, "hurriedly thrown into a state of defence during construction." And there is one further significant discovery. At a time not very distant from these events the defences of the Phase Two enclosure were, in part, *deliberately demolished*.

Do these archaeological facts fit into the pattern of events briefly described by Tacitus? Wheeler thinks they do, and his case is a strong one, from the standpoints both of history and strategic probability. Let us recapitulate. In A.D. 47-8 Ostorius had advanced into Flintshire and had reached the sea, when news reached him of a rising among the Brigantes (see p. 116). The rising died down, and Ostorius resumed his war with the Silures, defeating Caratacus, who escaped to Brigantia, but was handed over to the Romans by the pro-Roman Cartimandua. This was in A.D. 51, at which time the Brigantes were ostensibly friendly to Rome. Later, however, Venutius, whom Tacitus describes as being "pre-eminent in military skill", quarrelled with his wife, Cartimandua, after which he assumed a more hostile attitude towards Rome. At first, however, the rival factions fought among each other. Cartimandua, as has been described, captured the relatives of Venutius, whose followers responded by invading her territory. "This", writes Tacitus, "we had foreseen; some cohorts were sent to her aid and a sharp contest followed, which was at first doubtful, but had a satisfactory end." This happened during the feeble governorship of Aulus Didius in about A.D. 58.

41. Caerleon. Foundations of Roman legionary barracks.

42. Caerleon. The amphitheatre, probably used for troop exercises.

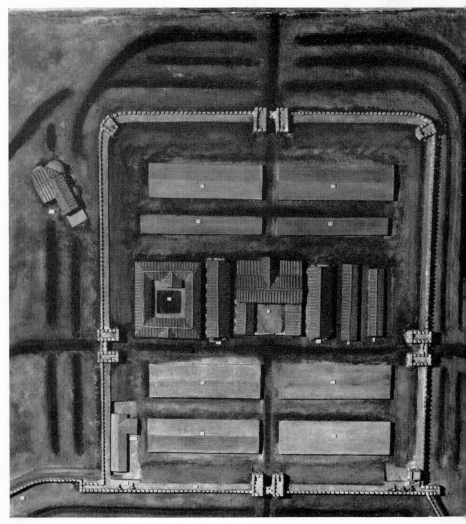

43. Model of the fort at Balmuildy on the Antonine Wall. This is the second century fort standing on the site of an earlier Agricolan structure.

Incidentally, Wheeler includes in his report an intriguing foot-note, in which he speculates whether perhaps Cartimandua was perhaps not a Brigantian, but a Belgic princess from southern Britain. And in seeking refuge in Brigantia, was Caratacus per-haps relying on old family or racial ties? We have heard of Camulodunum in Essex, capital of the Trinovantes. There was another Camulodunum in Brigantia, named after the same Belgic war-god. (It may possibly be the hill-fort of Almondbury, near Huddersfield.) There is also a Welsh legend in which Arywedd Foeddaway, who, says Wheeler, "represents Cartimandua, is a second cousin of Caradawe or Caratacus". And he adds: ". . . the Cartimandua-Venutius impasse is more easily intelligible if Cartimandua be regarded as an exile from the southern lands of cakes and wine, married incompatibly to a skin-clad rancher from the north, and thoroughly tired of unmitigated mutton" (the Brigantians were cattle-raisers).

But back to Tacitus. The next we hear is that "she [Cartiman-dua] grew to despise her husband, Venutius, and took as her con-sort Vellocatus, whom she admitted to share the throne with her". As a result war again broke out, and this time Venutius *"calling in aid from outside* [our italics], and at the same time assisted by a revolt of the Brigantes themselves, put Cartimandua in an extremely dangerous position".

So once again the Romans had to intervene to rescue the troublesome Queen. One can imagine the comments of the legion-ary commander of the 9th on hearing that once again he had to intervene in Brigantia. "The throne", writes Tacitus, "was left to Venutius; the war to us."

So the stage is set for the final episode, the arrival of Petillius Cerialis in A.D. 71, who moved the 9th up to York, nearer Brigantian territory, and attacked it vigorously. "After a series of battles", we are told, "Petillius had operated, if not actually triumphed, over the major part of their territory." When did the culminating battle take place? We cannot be certain, but it must have been before the end of the governorship of Cerialis in A.D. 74. Where did it take place? Let us return to Stanwick and peer into Sir Mortimer's trenches.

In the smallest enclosure, the Tofts, we see an abundance of pottery of the decade A.D. 50-60. The same is true of the second,

L

larger enclosure which was an extension of the first. If Stanwick was, in fact, the stronghold of Venutius its extension and strengthening would be a natural consequence of the troubled period of intertribal strife. Tacitus tells us that Venutius was "pre-eminent in military skill". The Phase Two enclosure is an impressive piece of military engineering, if a little old-fashioned by the standards of contemporary hill-forts in the south and west. The rampart was 40 feet wide, with a front face skilfully revetted with a vertical dry-stone wall which had been at least 10 feet high—"probably nearer 15 feet", writes the archaeologist. The great ditch which Wheeler's diggers revealed was a formidable obstacle. It had been cut obliquely through the boulder-clay and then several feet into the limestone beneath, making a flat-bottomed cutting about 15 feet broad. Stone quarried from the bedrock had been used to build the wall. This wall and ditch, encircling the Phase Two enclosure except at one point where the brook gave protection, was about two miles in circumference.

It was pierced on the western side by a gateway, near which several interesting objects were found, of which more later.

At a time not long after the building of the Phase Two enclosure the builders of Stanwick raised yet another, and much longer line of identical defences three and a half miles in circumference and enclosing more than 600 acres. The work was probably carried out towards the latter end of the decade A.D. 60-70. Why was it made? What was the reason for enclosing such a huge area, far larger than would be needed merely to accommodate troops alone? It could only have been intended to protect a large tribal group with its families and livestock. And one remembers the passage in Tacitus in which he says that Venutius "called in aid from outside". . . . Was this the rallying-point of the Brigantes and their allies, preparing to make a last stand as the Romans drew nearer?

Geographically the site would meet the strategic requirements of a skilful commander, who, after the break with his pro-Roman wife, had moved northward to be out of reach of Roman raids. "It was", writes Wheeler, "in the logical order of events that, in the fifties of the first century, while Cartimandua continued to dally with the Romans from the traditional southern capital, King Venutius and his anti-Romans should set up the standard of

resistance in the remoter north." For such a purpose Stanwick
had many advantages, standing as it does near the junction of
two main highways, one branching north-west across the Pennines to Carlisle, the other driving northwards to Scotland.

The huge size of the Phase Three enclosure presents a serious
difficulty. It would be impossible for Venutius to have manned
the entire three and a half miles of ramparts. Clearly it would be
necessary to move troops rapidly to threatened points on the
walls, but for this a central observation-post would be required—
a high place from which the British commander could survey the
whole area. The Tofts provides such a control-point. An interesting fact, noted by Wheeler, is that the ring of ramparts passes
inside the other knoll known as Henah Hill. If they had been
extended to include it the view of the defences from the Tofts
would have been masked at this one point.

But is there any further evidence which suggests that Stanwick
was the Brigantian stronghold? There is. Midway along the
southern rampart of the largest enclosure—the last to be built—
is an entrance gateway, the entire central portion of which was
dug out by Mr. Leslie Alcock and his staff, who removed 500 tons
of soil. It was a massive structure, cleverly designed for close-
range defence, with ramparts built above the general level of the
defences, enabling them to be enfiladed on both sides for a considerable distance. Archaeologists who are familiar with Iron Age
forts know what to look for, and in this case they expected to find
a causeway crossing the ditch.

There was no causeway, nor any artificial substitute for it; nor
any sign of a gate-structure or sockets for the gateposts. Digging
deeper still, the excavators discovered the reason: the ditch had
never been completed. The ancient diggers had dug down to the
bedrock and even begun to excavate it; large blocks of unfinished
stone, intended to be split up into smaller wall-blocks for the
revetment, lay scattered in the bottom of the huge trench. "The
picture of interrupted labour", Wheeler writes, "was complete
and eloquent."

The inference is clear. During the building of the gateway an
alarm had stopped the work. Hurriedly the excavators had
removed the intended causeway, thus joining up the ends of the
ditches and turning what had been planned as an entrance into a

strong-point. Nothing was found nearby save a few animal-bones, perhaps remains of the labourers' meals. There was no debris such as might be expected at the entrance to a fort, and which was, in fact, found near the entrance to the earlier, inner enclosure.

The mute drama of that unfinished gateway appeals so strongly that Sir Mortimer permits himself to say in his report: "We can almost see the tribesmen toiling vainly at their gate, almost hear the 9th Legion tramping up from its new fortress in York to one of its rare victories." Here were no skeletons with sword-cuts, as at Maiden Castle, nor were ballista-bolts found scattered about the site (though some day, perhaps, they may be found on another part of the vast site). But the unfinished, rock-cut trench tells its own story of marching men, neighing horses, and the blare of trumpets on the wind. . . .

There was other evidence which would take too long to de-scribe in a short chapter. Along considerable stretches of the Phase Two defences, the revetment of drystone walling, origin-ally 15 feet high, had been flung down into the ditch, where the stones still lay. After their victory, the Romans had "slighted" the defences. From an examination of the silt which lay between the layer of fallen stones and the rock beneath, Wheeler calculated that not many years had passed between the building of the walls and their destruction. Near the gate of the Phase Two enclosure, deep in the waterlogged soil of the ancient ditch, the archaeolo-gists found an Iron Age sword complete with its wooden scab-bard; a weapon which seemed to be of southern rather than northern provenance; had it belonged to one of Venutius's south-ern allies? Other objects were preserved in the sodden clay of the ditch; specimens of plants, such as willow, pond-weed, oak, ash, hazel and hawthorn, which enabled botanists to recreate the vegetation of this part of the North Riding in Brigantian times.

And there was one—only one—example of "lurid archaeo-logy". Lying in the clay of the ditch, near the entrance to the Phase Two enclosure, was a human skull bearing the marks of three hideous wounds. It had been detached from the neck below the fourth vertebra, probably by a sword-cut. No other bones were found nearby. It was evidently the skull of an enemy or captive who had been first executed with sword or axe and then beheaded. Probably it had been fixed on a pole above the gateway as a warning to others. The grisly *memento mori* looks out from the pages of Wheeler's scientific report along with the pottery, the flint scrapers and, of all things, a puff-ball. Before the archaeologists found it, the last man to see that skull was perhaps a Roman soldier who flung it into the ditch as he and his comrades stormed the stronghold of Venutius. (See illustration opposite p. 140.)

There seems little doubt that this was, indeed, the place where the Brigantian king made his last stand. After its fall Stanwick lay deserted and forgotten, while Cerialis and his legion moved on to the north.

CHAPTER TWELVE

FRONTINUS AND AGRICOLA

A N interesting aspect of the Great Invasion is the light it
throws on the Roman imperial system: the chain of command, the method by which its officers were selected and
appointed to particular posts. Of course, one would like to have
known more about the ordinary soldier: If only one document
had survived comparable to the ancient Egyptian story about the
charioteer Amenemope! Yet, apart from a few soldiers' letters—
to be quoted later—we have practically nothing from the other
ranks. The Roman historians, Tacitus, Suetonius, and others, tell
us something of the careers and personalities of high officers, but
when they mention the legionaries or their auxiliaries they
always write in the plural. The troops are brave, cowardly, loyal
or mutinous, but one sees them always *en masse*; hardly ever as
individuals.

We are left with the officers—and the higher echelons at that.
Yet there is a special interest in these careers, which enable us
to see the Roman administrative machine in operation. For
example, if one studies the official careers of five men, Vespasian,
Suetonius Paulinus, Petillius Cerialis, Julius Frontinus and
Julius Agricola, all of whom at some time served in Britain, one
can detect an intelligible and intelligent pattern of appointments,
based on personality and experience gained in particular areas.
Vespasian comes to Britain as a legionary commander under
Aulus Plautius in A.D. 43. Nearly twenty years later Suetonius
Paulinus, after a successful campaign in the Atlas Mountains, is
sent to govern Britain at a time when another mountain-people,
the Ordovices, are giving trouble. Suetonius' first step is to invade
North Wales, and capture Anglesey. At the same time Agricola,
then in his early twenties, is serving under Suetonius as a military
tribune (subaltern) in North Wales, probably in the 20th Legion.
Also at this time another officer, Petillius Cerialis, of higher rank
than Agricola, commands the 9th Legion at Lincoln and takes
part in the unfortunate attempt to relieve Camulodunum.

Ten years after the Boudiccan revolt, Vespasian becomes Emperor. There is rebellion among the Ordovices of north Wales, and the Brigantes of north Britain. Vespasian sends Petillius Cerialis, who in the meantime has acquired much higher rank and considerable administrative experience, to govern the island in which he had once been a legionary commander; and Petillius bases his operations at first on the fortress of Lincoln, where he once commanded the 9th. At the same time Agricola, who had gained experience in other parts of the Empire, also returns to Britain, this time to command the 20th Legion, to which he had formerly been attached as a mere A.D.C. And he operates from the Chester area, the same region with which he became familiar when he served under Suetonius ten years earlier.

At the end of his term of service under Cerialis, during which he operated on the left wing of the Roman advance into Brigantia, Agricola returns to Rome to take up a still higher appointment, this time as Governor of the Province of Aquitania, a large area of what is now south-western France, stretching approximately from Lyons to the Atlantic coast, and from the Loire to the Spanish frontier. Aquitania is almost as large as Britain, but not so important, because whereas Britain is garrisoned by four legions and comes nominally under the control of the Emperor (who is Commander-in-Chief), Aquitania contains no troops. The governorship of this Gaulish province was a civilian appointment. Incidentally, Agricola may well have been appointed to govern it because he was himself a Gaul.

Meanwhile in A.D. 75 Cerialis returns to Rome, his place as Governor of Britain being taken by Julius Frontinus. We do not know much about him, except that he was the author of a treatise on aqueducts and on strategy. Tacitus, in his *Agricola*, mentions him briefly. After describing the achievements of Cerialis against the Brigantes, he says: "But Julius Frontinus shouldered the heavy burden, and rose as high as a man could then rise. He subdued by force of arms the strong and warlike nation of the Silures, laboriously triumphing not only over a brave enemy, but over a difficult terrain."

Frontinus may well have served in Britain earlier; we do not know. But certainly he tackled the turbulent Welshmen, still unsubdued after thirty years, with impressive efficiency. We may assume that his predecessor, Cerialis, had broken Brigantian resistance and secured the north, probably as far as the Tyne-Solway line. Cerialis certainly reached Carlisle, where pottery of his time has been found. Frontinus, therefore, was free to deal with the long-standing problem of the hill-tribes beyond the Severn—the Silures, who had given so much trouble to Ostorius Scapula twenty-five years earlier. There is no written record of his conquests; we can read it, however, in the pattern of forts on the map of Roman Wales, and in the excavation reports of archaeologists such as Nash-Williams, Richmond, Wheeler and others. Evidently Frontinus realized that frontal penetration of the frontier was not practicable. Instead, following the example of Paulinus, he used sea-power. First he appears to have occupied the plain of Glamorgan, and moved the 2nd Augusta Legion, previously stationed at Kingsholm, near Gloucester, to a strategic site on the lower reaches of the Usk, now called Caerleon, a Welsh word meaning *Castra Legionis*—"The Camp of the Legions".

From here he could advance up the river valleys and thus, in Richmond's words, "penetrate and outflank the Black Mountains and force open the gateway to Brycheiniog by way of the upper Wye and the Usk". Westward of the Silurian territory (roughly Monmouth and Glamorgan) lay the land of the Demetae, who may not have been hostile to the Romans, who did not penetrate their country and police it with forts in the valleys, but encircled it. Mid-Wales probably presented few difficulties, being then too wild for habitation.

The method Frontinus adopted was simple and effective; it was the standard Roman system which was used in "pacifying" enemy territory. "The front line was held by regiments of auxiliary troops, from 500 to 1,000 strong, quartered in forts ranging from 3 to 7 acres in extent. Between and sometimes beyond the forts were smaller fortified posts which can best be described as military police stations. Behind the auxiliaries lay the great fortresses which formed the headquarters of the legionary troops to whom primarily Rome looked for the maintenance of her great military traditions. Behind the legions . . . sprang up the towns."[1]

A glance at the Ordnance Survey Map of Roman Britain will

[1] Wheeler, R. E. M., *Prehistoric and Roman Wales*, The Clarendon Press, 1925.

show this system was applied to Wales. At *Isca* (Caerleon) on the Usk is the legionary fortress, the most powerful piece on the chessboard. Northward, along the Usk Valley, lie the auxiliary fortresses of *Burrium*, *Gobannium* (Abergavenny), Pen-y-Gaer, *Cicutio* (Y Gaer), and *Alabum* (Llandovery). On goes the strategic road, linking these forts with the Roman gold-mines at Dolau Cothi, the fort at Llanio (*Bremia*) and so to the coast. From *Cicutio* (Y Gaer) another road runs almost due south through Merthyr Tydfil and what are now the mining areas, along the vale of the Taff, to Cardiff. Here, in Roman times, was another string of auxiliary forts: Pen-y-Darren, Heol-ddu-uchaf and Gelligaer. Further west another road ran south-westward along the valley of the Towy to Neath—recently identified as the Roman fort of *Nidum*; along this valley also were small forts, at Coelbren and Hirfynydd. Still further west lay the fort of *Maridunum* (Carmarthen) linked by a coast road with Neath and a valley road with Llandovery. South Wales was gripped tight by these military roads, like a man in a rope net—the forts being the knots in the rope.

What bitter fighting preceded the founding of these permanent forts we shall never know, for history tells us nothing. All that remain are the old roads, now widened, glossed with tarmac and streaming with motor traffic; and, here and there, a pattern of low earth banks marking the forts of Rome's auxiliary troops. In one or two cases inscriptions enable archaeologists cautiously to identify the *auxilia* who served in particular forts. For instance, the 2nd Cohort of Asturians, originally recruited in north-west Spain, were stationed for a time at *Bremia* (Llanio, in Cardiganshire). The 1st Cohort of Nervians, who came from the district between the Lys and the Sambre, in France, were stationed at Caer Gai, in Merionethshire. The Cavalry Regiment of Spanish Vettonians, whose homeland was between the Guidiana and the Douro, served for a time in the fort at Brecon, and the 1st Cohort of Sunici, from Lower Germany, left two inscriptions, one at Caernarvon and another at Holt in Denbighshire.[1]

Mightiest of all, and most impressive to the lay visitor, is the legionary fortress at Caerleon. The remains which one sees today

---

[1] See V. E. Nash-Williams, *The Roman Frontier in Wales*, University of Wales Press, Cardiff, 1954.

—substantial stone-built barracks, an amphitheatre, and the massive fortress walls—date from a much later period, for Caerleon remained a legionary base for several hundred years. But when Frontinus threw up the first defences beside the Usk in about A.D. 74 they would be of earth and timber. Caerleon will be discussed in a later chapter on the Army of Occupation.

When, in A.D. 78, Frontinus returned to Rome, the Silures had been finally subdued; from the Bristol Channel to the Berwyn Mountains Wales was firmly gripped by the conquerors. But behind those mountains the Ordovices of Flintshire, who had defied Ostorius Scapula and Suetonius Paulinus, still held out. It was the first task of the new Governor to conquer them. That Governor was Agricola.

A Gaul from Fréjus, on the Riviera coast, Agricola was born within sight of the Mediterranean and accustomed, as a child, to the vineyards and olive groves of southern France. Britain, as a country, could hardly have attracted him. *Forum Julii*, his birthplace, was one of the *coloniae* for retired soldiers which were founded in many places throughout the Empire. In Provence there was a cluster of them; Orange, built for men of the 2nd Legion, Arles for soldiers of the 6th, Narbonne for the 10th, and so on. They were splendid cities, though small by modern standards; their theatres, amphitheatres, baths and aqueducts can be seen to this day, evidences of a civilized, comfortable life lived in the sun. By contrast, Britain, with its wet and windy skies, untamed landscape and uncultivated tribesmen, must have seemed a barbarous land.

By the time he came to take up his Governorship, Agricola knew Britain well. As a schoolboy at Masilla (Marseilles), he could have talked with men who had taken part in the Claudian invasion of Britain, which occurred three years after he was born. Perhaps, however, at that time he was not particularly interested in political and military affairs, since we are told by his biographer that "in his early manhood he was tempted to drink deeper of philosophy than a Roman and a Senator properly may, but his mother, in her wisdom, damped the fire of his passion". Masilla was a Greek colony, and the Romans, though admiring the Greeks, feared and distrusted their sceptical, speculative intelligence.

Inevitably, as the scion of an old and famous family (both his grandfathers had been procurators of the Caesars), the young Agricola arrived in Rome and began his "Senatorial career". Like other young men, he was first attached to a legion. The year happened to be A.D. 61, when Suetonius was campaigning in north Wales and the Iceni burned Camulodunum. So Agricola, then aged twenty-one, got his first taste of military service in Britain. "Neither before nor since", writes Tacitus, "has Britain been in a more uneasy or dangerous state. Veterans were butchered, colonies burned to the ground, armies isolated. We had to fight for life before we could think of victory."

Suetonius, apparently, had selected Agricola to be tried out on his staff. The young man "got to know his province and be known by the army. He learned from the experts the best models to follow." He "was no loose young subaltern, to turn his military career into a debauch; nor would he make his staff-captaincy and his inexperience an excuse for asking long leave with its relaxing pleasures".[1] So writes Tacitus, anxious to present his hero as a model of Roman virtue. One hopes that Agricola was not quite such a prig.

His first military service completed, he returned to Rome and shortly afterwards married Domitia Decidiana, also of an illustrious family. Next he became *Quaestor* to the Governor of the province of Asia (Western Asia Minor), and during this period his wife bore him a daughter—a very important event to historians, because Tacitus subsequently married her. With a writer in the family, it was only natural that he should write his father-in-law's biography; that is why the present chapter contains rather more human detail than the rest of this book. Writers on Roman Britain should all be grateful to the daughter of Domitia Decidiana.

Agricola was lucky to survive the reign of Nero, when to be a Senator was to invite murder. "He understood the age of Nero", writes Tacitus, "in which you were a philosopher if you lay low." Tribune of the Plebs, Praetor, the usual offices came his way, and he filled them with quiet efficiency, "steering clear of extravagance, but not missing popular approval". Tragedy came during the Year of the Four Emperors, when men of Otho's fleet,

---

[1] Tacitus, *Agricola, op. cit.*

turning pirates, plundered Liguria and murdered Agricola's mother on her country estate. As he was setting out to attend the funeral ceremony, news reached him of Vespasian's bid for power. Agricola joined Vespasian's party, and the general Mucianus "sent him to hold levies, and, when he had performed the task ... put him in command of the 20th Legion".

The 20th, as we know, was in Britain. So once again Agricola returned to the island, landing, presumably at Richborough or Dover, and riding hard along the Watling Street to join his legion. Where it lay at this period is uncertain; it was certainly not at Chester, which was founded later, but it must have been somewhere in the central sector, possibly at Uriconium (Wroxeter). The young legate had a hard task ahead of him. The 20th was notoriously tough; it had sent detachments to Europe to fight on the side of Vitellius. It had only very reluctantly taken the oath of loyalty to Vespasian. The Governor of Britain, Vettius Bolanus, was, according to Tacitus, incapable of controlling his army; for a twenty-nine-year-old officer, fresh out from Rome, to gain the respect of 6,000 troops who had been allowed to run riot by a weak Governor could not have been easy. But somehow Agricola managed it, apparently by a combination of firmness and diplomacy. "He showed a rare self-denial; he let it appear that he had found in his legion the loyalty he created."

Under Petillius Cerialis he gained valuable military experience. Operating on the west side of the Pennines against the Brigantes, he led his legion with such skill that, at times, Cerialis "divided the armies with him, to test his quality, and when he had stood the test, sometimes put him in command of larger forces" (Tacitus).

In his early thirties he returned to Rome and shortly afterwards became Consul—the usual prelude to a governorship. One can imagine that the old Emperor, who in his youth had himself commanded a legion in Britain, may have questioned the young commander on the state of affairs in the island. There was now no question of consolidating the existing frontier. Throughout the reigns of the Flavian Emperors, Vespasian, Titus and Domitian there was a consistent forward movement.

It must have been clear to the Roman High Command that there could be no hope of securing a permanent hold in Britain

until both Wales and Scotland had been occupied. The policy of
supporting friendly "buffer states" had failed. Meanwhile, as
Frontinus fought his way into South Wales and established his
chain of forts, Agricola was sent to gain administrative experience
as Governor of Aquitania.

Four years passed, during which he governed an area stretching
from the Loire to the Pyrenees and from the Rhone to the
Atlantic coast. For Frontinus, in Britain, they were years of hard
living and hard fighting; the army advancing, slowly and pain-
fully, along the stony valleys of Monmouth, Brecon and Carmarthen; ambushes, night attacks, treachery and death. Then,
in A.D. 78, his four-year service over, he returned to Rome.
Vespasian was then sixty-nine and nearing his end. He recalled
Agricola and sent him to Britain, this time as Governor.

Shortly before Agricola's arrival the Ordovices had almost
annihilated a squadron of Roman cavalry and this triumph put
heart into them. "The war-party", writes Tacitus, "welcomed the
lead, and only waited to test the temper of the new Legate."
It was already autumn, the campaigning season almost over and
the auxiliaries scattered over the province. The legionaries,
assuming that there would be no more fighting that year, were
looking forward to returning to their comfortable winter quarters.
They were astonished when suddenly ordered into action.

Agricola was unable to concentrate the full force, but, rapidly
assembling a mixed unit of legionaries and auxiliaries, marched
them into Snowdonia (perhaps along the line of penetration
through Cerrig-y-druidion and Bettws-y-Coed), "himself in the
van, to lend his own courage to the rest by sharing their peril".
The Ordovices, who had not dared to meet him on the plain,
were defeated in their own mountain stronghold. "He cut to
pieces", writes Tacitus, "the whole fighting force of the nation."
When he reached the Menai Straits he picked from his auxiliary
troops those who had experience of rivers and made them swim
across, with arms and horses under control beside them. The
enemy, who were unprepared for such tactics, were taken by
surprise.

> They sued for peace and surrendered the island, and Agricola,
> in a flash, found himself enjoying reputation and respect. Had he
> not, at his very first entrance to the province, deliberately chosen

a difficult and dangerous enterprise, at a time usually devoted to pageantry and ceremonial visits?[1]

Agricola completed what Frontinus had begun, and in the years that followed a chain of auxiliary forts was built in Flint, Denbigh and Caernarvon, similar to those in the south; and a second legionary fortress, at Chester, provided the basic support for the auxiliaries stationed in the north, as Caerleon did for those in the south. The Roman name for the town was *Deva*. The site was well chosen, looking south-westward towards Wales and north-eastwards towards Lancashire and the north. Agricola probably knew the site from his earlier days under Suetonius, but until his Governorship it had not been a permanent base. Now, as the men of the 20th Legion raised their banks and palisades and dug their trenches beside the Dee, the final pattern of the Roman occupation began to emerge: three powerful legionary bases, at York, Chester and Caerleon—to which the 2nd Augusta was transferred from Gloucester—screened by a chain of small auxiliary forts and a network of military roads.

It was now A.D. 79; a generation had grown up which was unborn when Aulus Plautius landed. From the Kent coast to the Isle of Anglesey, from Cornwall to Carlisle, the land was Roman. From the Ouse to the Thames there were well-engineered roads; planned towns were taking the place of the old Celtic hill forts; red-roofed villas with colonnades and porticoes, prosperous, undefended farms and homesteads, thriving ports and harbours had risen under the *Pax Romana*. Northward of a line stretching roughly between the Mersey and Humber, Brigantia had been subdued, but not pacified; still further north, beyond the Tyne and the Solway, lay unexplored territory, inhabited by hostile tribes of unknown strength, who might at any time descend on the Romanized south. No one knew what lay beyond the fells of Northumberland, the region which the Romans called the Caledonian Forest. Agricola, who had campaigned in the north with Cerialis, knew that this objective still remained—to see what lay beyond the Cheviots, to explore the coast with his fleet, to discover whether or not Britain was truly an island; to establish a permanent northern frontier. Only then would the conquest of Britain be complete.

[1] Tacitus, *Agricola, op. cit.*

CHAPTER THIRTEEN

INTO SCOTLAND

AGRICOLA'S victory in north Wales had been swift and brilliant. Yet, in reporting his success to Rome, he forbore to use the usually "laurelled despatches" with which it was customary to announce a major triumph. In fact, he affected to regard the episode as a police action rather than a major military operation. This, as Mr. A. R. Burn comments in his fascinating little book, *Agricola and Roman Britain*,[1] must have "set the troops speculating with considerable interest on what he *would* regard as a major operation".

His subsequent action, before he mounted his big offensive on the north, is in striking contrast to that of Suetonius after his victory over Boudicca. The new Governor was more than a brave and skilful general. In Aquitania he had governed with wisdom and justice. "It is a common belief", says Tacitus, "that soldiers lack the finer points of intelligence", but adds that Agricola, "even when dealing with civilians", had enough good sense to be natural and just. When he sat as judge of the assizes, which was one of his duties, he was "serious and austere, though still inclined to mercy. When duty had had its due, he put off the official pose, harshness, arrogance and ceased to be part of his make-up. He succeeded where few succeed; he lost no authority by his affability, no affection by his sternness."[2]

In Britain he showed similar qualities of moderation and mercy. Whereas Suetonius had allowed his troops to murder and pillage after the Iceni had been crushed, Agricola kept his army in firm control, and checked abuses which had sprung up under former Governors. He had "learned from the experience of others that arms can effect little if injustice follows in their train. He resolved to root out the causes of war. Beginning with himself and his staff, he enforced discipline in his own household first—a task often as difficult as the government of a province. He made no use of freedom or slaves for official business. He would not be

[1] English Universities Press, 1953.   [2] Tacitus, *Agricola, op. cit.*

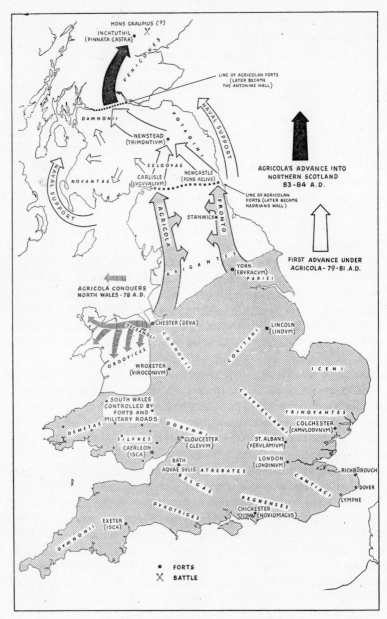

Agricola's Campaigns, A.D. 78–84.

influenced by personal feelings, recommendations or petitions in choosing his centurions and men. The best, he was sure, would best justify his trust."

A number of lucrative "rackets" had been operated by certain Roman officials; one of them was to levy a tribute of corn from tribes known to have none, though the Roman granaries were full. When the tribute could not be met, it was then "suggested" that the tribe should buy the Romans' corn and then sell it back to them. Of course, the corn was never moved from the granaries during this transaction. The only movement was of cash—from the tribe to the pocket of the official. These and other extortions Agricola stamped out, easing the levy of corn and tribute and distributing the burden more fairly.

This portrait of the just and magnanimous Governor, brave in war and merciful in peace, may well be overdrawn. Tacitus was writing of his wife's father and no doubt anxious to present him as a model of true Roman virtue. In such portraits the blemishes which modern biographers admit in their subjects were not permitted. Yet the irritation sometimes aroused by the smug narrative should not tempt us to be over-sceptical. Because the faults are not mentioned, it does not follow that the virtues were not real enough. Tacitus was a great historian who knew his subject intimately; and he was certainly no sycophant.

Irritation is, perhaps, more justified by the historian's aloof unconcern with geographical detail. Dining with his father-in-law in Rome, he must have heard Agricola re-live his British campaigns again and again; speaking of the tribes he had fought, the routes he took, the rivers crossed, and of "hairbreadth 'scapes i' the imminent, deadly breach". Yet Tacitus gives only the broadest outlines of the successive campaigns which carried the Romans from the Pennines to the remote highlands of Scotland. So once again we have to turn to the archaeologist to help fill in the details. Much has been learned in recent years. Since 1946, writes Mr. S. N. Miller, "our knowledge of Roman Scotland has been further extended by a rapid succession of discoveries, some of them of an unexpected kind, due to personal initiative and to excavations carried out under various auspices. . . ."[1]

[1] *The Roman Occupation of South-western Scotland*, by Clarke, Davidson, Robertson, St. Joseph, edited by S. N. Miller, Glasgow Archaeological Society, 1952.

M

Some of these discoveries have been made through the help of that recent ally of archaeology—the aeroplane. Aerial photography of ancient sites—of which Dr. St. Joseph is a pioneer—has notably increased our knowledge of Roman Britain, and this knowledge is being continually extended. The advantage of the aerial method, is that by photographing a landscape under suitable conditions of light the outline of walls, roads, fields which are invisible at ground-level appear on the photographic plate. Subsequent investigations of the site almost invariably confirm the truth of the picture.

To return again to Tacitus. He tells us that by the summer, following the conquest of north Wales, he had "concentrated his army". We have seen that when the Governor arrived in the previous autumn the normal campaigning season was over. The lightning attack on the Ordovices had been mounted by mixed units rapidly assembled for the task. But now Agricola deployed his forces for a major operation. Chester (*Deva*), which now became the base of Agricola's old legion—the 20th—seems the most likely focus of concentration. Westward, it overlooked the newly-conquered territory of the Ordovices. North-eastward, it looked towards the coastal corridor between the Pennines and the sea. Agricola, of course, was familiar with this route, having traversed it when he operated on the left flank of Cerialis when the latter was invading Brigantia. "There is no doubt", writes Richmond, "that it was Agricola who rounded off the consolidation of northern Britain, and that much of his work took place on the west coast, though his hand is also traceable in County Durham and between Tyne and Solway."

In the spring or early summer of A.D. 79, Agricola moved out, almost certainly from Chester, on the first of his five great campaigns. We can imagine him, mounted, and wearing the splendid armour of a general, leading a great host "in all the pride and panoply of glorious war". The magnificence of legionary armour and equipment—even that of the private soldiers—would have astonished us could we have seen a legion on the march. The helmets and cuirasses of burnished steel, often inlaid with polished bronze, flashed in the sun; the standards swayed above the heads of the marching legionaries, each man with his big shield at the back, short fighting-sword slung from a strap over the shoulder, and long, slender javelin in hand. Plumes nodded, horses neighed, centurions barked their orders as the long column moved across the plain of Cheshire to the crossing of the Mersey.

First came a squadron of auxiliary cavalry with baggage. Then followed the legion with its own baggage at the rear. At the rear and on the flanks were more auxiliary horsemen. Such was the order of march in "safe" territory. In hostile country the order was different; if there was danger of ambush, archers and lightly armed troops skirmished ahead. Then came a full-strength detachment of legionary foot and horse, followed by engineers and road-makers, and the officers' baggage (protected by cavalry). Next followed the main force, preceded by 120 legionary cavalry, engineers with siege-engines, the general and his cohort commanders and guards, in front of the Eagle, with trumpeters behind. Then a legion, marching six deep, and its baggage carried by pack-animals and servants. Finally there was a force of legionary horse and foot bringing up the rear.[1]

Agricola "was present everywhere on the march", writes Tacitus, "praising discipline and checking stragglers. Himself he chose sites for camps, himself reconnoitred estuaries and woods; all the time he gave the enemy no rest, but constantly launched plundering raids." The reference to estuaries seems to indicate the west-coast route through Lancashire, across the Mersey and the Ribble—where, at Ribchester, there was an early fort—then northward along the valley which divides the Pennines from the fells of Westmorland and Cumberland to Carlisle. On the Map of Roman Britain this valley is thickly studded with forts—Brougham, Plumpton Head, Salkeld Gate, Old Penrith, Petteril Green, Barrock Fell—some of which are of later date, but clearly showing the line of penetration.

The same method used in "pacifying" Wales was applied in the north: seal off the river estuaries with forts, deny the hillmen access to their lowland food-supply, and build auxiliary forts along the main passes. Along the road which crosses the Pennines between Brougham and Greta Bridge there are five forts, three fortlets, five signal stations, one temporary camp and one

[1] This description is modelled on that given by Arrian a century after Agricola. Arrian was writing about the offensive against the Alans of the east; but the formation which Agricola adopted was probably similar.

"practice camp" (used for troop-training); and there may have
been more. The little red squares and circles on the map are
eloquent. This was the line of the later Roman road linking the
two parallel routes into Scotland; the westward route from
Mamucium (Manchester) through Ribchester, Carlisle, and over
Beattock to the Clyde Estuary; and the eastern route from York,
through Catterick, Piercebridge, Corbridge, Newstead and the
Firth of Forth.

While Agricola advanced along the west coast from Chester
at the head of the 20th, the 9th almost certainly supported him on
the eastern side of the Pennines. We know the name of the
commander of the 9th at this time, Caristanius Fronto, from
Antioch, in S.E. Asia Minor. Fronto was one of the "new men"
discovered by Vespasian, who had probably met him when
fighting the Jews in Judea. As a young man, Fronto had commanded the Bosphorus Horse, a cavalry unit stationed on the
Euphrates frontier, near Europos. It had been recruited from
among the semi-barbarians of what is now southern Russia—an
indication of the far-reaching limits of the Roman Empire.

Fronto is not mentioned by Tacitus or any other Roman
historian. We only know of him through the formal inscription
found at Antioch, recording his career. Yet much may be learned
from this, brief though it is. He was probably descended from a
soldier who served under Caesar during the revolutionary wars,
and who, from the days of Augustus, had been settled in the
Roman colony of Antioch. "It is . . . probable that he first
attracted Vespasian's notice during the Jewish campaign, and
that his horsemen were among the troops who marched in
Vespasian's interests; the regiment next turns up on the Danube.
Caristanius was among the new senators created perhaps in 70,
and later promoted to praetorian rank. . . ."[1]

It was this young officer, born on the Levant and having
commanded Crimean horsemen in the hot, barren deserts of
Mesopotamia, and who had subsequently served on the Danube
frontier, who came to Britain and took over command of a legion
at York. How he must have complained of our weather!

How did Fronto and the 9th Legion keep in touch with
Agricola's forces on the west coast? Today there would be radio-

[1] Burn, A. R., *Agricola and Roman Britain, op. cit.*

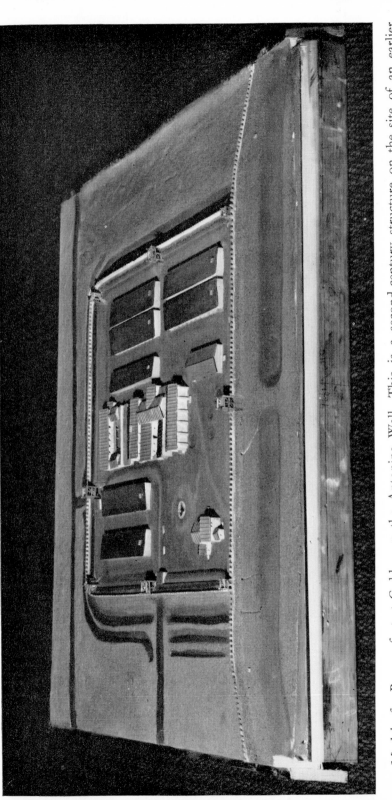

44. Model of a Roman fort at Cadder on the Antonine Wall. This is a second-century structure on the site of an earlier Agricolan fortress. Note headquarters buildings in the centre with barrack blocks on either side.

45. The road to Hadrian's Wall: view near Ebchester. The wall lies beyond the distant ridge.

telephonic communication. But the Romans also had a swift and efficient means of transmitting messages. Signal-stations, remains of which survive in many parts of northern Britain, flashed fire-signals from point to point. One can see representations of such signal-towers on Trajan's column. To send a message across the Pennines in A.D. 79 probably took little longer than putting in a trunk-call from Liverpool to York today.

In following Agricola's advance, it is tempting to let imagination run riot. Here we will adhere purely to the facts as revealed (*a*) by Tacitus and (*b*) by archaeology. In A.D. 79, the second year of his Governorship, he appears to have reached the Tyne-Solway line, the narrowest point of northern Britain, subsequently to be crossed by Hadrian's Wall. Along the line of the ancient Dere Street, between Corbridge and Carlisle, archaeologists have found remains of forts containing "Flavian" pottery dating from Agricola's period. *Corstopitum*, near Corbridge, later to become a main supply base for Hadrian's Wall, has an earth-and-timber fortress of Agricolan date which may well have been his winter quarters in A.D. 79-80:

> . . . the first Roman fort at Corstopitum seems by the associated remains to belong to the period of Agricola's governorship, but that fort represents the period when active operations in the field were over, and the Romans were securing their hold on the country by a series of permanent stations, each containing an infantry battalion (*cohors*) or a cavalry regiment (*ala*).[1]

Further west, along Dere Street, were other forts of Flavian date . . . "rectangular earthworks surrounded by ditches and enclosing timber buildings". And Birley adds that Corstopitum's "first garrison was probably the Gallic cavalry regiment known as the *ala Petriana,* to judge by the tombstone of a standard-bearer of that unit, now to be seen in Hexham Priory; that must have come from one of the cemeteries at Corstopitum; the regiment was 1,000 strong, the only one of that size in the army of Britain, and its presence at Corstopitum emphasizes the military importance of the site at that period."[2]

"The fourth summer", writes Tacitus, "was spent in securing

[1] Birley, Eric, M.B.E., M.A., F.S.A., *Corbridge Roman Station (Corstopitum) Northumberland*, H. M. Stationery Office, 1954.

[2] Birley, *op. cit.*

the districts already overrun, and, if the valour of our armies and the glory of Rome had not forbidden a halt, a place for halting was found inside Britain itself. Clyde and Forth, carried inland to a great depth on the tides of opposite seas, are separated by a narrow neck of land. This neck was now secured by garrisons, and the whole sweep of the country to the south was safe in our hands. The enemy had been pushed into what was virtually another island."

Here, most unusually, Tacitus actually gives us points of geographical reference—the estuaries of the Forth and Clyde. Archaeology confirms the truth of his statements. At numerous points along the line are forts, of which the most prominent remains are those of the later, "Antonine", period, i.e. built along the line of the wall erected in the reign of Antonius Pius at about A.D. 139. But under these later forts, at Cadder, Balmuildy, Old Kilpatrick and elsewhere, Flavian pottery indicates that Agricola's men had been there some sixty years earlier. The "Antonine" structures had, in fact, been built on or near the foundations of Agricola's, just as his forts between the Tyne and Solway were replaced, in A.D. 120, by the permanent frontier defences of the Emperor Hadrian. Their sites had been well chosen.

The truth of Tacitus's comment is here borne out: "It was observed by experts that no general had ever shown a better eye for ground than Agricola. No fort of his was ever stormed, ever capitulated or was ever abandoned. They were protected against long-protracted sieges by supplies renewed every year. And so winter in these forts had no terrors. Frequent sallies were made, and every commandant could look after himself."

The modern historian or archaeologist, starved of documentary evidence, scans Tacitus's comments very closely, searching for the slightest clue which will help him. "And so winter in these forts had no terrors." What terrors? Was Tacitus referring obliquely to the forts built in the wild Pennines by Petillius Cerialis? Does this sentence, perhaps, hint at some grim moment when a relieving detachment of auxiliaries, marching up to some lonely fortress in the Yorkshire wolds, previously cut off by snow, found only the burned-out hutments and the skeletons of the dead? Or did they sometimes meet demoralized fugitives,

overcome by fear and hunger, who had surrendered their position
in order to save their lives?

The fifth campaign opened in A.D. 82, when Agricola "began
with a sea passage, and in a series of successful actions subdued
nations hitherto unknown. The whole side of Britain that faces
Ireland was lined with his forces. . . . Agricola had given welcome
to an Irish prince, who had been driven from home by a rebellion;
nominally a friend, he might be used as a pawn in the game. I
have often heard Agricola say that Ireland could be reduced and
held by a single legion and a few auxiliaries . . . " writes Tacitus.

Until just before the Second World War archaeologists had
been unable to substantiate the truth of this statement. In eastern
Scotland, from the Cheviots through Roxburgh, Peebles, Mid-
lothian, Kinross and Perth, they had been able to trace a clear
line of advance. There was a Roman road running from Corbridge (*Corstopitum*) through High Rochester (*Bremenium*) to
Newstead (*Trimontium*), Inveresk on the Firth of Forth, and thence
through Camelon, near Falkirk, to Dunblane, Ardoch, and the
Gask Ridge to Inchtuthill on the Tay. In several of these places
Flavian pottery indicated the line of Agricola's eastern advance
into Scotland. At Newstead, on the Tweed, Dr. Curle discovered
a large Roman fortress, probably built under the guidance of
Caristanius Fronto, which yielded the finest collection of Roman
military equipment found in Britain; a large part of the finds
were Flavian, including parade helmets, horse-harness, portions
of leather tents, pick-axes, blacksmiths' and carpenters' tools. (See
illustrations 25 and 27.) There were also wooden writing-tab-
lets, and their metal pens or *styli*, which scratched the now-vanished
wax surface; there were great jars which had originally held
wine or oil. And there were wooden chariot-wheels with iron
tyres shrunk on, excellently made in the traditional Celtic way.

Such was the picture up to 1937, a single line from Corbridge,
over Cheviot and so by Newstead to the Firth of Forth and
beyond. Yet, writes, Mr. S. N. Miller, "even for the period before
the frontiers had settled into a uniform system of transverse
lines, an unsupported penetrative line of that length seemed a
hazardous way of controlling so wide a tract of difficult country
so recently overrun".[1]

[1] *The Roman Occupation of S.W. Scotland, op. cit.*

Had there been a western line of advance, parallel to the well-known route unto Perthshire? Tacitus had said that "the whole side of Britain that faces Ireland was lined with [Agricola's] forces". But where was the archaeological evidence? "Until 1946", writes Mr. Miller, "no site on the western road from Carlisle to the Firth of Forth was known from the evidence of datable objects to have been occupied by Roman troops in the Flavian period." Yet since Mr. Clarke's exploration of the fort at Milton in that year abundant evidence has been forthcoming. Some of these forts have been first discovered on the ground. Others were first identified from the air. Flying low over the hills of Dumfries, Lanark and Stirling in late afternoon, when the low-slanting sun shadowed the faint line of embankments, or with highly-sensitive plates which registered the colour-variations of crops growing above hidden foundations, Dr. St. Joseph has identified the unmistakable "playing-card" plan of numerous Roman forts, invisible from ground-level. Many of these forts date from the reoccupation of Scotland under Antonius Pius; but some, on investigation, have yielded Flavian pottery and mark the progress of Agricola.

The picture is fascinating and somewhat bizarre. The aircraft drones over the quiet fields and disappears. Weeks or months later some bewildered farmer in Lanark is requested to give permission to dig on his land. Months afterwards the archaeologists arrive; and the next thing he knows is that pieces of pottery are being dug up, washed and scrutinized to prove that nearly 1,900 years ago one of Agricola's cavalry cohorts camped on his property.

In the entire history of Roman archaeology in Britain there has probably been nothing comparable to the discoveries made in south-western Scotland during the past twelve years. A whole new vista has been opened up; a line of forts stands revealed. In spite of all that my respected and scholarly friends tell me, I refuse to believe that archaeology is not sometimes romantic.

CHAPTER FOURTEEN

THE LONG MARCH ENDS

To trace the course of Agricola's invasion of Scotland, supplementing Tacitus's vague description with hard archaeological fact, is a fascinating exercise, all the more exciting because of the mass of fresh evidence which keeps pouring in from Scotland. There is now no doubt that Agricola's army advanced into southern Scotland by two routes, which converged near the Forth Estuary, from which a single road ran northward from the isthmus, east of the mountain barrier. The eastern route, from Corbridge, up through High Rochester, Cappuck, Newstead and Inveresk, has been known for a long time. The western route—as was indicated in the previous chapter— can be traced in a chain of military works nearly all of which have been identified during the past twenty years. About ten miles north of Carlisle (Roman *Luguvalium*) lies Netherby, best known to many of us from Scott's *Lochinvar*:

> There'll be racing and chasing on Cannobie Lee
> But the lost bride of Netherby ne'er did they see. . . .

But it was also known to the Romans as *Castra Exploratorum*: they built a fort there. Almost due west from this point a road ran to Birrens, where the Society of Antiquaries of Scotland has identified two Romans forts and two marching-camps. North-westward of Birrens (*Blatogulgium*) the old road passes another fort and two marching-camps at Burnswark. Still further north, Mr. O. G. S. Crawford established that the entrenchment at Torwood Muir, near Lockerbie, marked another marching-camp. Here the ancient road divided; one spur ran almost due north to Tassieholm, Beattock, Redshaw Burn and Little Clyde (identified by Mr. O. G. S. Crawford). The other road went west to Carzield, Dalswinton, Barburgh Mill, Carronbridge and Durisdeer to join the other road at Crawford, where Dr. St. Joseph made a cut across an earthwork and discovered Roman pottery. Mr. Crawford, in an aerial survey, revealed a signalling-station near the

Devil's Beeftub, near Moffat, and the post at Redshaw Burn. Subsequently Dr. St. Joseph dug them and found that they were Roman.

North of Crawford the road again divides, one branch striding north-eastward towards the Firth of Forth, where, at Inveresk, there was a fort—the other going northward to Castledykes (brilliantly excavated by Miss Anne Robertson) and then north-westward through Bothwellhaugh to the Clyde. Many of these forts dated from the Antonine period (A.D. 139) but in some, such as Milton, Birrens, Castledykes, Loudoun Hill, pottery of Agricola's time has been found. Scotland has every reason to be proud of her archaeologists—including those of the past. For instance, over 200 years ago William Roy a military surveyor and geodesist, was employed after the Battle of Culloden in surveying the Scottish Highlands. An enthusiastic antiquary, he was fascinated by Roman military works, which were better preserved in his day than in ours. His *Military Antiquities of Scotland*, published in 1793, contains beautifully-drawn plans of Roman forts and roads, including a road through Annandale to the upper Clyde, on which scholars of the late nineteenth century threw doubts, alleging that there was no conclusive proof of any Roman site along it. But now Roy's successors have proved him right. There was such a road.

"The works from Milton to Crawford", writes Mr. S. N. Miller, "which are unquestionably Roman, are already sufficient to complete the proof that the old road traceable through Annandale and Upper Clydesdale is a Roman road. . . . Over long stretches of uncultivated land the metalled track and the subsidiary structures, with the pits from which the material for the road was obtained, are well enough preserved to illustrate in many particulars the methods of the Roman road-builders in the frontier area. . . ."[1]

Roy pointed out another interesting fact: that the Roman marching-camps in Scotland were of two sizes; the larger size (of about 100 acres) occurs only along a single route leading northward from the Forth-Clyde isthmus. South of this line the forts were smaller—about 50 acres, and are found along *two* different routes, an eastern route, as at Towford and Channelkirk,

[1] Miller, S. N., *The Roman Occupation of S.W. Scotland, op. cit.*

and a western route, as at Torwood Muir and Cleghorn. Roy considered that the probable explanation was that the force which entrenched the large camps north of the isthmus advanced in one column; below that line they had advanced in two columns. Modern research has confirmed this theory.

The fascination of this subject is perpetual. For more than 200 years antiquaries have studied their Tacitus, and then tried, with the limits of their topographical and archaeological knowledge, to solve the problems presented by that historian's maddening vagueness. In 1958 we are still speculating. But the pattern is now much clearer.

To recapitulate: in A.D. 79 Agricola was campaigning in northern Britain, pushing up to the Tyne and Solway, establishing there a line of forts along Dere Street, near which, forty years later, Hadrian would build the Wall. It was in this year, on one of these northern roads, that he received news that he now owed allegiance to a new Emperor. Vespasian was dead; Titus, his son, had assumed the purple. The troops were paraded with full ceremonial, told the news, and called upon to swear allegiance to Titus, an affable, easy-going man who had served with distinction in Judea under his father. One wonders if, later, Agricola heard how Vespasian died; of how, as he lay on his death-bed, the old warrior turned to his companions and said with a smile, "Alas, I am turning into a god"; of how, when death took him, he struggled to his feet, gasping, "A Generalissimo ought to die standing"—and did so. It was then twenty-six years since Vespasian had campaigned in the same island where now the legions saluted his son as "Imperator".

In A.D. 80-1 Agricola raided as far as the Tay, but in A.D. 81, before winter came, he consolidated the Forth-Clyde isthmus—the narrowest part of the British Isles—with a chain of forts, at Croy Hill, Bar Hill, Old Kilpatrick, Camelon, Rough Castle and elsewhere. These forts—or, rather, their Antonine successors—can still be traced in places along the line of the Antonine Wall. Sixty years later, when that wall was built, they were reoccupied and permanent forts built on their foundations. But archaeologists have proved, from pottery found on the sites, that they were first built by Agricola.

In A.D. 81, Titus died at the age of only forty-two, and was succeeded by his brother, Domitian, then nearing his thirtieth birthday. Again there would be the parades, the swearing-in of the legions, not only of the troops in the field, but those left behind in the fortresses at Caerleon, York and Chester. During the winter the Governor no doubt went south to attend to official business, and to spend some time with Domitia, his wife, and small daughter, who was now in England. The official residence may have been at York or London—which by this time had become more important than Camulodunum. We do not know.

The succession of the new Emperor probably raised problems for Agricola. He had already been Governor for four years, the normal term. He might be recalled before his task was completed. Again, Titus wanted legionary drafts from Britain for his forthcoming campaigns in Germany. He, personally, would be crossing the Rhine in the early part of the following year. He ordered Agricola to send him detachments of the 9th and the 2nd Adiutrix, promising in return to despatch newly-recruited German levies to Britain, and to allow the Governor to recruit Britons. There would probably be much official correspondence. In the end Agricola's term of office was extended. But when he returned to Scotland in the spring of A.D. 82 he did not embark on a major campaign. Instead, he sailed along the west coast and explored the sea-lochs north of the Firth of Clyde. This was the campaign in which, Tacitus tells us, "Agricola began with a sea passage, and in a series of successful actions subdued nations hitherto unknown. The whole side of Britain that faces Ireland was lined with his forces." He seems to have occupied Galloway.

When, in A.D. 83, the year of his sixth campaign, the Governor arrived in Scotland, the troops knew that a big new offensive was afoot. All along the Forth-Clyde line, where, for two winters, auxiliary cohorts had been dug in,[1] orders were given to abandon their camps and march to the base where the main force was concentrating—probably near Falkirk. They arrived to join the 30,000 men who were preparing for the northward march. There was the 20th, of course. There was the 9th—much below strength,

---

[1] This seems probable from the fact that archaeological evidence indicates that the forts were occupied for only a short time. Agricola must have stripped the garrisons to supplement his main army.

46. *Above:* South gateway to Housesteads Fort on Hadrian's Wall, showing
grooves made by cart and chariot
wheels.

47. *Left:* The Emperor Hadrian,
who built the great wall in Northumberland.

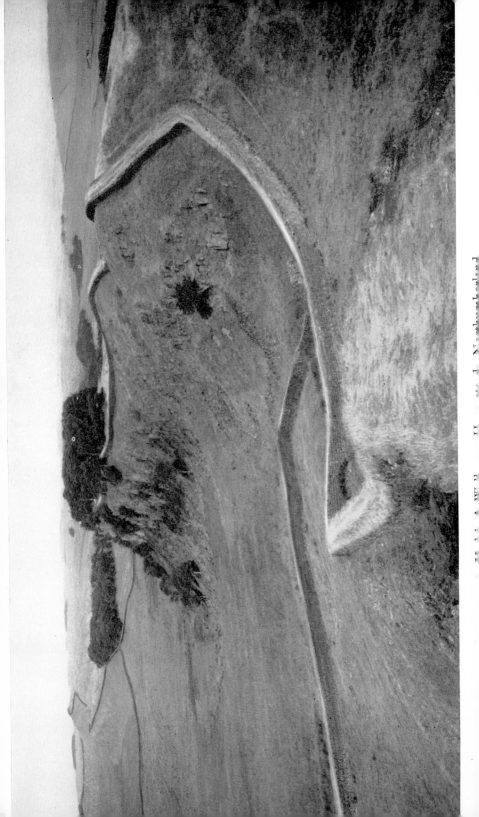

Yeavering Bell, near Wooler, Northumberland

because a detachment, under Roscius Aelianus, had been sent to the Rhine. There was the 2nd Adiutrix, also reduced in strength, and numerous auxiliary cohorts, both cavalry and infantry. Presumably the 2nd Augusta remained at Caerleon to keep watch on the south.

So, says Tacitus, "in the summer which saw the sixth year of his command in Scotland, Agricola embraced in his schemes the states that lie beyond the Forth. Fearing a general rising of the northern nations and threatening movements by the enemy on land, he used his fleet to reconnoitre the harbours. It was first brought in by Agricola to bring up his forces to the requisite strength. Its continued attendance on him made an excellent impression."

Agricola pushed forward along that single eastern road, from Falkirk to Stirling, and then through Strath Allan and across Strathearn, with the Ochill Hills at his back, the Firth of Tay gleaming on his right, and, away to the north-east, the forbidding mass of the Grampians, The lowland tribes, the Novantae, the Segolvae, the Votandini, the Damnoni of the Forth-Clyde isthmus, had yielded to him. Ahead, hidden in their dark hills, were the *Caledones*, whom he was determined to bring to battle. He could have had no illusions concerning the task which faced him. During the preceding two years, reconnaissance must have revealed the tangle of mountains and glens in which the enemy lurked, the Caledonians whose "reddish hair and large limbs . . . proclaim a German origin" (Tacitus). Their great leader was Calgacus, a name meaning "swordsman".[1]

These would be the Celtic aristocracy, "tall, fair or red-haired chiefs in primitive tartan, their shields and helmets gay with enamel, drove their pairs of small, tough, fast-moving ponies; they were followed by thousands of half-naked, barefoot infantry, bearing small, square, wooden shields, with a metal boss over the handgrip, and spears, with a knob at the butt-end, which could be clashed with a terrifying noise".[2]

From remains of forts lining Agricola's march, we can appreciate his strategic plan. It was the familiar method which had already been used with success in Wales and northern England. From Dunblane, through Strath Allan to Auchterarder, across

[1] It occurs in Ireland too, "Calgaich".   [2] *Agricola and Roman Britain, op. cit*

Strathearn to Perth and thence north-eastward along the valleys of the Tay and the Isla, runs a broad, low, valley system, into which debouch narrow glens leading to the mountainous hinterland. At the mouths of these glens Agricola planted his forts, manning them with small detachments of auxiliaries; their purpose was to seal off the glens and deny the Caledonians access to the lowlands. There is one at Bochastle, by Callendar, another at Dalginross in Glen Artney, and a third at Fendoch at the entrance to the Sma' Glen. Fendoch, incidentally, is the only Agricolan fort so far discovered which has not been overlaid by later works. It was brilliantly excavated by Professor Richmond and is the only completely excavated Agricolan fort.

Further east, in the line of Agricola's advance, are other forts, marching-camps and signal-stations, e.g. at Dunblane, the big, multiple-banked fort at Ardoch, the line of signal-stations along the Gask Ridge, and the forts at Bertha and Grassy Wells. The large number of these signal-stations, the foundations and post-holes of which still remain, shows that the Romans were sensitive about the communications; and one can well understand why. The forts, each with its small contingent of troops, were highly vulnerable to attack by the hillmen, unless reinforcements could be brought rapidly to the scene. These timber signal-towers, examples of which are shown on Trajan's column, formed an essential part of the Roman military system. By day signals were passed by flags; by night beacons were lit. What happened in rain or mist we are not told.

Tacitus mentions that one of these forts was attacked, though not taken; but probably the Caledonians were trying to break through Agricola's line of communication and get at his rear. Failing in this, the Caldeonian chieftain, Calgacus, who, like Caratacus and Venutius, seems to have been a bold and cunning strategist, decided to adopt another plan: to wait until the Romans reached more open country, and then, moving in several columns, there was a chance that some might get through to attack their rear. This plan, apparently, reached the ears of Agricola, presumably through captured prisoners. He called a staff conference.

> There were cowards in the council [writes Tacitus] who pleaded for a "strategic retreat" behind the Forth, claiming that "evacuation is preferable to expulsion". But at that juncture Agricola

learned that the enemy was about to attack in several columns. To avoid encirclement by superior forces, he himself advanced with his army in three divisions.

One of these divisions contained the depleted forces of the unlucky 9th. Watching from the hills as the Romans moved along Strathmore, Calgacus may have observed that this division was smaller than the other two. He waited until it had camped for the night. One can imagine the usual Roman drill, as described by Vegetius: the throwing up of embankments, the pitching of tents and posting of sentries, the tired legionaries unbuckling their armour and lying down to sleep. Then Calgacus struck, in a manner which Tacitus has described so vividly that it would be an impertinence to paraphrase him:

> Striking panic into the sleeping camp, they cut down the sentries and broke in. The fight was already raging inside the camp when Agricola was warned by his scouts of the enemy's march. He followed close on their tracks, ordered the speediest of his cavalry and infantry to skirmish up to their rear, and finally made his whole army join in the battle-cry. Dawn was now breaking and the gleam of the standards could be clearly seen. The Britons were dismayed at being caught between two fires, while the men of the 9th took heart again; now that their lives were safe they could fight for honour. They even effected a sally, and a grim struggle ensued in the narrow passage of the gates. At last the enemy broke under the rival efforts of the two armies—the one striving to make it plain that they had brought relief, the other that they could have done without it. Had not marshes and woods covered the enemy's retreat, that victory would have ended the war.

The victory had an exhilarating effect on the Romans' morale: "The army protested that no obstacle could bar its brave advance. 'We must drive deeper and deeper into Caledonia and fight battle after battle till we have reached the end of Britain.' Even the conservative strategists of yesterday were forward and boastful enough after the victory." The Britons, however, were equally confident, "putting their wives and children in places of safety and ratifying their league by conference and sacrifice".

Thus ended the campaign of A.D. 83, "with the temper of both parties raised to fever heat". But now it was time to establish winter quarters. Agricola led his army to a point where the Tay curves westward near what is now Meiklour Park. A little further upstream to the east of Caputh it makes an elbow turn, where, on the high ground above the river, Agricola established the only legionary station in Scotland, comparable in size to Caerleon and York. The Romans named it *Pinnata Castra*; today it is a disused golf-course marked on the map in very small letters as *Inchtuthill*. In 1952 Dr. St. Joseph and Professor Richmond proved it to be Agricolan. It is still being excavated.

Here one legion, probably the veteran 20th, was left to winter in the north, with some auxiliaries, while the 2nd and the 9th returned to their bases. Agricola also went south. He had much administrative and judicial business to attend to. A new Law Officer, one L. Iavolenus Priscus, had been sent out to help him with legal matters. Then there had been trouble in Cumberland, where a contingent of raw German levies, the Usipi, sent out by Domitian, had mutinied, seized a ship, and sailed round Scotland until they were eventually captured by the Frisians and sold as slaves. But Agricola had more personal troubles. His wife, after twenty-one years, had given birth to another child, a son; and the baby was ailing.

Meanwhile, in Scotland, the 20th at Inchtuthill, and the auxiliary cohorts scattered in their isolated forts in the glens, endured the bitter northern winter, when snow blocked the passes, when the clenched hand stiffened on the spear-shaft, and the frozen earth blunted the trenching-tools as the troops dug in. One imagines the patrols: the columns of marching men, black against the snow; the centurion's breath steams on the air as he curses his men into line, and the horses stumble as the cavalrymen clatter through the glens, eyes alert for an ambush. And there would be night alarms, when the beacon-fires flashed from tower to tower along the Gask Ridge, and men turned out to bring relief to some threatened fort.

The snow melts, spring returns to the glens, and the 9th and the 2nd Adiutrix move out of their quarters at York and Chester and march northward again. Agricola is with them riding through Northumbria and the Lowlands, pausing for a night's rest and perhaps finding time, between official despatches, to write a few lines to Domitia concerning the sick child. Meanwhile, in Caledonia, Calgacus has rallied the tribes for a major battle with the invaders. "They had realized at last", writes Tacitus, "that common action was needed to meet the common danger, and had sent round embassies and drawn up treaties to rally the full force of all their states. Already more than 30,000 men made a gallant show, and still they came flocking to the colours—all the young men and those whose 'old age was fresh and green', famous warriors with their battle honours thick upon them".[1]

It was A.D. 84, the seventh year of Agricola's campaigning, and the last.

He began "by sending his fleet ahead to plunder at various points up the coast and thus spread uncertainty and terror and, with an army marching light, which he had reinforced with the bravest of the Britons and those whose loyalty had been proved during a long peace, reached the Graupian Mountain, which he found occupied by the enemy". Either before he set out or on the long march, news reached him that his son, born in the previous year, had died. "This cruel blow", writes his son-in-law, "drew from him neither the ostentatious stoicism of the strong man nor the loud expressions of grief that belong to women."

For Agricola, the challenge of high responsibility may have dulled the edge of private grief; the final battle with the Caledonians was approaching, and perhaps the end of his long labours. Yet at times, when the mind unclenched from its task, the sickness of the heart would return. His first child, a boy, born within a year of the marriage, had died in Asia. The second, a daughter, had happily survived and was now a young woman, married to Tacitus. He had no heir until, after twenty-one years, his wife had borne him another son. Now the child was dead, and while Agricola led his legions towards the mountains, Domitia, far to the south, was left alone in the empty splendour of the Governor's Palace.

We do not know where the battle took place. Tacitus names the field of combat *Mons Graupius*—the "Graupian Hill". It seems to have been near the sea. The British took up their position on hills which rose steeply in places and in others swept smoothly down to a level plain. The Caledonian's chariots—the aristocratic arm—were in the centre, with infantry on the hills "in tier after tier", says Tacitus, "an imposing and also a daunting spectacle".

---

[1] Tacitus, *Agricola, op. cit.*

N

In front was a screen of half-naked, barefoot infantry with their swords and small, square shields. Agricola estimated the total enemy strength at 30,000. Against them Agricola brought some 20,000 men,[1] drawn up in two lines. In the first line stood 8,000 auxiliary infantry, with 1,500 cavalry on either wing. The line would have extended for about two miles.

Behind it, with their backs to the entrenchments of the camp, stood the three legions, each with its eagle gleaming above the ranks of heavily-armoured men, about 10,000 in all, with further cavalry wings held in reserve. The men dressed ranks, each company under its centurion, each auxiliary cohort under its commander. Then Agricola rode along the ranks and encouraged his veterans. Before marshalling them in battle order, he had assembled and addressed them. Tacitus, of course, was writing the conventional "eve-of-battle oration", but at least he knew Agricola, who could have told him what he actually said:

> This is the seventh year, comrades, that you by your valour, by the divine blessing of Rome and by my loyal efforts have been conquering Britain. All these campaigns, all these battles, have made great demands—on courage in the face of the enemy, on patient toil in face of Nature herself. . . . And so we have passed the limits that held back former Governors and their armies. Our grip on the ends of Britain is vouched for, not by report or rumour, but by our encampment here in force. . . . How often on the march, when you were making your weary way over marshes, mountains and rivers, have I heard the bravest of you exclaim, "When shall we find the enemy? When shall we come to grips?" Well, here they are, dislodged from their lairs. The field lies open, as you so bravely desired it. . . ."

He went on to encourage the troops by recalling their many battle honours, and their previous victories in Britain. He even made the typical general's joke—no doubt greeted with much laughter: "These are the Britons with the longest legs", he said, "the only reason they have survived so long." And he ended by exhorting his men to "have done with campaigning, crown fifty years with one day of splendour, convince Rome that, if wars have dragged on or been permitted to revive, her soldiers were not to blame!"

[1] Several thousands had been left to garrison forts along the line of march.

Tacitus says that "a wild burst of enthusiasm greeted the end of this speech. The troops were mad for action and ready to rush into it." But the historian gives to Calgacus, the Caledonian general, an even better oration, a speech of almost Shakespearian splendour:

> Battles against Rome have been lost and won before, but never without hope; we were always there in reserve. We, the choice flower of Britain, were treasured in her most secret places. Out of sight of subject shores, we kept even our eyes free from the defilement of tyranny. We, the last men on earth, the last of the free, have been shielded till today by our very remoteness and the seclusion for which we are famed. . . . But today the boundary of Britain is exposed; beyond us lies no nation, nothing but waves and rocks and the Romans, more deadly still than they. . . . Brigands of the world, they have exhausted the land by their indiscriminate plunder, and now they ransack the sea. . . . East and west have failed to glut their maw. They are unique in being violently tempted to attack the poor and the wealthy.

He pours scorn on the Roman Army:

> Look at it, a motley agglomeration of nations, that will be shattered by defeat as surely as it is now held together by success. . . . Most of them have no country, or, if they have, it is not Rome. See them, a scanty band, scared and bewildered, staring blankly at the unfamiliar sky, sea and forests around! The gods have given them, spellbound prisoners, into our hands.

And he ends with the famous, bitter taunt, flung against a system which brought peace, order and civilization at the price of barbarian freedom:

> *They create a desolation, and call it peace!*

The battle opened with an exchange of missiles; the Caledonians showing great skill in parrying the shots with their swords or catching them on their shields. It was the veteran Batavi from the Netherlands and the Tungrians of Belgium who took the first shock of battle. Agricola ordered them to close with the enemy and fight it out at the sword's point. "The manœuvre was familiar to those old soldiers, but most inconvenient to the enemy with their small shields and unwieldly swords—swords without a thrusting point. . . . The Batavi began to rain blow after blow, push with the bosses of their shields and stab their enemies in the face. They routed the enemy on the plain and pushed on uphill."[1]

The legions had not moved. Agricola was keeping his crack troops in reserve. Meanwhile, as the British infantry gave way before the Batavi, the Roman cavalry routed the Caledonian chariots, and then, swinging round, plunged into the infantry battle. But the Britons stood their ground and brought the Roman onslaught to a standstill.

> By now [writes Tacitus] the battle looked anything but favourable to us, with our infantry precariously perched on the slope and jostled by the flanks of the horses. And often a stray chariot, its horses panic-stricken without a driver, came plunging in on flank or front.

Higher up the hill were masses of Britons who had not yet joined in the fight. Now they began slowly to descend and take the Romans in the rear. Anticipating this move, Agricola gave the order for his cavalry reserves to block their path. The trumpets sounded, and the auxiliary horsemen, gripping their lances, hurled themselves into the advancing British infantry. "He thus broke and scattered them in a rout as severe as their assault had been gallant."

It was the critical moment of the battle; the Caledonians, losing their cohesion, split up into small groups. They began to waver and then scatter. Then Roman discipline triumphed. While the enemy were in disorder, the Roman troops retained their fighting formations. "Our squadrons, obedient to orders, rode round from the front and fell on the enemy in the rear. The spectacle that followed over open country was awe-inspiring and grim. Our men followed hard, took prisoners and then killed them as new enemies appeared. . . . Arms, bodies, severed limbs lay around and the earth reeked of blood; and the vanquished now and then found their fury and courage again."

Still the legions had not moved, nor was there now any reason to use them, for now it was a cavalryman's battle. The Britons, retreating to the woods, tried to rally, but Agricola,

---

[1] Tacitus, *Agricola, op. cit.*

ringing the woods with his horsemen, while others dismounted, discarded their equipment and scoured the forests. Finally, the Britons, despairing at seeing the Romans still firm and steady while they were disorganized and leaderless, made their escape into the hills. When night came Agricola was master of the field, 10,000 of the Britons fell; on the Roman side (according to Tacitus) only 367.

Thus ended the last battle of the Great Invasion, forty-one years after Aulus Plautius landed in Kent. It was not, of course, the end of fighting, for in later centuries the tribes of northern Britain rose again and again, and Scotland was lost and re-occupied several times, until finally the Romans abandoned hope of holding it, and retreated to the Tyne-Solway line, where they established the permanent northern frontier of the Empire.

After Mons Graupius, the Caledonians were broken for a generation, and the northern frontier was secure for a time. The Romans never again advanced beyond the line which Agricola had won. The invasion, as such, was over.

EPILOGUE

THE invasion was over; the occupation only beginning. Britain was to remain a Roman province for another three centuries, during which, in the words of Sir Winston Churchill, the island "enjoyed in many respects the happiest, most comfortable and most enlightened times its inhabitants have had" —words which should be carefully weighed by those who still cling to the ancient fallacy that the Romans were oppressors, holding down a sullen, captive people.

Those 300 years were the sum of the achievement of such men as Plautius, Suetonius, Frontinus, Cerialis and Agricola. Even in Agricola's time British tribesmen were fighting loyally on the side of the Romans against Calgacus. National exclusiveness, patriotism, based on race or geography, hardly existed. In the second century the people of southern and central Britain, if not of the north, were proud to call themselves Romans, as were the Spaniards, the Gauls, the Syrians, even—in moments of emergency—the Jews. The Apostle Paul was glad to claim Roman citizenship and protection when threatened with death by his own countrymen.

The massacres after Boudicca's revolt, the sympathy one feels for Caratacus and Venutius, the revulsion from the slaughter at Mons Graupius must be balanced against those peaceful, prosperous 300 years. The Iceni, the Silures, the Ordovices and the Caledonians fought bravely, but for what? Tacitus gives their leaders brave speeches full of the noblest sentiments; but they are really the sentiments of a Roman author who was probably too close to the Roman system to value its merits, while being only too conscious of its defects. His sympathy for the conquered may be only a literary device to heighten the dramatic conflict of his narrative; or it may represent the sentimental nostalgia for the primitive to which highly civilized men often fall victim. The myth of the "noble savage" dies hard, even today; but it *is* a myth. If the British had triumphed, Britain would have remained a savage land in which a few semi-barbaric chieftains enjoyed hereditary privilege, while the mass of their subjects lived in near-squalor.

But if the south, Midlands and west became Roman, the far north did not. It remained, for three centuries, a frontier zone. Perhaps, if Agricola had been permitted to occupy and fortify the whole island, there would have been no further trouble. Tacitus believed this, but he was prejudiced. He paints a sombre picture of the battlefield after the victory at Mons Graupius:

> The next day revealed the quality of the victory more distinctly. A grim silence reigned on every hand, the hills were deserted, only here and there was smoke seen rising from chimneys in the distance, and our scouts found no one to encounter them.

The way to the north lay open; but summer was almost spent, and Agricola could only take ship and coast round Britain. "The forces allotted were sufficient, and the terror of Rome had gone before him. Agricola, marching slowly in order to inspire fresh nations by his very lack of hurry, placed his infantry and cavalry in winter quarters. At the same time the fleet, sped by favouring winds and fame, took up its quarters in the harbour of *Trucculum*, from which it had set out to coast all the neighbouring stretch of Britain and to which it now returned."

It is an impressive picture, which loses nothing by a great writer's choice of words. But the hard facts suggest a different story. Agricola had spent seven years in Britain, and the island had held down four legions and numerous auxiliaries, scattered in forts from the Severn to the Tay. The cost of garrisoning the island must have been tremendous. Agricola, the "man on the spot" only saw the local situation. Domitian, in Rome, was aware of the whole imperial picture; messages came to him from the governors of the Rhine provinces, urgently calling for reinforcements. And the Rhine was much nearer Rome than Britain. When he returned to his winter quarters, Agricola received orders to return to Rome. Moreover, Domitian had decided to reduce Britain to a "three-legion" province. The 2nd Adiutrix was recalled, leaving only the 2nd Augusta at Caerleon, the 9th at York, and the doughty 20th at Inchtuthill. Later the 20th was ordered to leave its newly-won territory and return to its old base at Chester.

Towards the autumn of A.D. 84, with his wife, Agricola embarked, probably at Richborough. The white cliffs of the Kent coast grew fainter as the galley dug its bows into the Channel swell. Was Domitia standing beside her husband as he bade farewell to the island which, three times in his lifetime, he had entered with high hopes—first, as a young subaltern under Suetonius, second, under Cerialis as legionary commander, third and finally-as Governor? Or was she in her cabin, offering, between bouts of seasickness, heartfelt thanks to the gods for the fact that she would never see the accursed island again?

There remains only to add a few summarizing notes and a brief impression of the Roman army of occupation. Looking back over the history of the invasion, the first point which strikes one is the length of time—forty-one years—between the Claudian invasion and Agricola's final victory at Mons Graupius. From the Roman record in other lands, e.g. Gaul, it seems clear that, if they had intended originally to conquer the whole of Britain, they would have done so much more quickly. But they probably had no such intention. After overrunning the island up to the line of the Fosse Way, they almost certainly intended to draw their frontier between the Humber and Severn. Then, when the Silures gave trouble, they were forced to push the frontier forward in order to protect their newly-won territory. Hence the foundation of the legionary fortress at Gloucester.

When the Iceni revolted, and, in the words of Tacitus, "we had to fight for life before we could think of victory", there was a serious suggestion that the island should be totally abandoned. This may have been the reason why Seneca and other high officials were so anxious to call in their loans to the British chieftains, one of the acts which touched off the revolt which almost lost the Romans Britain.

Later they found it imperative to subdue Wales, and when the intertribal feuds within the Brigantian canton threatened their security, it was necessary to advance beyond the Humber to the Ouse, and then northward of York to take in all northern Britain to the Tyne-Solway line. Even this was not enough. Perhaps among the allies who rallied to Venutius at Stanwick were tribes from beyond the Solway; the defeat of these tribes by

Cerialis would open a wound which could not be healed. Hence the necessity to invade Scotland. It was a kind of "chain reaction".

The story of the three centuries which followed Agricola's governorship would provide ample material for another book. Here I shall refer only to the army of occupation which guarded and policed the frontiers during those centuries. "Army of occupation" is not an accurate description, since it suggests a force holding down a subject population against its will. Its function was, in fact, to protect the peaceful, Romanized hinterland from any possibility of attack from without. Scotland was always a severe problem. In the time of Hadrian (c. A.D. 120) the Romans built a great wall stretching from the Tyne to the Solway, linking a chain of forts, fortlets and "mile-castles", with gates at intervals.

Even today, when most of it has disappeared, and even the best-preserved remains survive only to a height of about 6 feet, Hadrian's Wall is the most splendid Roman monument in Britain, and perhaps the finest Roman military structure in the world. Over seventy miles long, it linked the estuaries of the Tyne and Solway, and there was a chain of ancillary forts along the Cumberland coast. The eastern forty-five miles were closed by a stone wall, 10 Roman feet wide and 16 feet high from the ground to the top of the rampart walk; westward lay a turf rampart, 20 feet wide at the base and 12 feet in height. Where the ground north of the Wall was sufficiently steep (as in the section near Housesteads) there were no additional defences. At other places the wall was fronted by a deep ditch, and behind it lay the *vallum*, a flat-bottomed ditch with a continuous mound on each side of it, running at various distances from the wall, with a strip of "no-man's-land" between.

At every Roman mile there there was a "fortlet" attached to the Wall, with two turrets between each, and along the top of the Wall was a sentry-walk. "These parts of the defences", writes Richmond, "were designed to prevent infiltration. The second problem was the defence against attacks. For this purpose each mile-castle was provided with a wide sally-port, through any of which the fighting garrisons stationed behind the Wall might issue to encircle attackers and drive them against the barrier, like hunters using a corral. Thus employed, Roman discipline and tactics could be made to tell."[1]

At first the supporting forts were some distance behind the Wall, but later they were moved up to the barrier itself; and most of these can still be seen at such places as Birdoswald, Carvoran, Housesteads, Carrawburgh, Chesters and elsewhere.

Within these well-built forts, each with its barracks, stables (where necessary), headquarters building, commandant's house and other ancillary structures were quartered the auxiliary troops whose task was to preserve the Roman peace on the frontier. They came from many parts of the Empire. For instance, Housesteads, was occupied for a time by the 1st Cohort of Tungrians, an infantry battalion first raised in the district of Belgium whose centre is the modern Tongres. At Chesters, not far away, was a cohort (1,000 strong) of Asturian cavalry, originally recruited in Spain. Another unit, stationed at Chesters for a time, was the *cuneus Frisiorum,* recruited in Friesland (northern Holland). But some of these men came from much further afield. There were traders too, such as one Barates, who came from far-off Palmyra, in the Syrian Desert. He married a British woman and settled in Northumberland.

Adjoining each fort was the inevitable bath-house or club, and a settlement in which the womenfolk of the garrison lived, together with traders and retired soldiers who preferred to end their days where their active life had been spent, instead of returning to their distant homelands. There were also temples, altars and shrines, some to local gods, others to deities who hailed from Italy, Greece and the East. Mithras had many temples. The Persian sun-god was popular among Roman soldiers, and at Carrawburgh, near the Wall, archaeologists discovered a well-preserved temple to him, which even included a ritual pit, sealed by a heavy slab of stone, under which neophytes underwent their initiation. A fire was built above the stone to test the initiate's powers of endurance.

There are few places left where one can sense what the word "frontier" meant in the ancient world: not an artificial barrier between civilized states, which is what it usually means today, but the beginning of the beyond. Northumberland is such a place.

[1] Richmond, I., *Roman Britain, op. cit.*

Driving northward from Scotch Corner through what is now pastoral country, one sees on the skyline the dark ridge which was the Roman frontier. Near the pleasant little country town of Corbridge, overlooking the Tyne, lies *Corstopitum*, one of the main supply bases for the Wall, with its regimented lines of barrack blocks and its Museum full of military equipment dug from the site; pioneers' axes, cavalry harness, sling-bullets, helmet-fittings, armour, spears, swords, arrow-heads, ballista-bolts from the armourers' stores, and the weather-worn altars of exotic gods. Further north still you climb to the Wall itself, and, as you pass the line of ditch and *vallum* the ghosts of generations of helmeted sentries seem to greet you. You speed on across the bare uplands where the curlews cry, and the lonely road switchbacks over the fells, billowing on to the Cheviots: the same road which Agricola took, swept by the same bitter wind which tugged at his helmet-plumes, and which now buffets your car. In winter you may drive for fifty miles and not see another human being, through country which can have changed little in 2,000 years.

If you turn westwards along the line of the Wall itself, you may enjoy one of the most inspiring drives in all England. All the way to Chesters (Roman *Cilurnum*) you are on or near the Wall, and the triple line of ditch and embankment is clearly visible. From time to time the grey bulk of the ancient rampart rises from the dun-coloured fields like a submarine surfacing. Then for a time the line of ditches and *vallum* moves away to the left and above the road, marching across the undulating fields to where a jagged cliff rears up to the west. Beyond that, on a crag above the Irthing, lies *Borcovicium*, and, further west still, Greatchesters, Carvoran, Birdoswald, and the other forts. Turn about, and drive eastward along the Newcastle road and for a time you lose the Wall. Yet when you enter the straggling outskirts of the city it appears again. The noble line of the rampart has gone, but, across strips of waste land beside the road and under the front gardens of suburban villas the worn grey foundations of Hadrian's great monument are still there, marking the northern limit of an Empire which, in the south, reached the Upper Nile, and in the east the borders of Persia.

For a time the Romans tried to establish a frontier still further

north, linking the Firths of Forth and Clyde. It was built in
A.D. 142 under the orders of the Emperor Antonius Pius. This
Antonine Wall, however, was subsequently abandoned and the
Romans fell back on their old frontier between Tyne and Solway.
Substantial parts of the Antonine Wall still exist, particularly near
Falkirk and a little to the west of that town, where the deep ditch
and high, turfed bank remain little changed by time. But at
other places the rampart runs through factory yards, back
gardens, a cemetery and a golf-course. The forts, many of which
were founded by Agricola and subsequently reoccupied, were
built closer together than those behind Hadrian's Wall. Scanty
remains can still be seen at Old Kilpatrick, Bar Hill, Cadder
and other sites, but the objects found there, together with
the inscribed "distance-slabs" commemorating the legions
who built the wall, are now in the Glasgow and Edinburgh
Museums.

The story of the successive occupations, abandonments and
reoccupations can be read in the archaeological remains found in
the forts behind and in front of the two walls. At Housesteads
an office of the Headquarters Building, formerly occupied by
the Adjutant and his clerks, became, in more troubled times,
a workshop for making arrowheads, many of which were found
on its floor. At High Rochester, north of *Corstopitum*, charred
timber showed where the British tribesmen had piled brushwood
against the gates of the fort and burned them down. A few
hundred feet away, in the heather, lay a Roman stone "cannon-
ball" fired from a spring-gun against the attackers.

Evidence such as this—and there is much—dates from the
troubled days, when the Romans and the Romanized British
were desperately fighting off attacks from the northern barbarians,
when internal struggles and external pressure were causing the
frontiers to crumble, and Rome was fighting on many fronts, of
which Britain was not the most important. The picture one wishes
to leave in mind is of the relatively peaceful Britain of the first,
second and third centuries, when, for generation after generation,
the legions kept guard from their fortresses—the same legions
which had conquered Britain, the 2nd Augusta at Caerleon, the
20th at Chester, and the 9th (later replaced by the 6th) at York.
From these ran well-made roads linking the auxiliary forts along

the Welsh mountain passes, in the Pennines, and along the borders of what is now Scotland. These, in time, became permanent buildings of stone, with tiled roofs; each with its commandant's house, its general headquarters building, its barracks and baths.

In times of peace they were little more than police stations. Their officers would be posted to them from abroad, and in time some of these men would return to Rome or be transferred to other provinces of the Empire. But among the common soldiers many formed attachments with British women and, when their time had expired, drew their gratuities, married (they were not permitted "official" marriages with foreign women until they became Roman citizens) and settled with their families beside the Usk, or the Ouse, or the Tyne.

In time substantial civilian settlements grew up beside the fortresses, small towns known as *vicae*, with shops and places of entertainment. Then there were the temples; some dedicated to Roman gods, some to local deities, others to the gods of Egypt and Asia. Isis had her worshippers, and Mithras, who came from Persia, his temples. Many altars have been found, set up by Roman soldiers. Here is one from Birrens, a few miles northwest of Carlisle:

> To Jupiter, Best and Greatest, the 1st German mixed Battalion, 1,000 strong, surnamed Nervana, commanded by Lucius Faenius Felix, Tribune (dedicate this altar).

From *Trimontium* (Newstead) on the Tweed:

> To Apollo; dedicated by Lucius Maximius Gaetulicus, Centurion of the Legion.

From Auchendavy, in Scotland:

> To Mars and Minerva, Guardians of the Parade-Ground, (?) to Hercules, to Epona, and to Victory; dedicated by Marcus Cocceius Firmus, Centurion in the Legion 11 Augusta.

On the moors near Stanhope, in Weardale, Durham, the following memorial was found, evidently set up by a Roman officer to commemorate a successful hunt:

> Sacred to the Invincible Silvanus; Gaius Tetius Veturius Micianus,

Commandant of Sebosius' Horse, set this up gladly, in discharge of his vow, for the capture of a magnificent boar, which many before him had failed to catch.

And there is this pathetic tombstone, found at York, and set up by a soldier of the Sixth Legion:

> To the Gods, the Shades; For Simplicia Forentina, a Most Innocent Being, Who Lived Ten Months. Her Father, Felicius Simplex, of the 6th Legion, Dedicated This.

These were the permanent memorials, set up as a tribute to the gods, or in solemn memory of a dear friend or relative. The impermanent memorials—the letters, bulletins, despatches which formed the daily traffic of life—have totally vanished. Now and again archaeologists come upon wooden writing tablets originally covered in wax on which letters were written with a sharp stylus; but the writing has usually perished. In Egypt, however, where the dry climate has preserved them, some documents on papyrus have survived; these range from regimental orders to soldiers' letters home. Such letters must have also been written from Britain, and therefore it may be appropriate to quote three of them. The first is from a young marine:

> Claudius Tarentianus to his father Claudius Tiberianus.
> I went by boat and with your help I enlisted in the Fleet, lest I seem to you to wander like a fugitive, lured on by a bitter hope. I ask and beg you, father, to send me by Valerius a battle-sword, a . . . pick-axe, a grappling-iron, two of the best lances you can get, a cloak, my trousers so that I may have them (since I wore out my last pair before I went into the Army and my trousers were put aside new). And if you are going to send anything, put an address on everything and describe the seals to me by letter in case anything gets changed on the journey. . . . I sent you two jars of olives, one in brine and one in black. . . . (?) I ask and beg of you, Father, to go to the Delta on a trading boat, by sea. . . . My mother, my father . . . Ptolemeus, all my brothers salute you. Salute Aphrodisia, Serenus the Clerk, your colleague Tarentius and all their comrades. I pray that you have good health for many years. Farewell.

Another, from the same soldier, reads:

> I received the things you sent me, including the short cloak, and

thank you for you have me free from care. Write to me about your health, and if the gods are willing I hope to live frugally and to be transferred to a cohort. But you can do nothing here without money, and letters of recommendation will be of no use unless a man helps himself. So I beg you, Father, to send me a reply promptly. . . .

Perhaps the most revealing is one from a young officer stationed in Alexandria who found himself short of funds, so that he could not keep up with his wealthier comrades. It is addressed to his mother:

I hope you are well, as I am. Please send me 200 drachmae. When Gemellus came I only had 20 staters left. Now I've none left, for I've bought a mule-car and that has taken all my money. Please send me a driving-coat, an overcoat, a jacket and a pair of cushions. And, dear Mother, *do* please send me my monthly allowance. You told me you would. "Before you go to camp," you said, "I will send one of your brothers," and yet you have sent me nothing. You promised you wouldn't leave me broke and yet you do. You treat me like a dog. Father came to see me and he gave me nothing at all. They all laugh at me in the barrack-room and say, "His father's a soldier and he doesn't give him any money."

Father promised me, "When I get home I'll send you all you want," yet he hasn't sent a thing. Valerius's mother sent him a pair of bandoliers, plenty of olive oil, a nice packet of fresh meat and 200 drachmae. Please send me some money and don't leave me like this. I've had to borrow money from one of my mates, and from my sergeant. My brother Gemellus wrote me a letter, but only sent me a pair of pants. I'm sorry I could not manage to see my brother when he came to see me, and he was sorry too. He sent me a reproachful letter because I went somewhere else. I'm writing so that you will know the truth about this. Please answer this letter quickly.

Give my greetings to all at home; Apollonarius, Valerius, Geminus, and all our friends.[1]

Your loving son.

How did the Roman Army spend its time in peace? Very much as a modern army does; in parades, drill, exercises and manœuvers. At several places in England, archaeologists have found

[1] Translated by Dr. John Morris.

camps which could not have served any military purpose, except that of training. There is one at Cawthorn, and another at Woden Law.

There would be the usual routine of the General's inspection, when armour and kit were polished, and the troops were put through their drill under the fierce eye of centurions and sergeants. At the end they would be stood at ease to hear the great man's words. If they were lucky, they might be golden words, like these, addressed by Hadrian to the 1st Pannonian Squadron in North Africa:

> You were quick to obey orders and you manœuvred well over the whole ground. Your javelin-throwing was accurate and good, and that in spite of the javelins being of a type difficult to grasp. Your spear-throwing too was in many cases excellent, and the jumping was neat and lively. I would certainly have pointed out to you any deficiencies if I had noted them—for example, if you had shown a tendency to overshoot your targets. But there has been no flaw of any kind. All your exercises have been carried out perfectly according to rule.[1]

One hopes that after such commendation Hadrian ordered the men a free allowance of wine.

Military life in Roman Britain was not all drill and manœuvres. Sometimes there was vigorous action in the north, ranging from skirmishes to serious border warfare. The chains of red squares on the Map of Roman Britain, marking the forts along the strategic highways, reveal how important the northern frontier was, and the numerous garrisons needed to man it. Below a line from York to Chester there is hardly any red on the map.

Above that line the forts come thick and fast. From York to Corbridge, from Catterick to Carlisle, from the Tyne to the Solway and down the Cumbrian coast, they are threaded like beads on a necklace. Two more strings hang like pendants from the Forth-Clyde line, and along that narrow isthmus, between the two estuaries, the red squares almost touch each other. Still further north a chain of forts stretches through Strathmore to Inchtuthill, though in later years these were abandoned.

If southern and central Britain can boast the majority of civilian

[1] Translated by J. Lindsay, *The Romans were Here*, *op. cit.*

settlements—towns such as Londinium, Verulamium, Silchester and Bath—it is to Wales and the north that we must look for the most numerous remains of Roman military occupation. A traveller in the second century A.D. would hardly see a single soldier in the south and west, save for a few on police duty or acting as escort to the Governor. But at Caerleon, Chester and York lay the legions, each within its stone-walled fortress-town where the armoured sentries stood guard at the gates. Within those walls straight, paved roads ran between blocks of buildings with brown-tiled roofs; near the centre stood the principium, the head-quarters building of the legionary commander and his staff; including his adjutant and a host of clerks. Here defaulters such as Marcus Arrius Niger would be put on a charge, and bank a proportion of his pay for his own and the Empire's good (while he gambled the rest of it in the regimental bath-house). In another part of the fortress stretched the neat lines of barracks. There would be the chapel where the standards were kept, and the hospital. Outside the walls were the parade-ground and amphitheatre—used, not only for sport, but for regimental exercises. Substantial remains of such fortresses still survive at Caerleon, York and Chester.

Apart from Hadrian's Wall—which strictly does not belong to the invasion period—the most impressive achievement of the Roman Army in Britain was the great network of roads which it built. Thousands of miles of these military highways still exist. Cars and lorries stream down the Watling Street, along which Suetonius hurried to intercept Boudicca. Along the Fosse Way, which lay behind Scapula's first frontier, along Irmine Street, which heard the hoof-beats of Cerialis's cavalry, along the road which marks Agricola's march into Scotland, the pulse of life still throbs. These roads, even more than the legionary stations and the lonely upland forts, are Rome's most enduring monument to the Great Invasion.

THE END

o

INDEX

Abbey Field, near Colchester, 101
Abergavenny (*Gobbanium*), 169
Achaeans (Ahhiyawa), the, 29
Aedui, the, 46, 52
Aelianus, Roscius, 189
Agamemnon, 25
Agricola, Julius, Governor of Britain, his drive into Scotland, 15, 105, 185-92, 204, 209; birth and early life, 36, 166, 170, 171, 172; in command of the 20th Legion, 70, 153; Tacitus's biography of him, 147, 148, 167, 171, 174, 175, 177, 193, 196; as Governor of Aquitania, 167, 173, 175; appointed Governor of Britain, 173; his defeat of the Ordovices, 173-4; his march to the north, 178-84, 203; his defeat of the Caledonians at Mons Graupius, 193-7; his recall to Rome, 199-200; also mentioned, 13, 14, 30, 123, 198, 201
Agricola and Roman Britain (A. R. Burn), 175, 180, 189
Agrippina, 119, 122, 128, 149
Aisne, River, 41
Aix-en-Provence, 37
Alcock, Mr. Leslie, 163
Aldbrough St. John, 154
Alexandria, 76, 207
Allobroges, the, 31
Almondbury, 154, 161
Alps, the, 26, 27, 28, 31, 35, 36, 37
Alsace, 41
Altamira, 21
Amenemope, 166
Ammianus, Marcelinus, 60, 70
Ancient Monuments Act, 155
Andate, grove of, 139
Anglesey, 122, 129, 130, 132, 140, 166, 174
Annandale, 186
Antioch, 180
"Antonine" period, 182, 186, 187
Antonine Wall, 187, 204
Antonius Pius, 182, 184, 204
Antonius Primus, 150
Appenines, the, 37
Aquitania, province of, 69, 167, 173, 175
Ardennes, the, 19, 43, 145
Ardoch, 183, 190
Arles, 36, 170

Armenia, 27, 111, 122
Arminius, 86
Arras, 43
Arrian, 60
Artois, 47, 97
Asia Minor, 37, 171
Atlas Mountains, 129, 166
Atrebates, the, 43, 46, 49, 125
Atrius, Quintus, 53
Auchendavy, 205
Auchterarder, 189
Augustus, Roman Emperor, 59, 69, 180
Auxilia, Roman, 63-4
Avebury, 25, 33, 42

Badbury Rings, 106
Balearic Isles, 64
Balkerne Gate, Colchester, 133
Balmuildy, 182
Barates, 202
Barberini, Palazzo, in Rome, 98
Barburgh Mill, 185
Bar Hill, 187, 204
Baring, 78
Barrock Fell, 179
Basingstoke, 125
Batavi, the, 88, 92, 94, 195, 196
Bath, 209
Battersea, 29
"Beaker Folk", the, 24, 25
Beattock, 180, 185
Bedriacum, 150
Belas Knapp, 24
Belgae, the, 31, 43, 45, 50, 57, 59, 105, 114, 115
Berkshire, 43
Bertha, 190
Berwyn Mountains, 115, 117, 170
Bettws-y-Coed, 173
Beveland, 88
Bigbury Woods, 53
Birdoswald, 202, 203
Birley, Mr. Eric, 61, 128, 181
Birrens (*Blatogulgium*), 185, 186, 205
Bishops Stortford, 57
Black Mountains, the, 168
Blandford, 109
Bletchley, 140
Bochastle, 190
Bodunni, the, 91, 93